SOLIDARITY AND JUS
AND SOCIA

C000041097

In this timely book, Ruud ter Meulen argues that the current trend towards individual financial responsibility for health and social care should not be at the expense of the welfare of vulnerable and dependent individuals. Written with a multidisciplinary perspective, the book presents a new view of solidarity as a distinct concept from justice with respect to health and social care. It explains the importance of collective responsibility and takes the debate on access to health care beyond the usual framework of justice and rights. Academics from a range of backgrounds, including sociology, ethics, philosophy and policy studies will find new perspectives on solidarity and fresh ideas from other disciplines. Policy-makers will better appreciate the contribution of family carers to the well-being of dependent and vulnerable people, and the importance of the support of solidarity in these types of care.

RUUD TER MEULEN is Emeritus Professor of Ethics in Medicine at the University of Bristol. He was Director and Professor in Philosophy at the Institute of Bioethics and the University of Maastricht (the Netherlands) before moving to Bristol in 2005. He is editor-in-chief of the volume *Rethinking Cognitive Enhancement* (2017) and has published more than 150 articles, chapters and books in medical ethics. He was a visiting Scholar at the Hastings Centre and the Brocher Foundation (Hermance, CH), and is currently President of the European Association of Centres for Medical Ethics (EACME).

CAMBRIDGE BIOETHICS AND LAW

This series of books was founded by Cambridge University Press with Alexander McCall Smith as its first editor in 2003. It focuses on the law's complex and troubled relationship with medicine across both the developed and the developing world. Since the early 1990s, we have seen in many countries an increasing resort to the courts by dissatisfied patients and a growing use of the courts to attempt to resolve intractable ethical dilemmas. At the same time, legislatures across the world have struggled to address the questions posed by both the successes and the failures of modern medicine, while international organisations such as the WHO and UNESCO now regularly address issues of medical law.

It follows that we would expect ethical and policy questions to be integral to the analysis of the legal issues discussed in this series. The series responds to the high profile of medical law in universities, in legal and medical practice, as well as in public and political affairs. We seek to reflect the evidence that many major health-related policy debates in the UK, Europe and the international community involve a strong medical law dimension. With that in mind, we seek to address how legal analysis might have a trans-jurisdictional and international relevance. Organ retention, embryonic stem cell research, physician-assisted suicide and the allocation of resources to fund health care are but a few examples among many. The emphasis of this series is thus on matters of public concern and/or practical significance. We look for books that could make a difference to the development of medical law and enhance the role of medico-legal debate in policy circles. That is not to say that we lack interest in the important theoretical dimensions of the subject, but we aim to ensure that theoretical debate is grounded in the realities of how the law does and should interact with medicine and health care.

Series Editors
Professor Graeme Laurie, *University of Edinburgh*
Professor Richard Ashcroft, *Queen Mary, University of London*

SOLIDARITY AND JUSTICE IN HEALTH AND SOCIAL CARE

RUUD TER MEULEN

University of Bristol

CAMBRIDGE
UNIVERSITY PRESS

CAMBRIDGE
UNIVERSITY PRESS

University Printing House, Cambridge CB2 8BS, United Kingdom

One Liberty Plaza, 20th Floor, New York, NY 10006, USA

477 Williamstown Road, Port Melbourne, VIC 3207, Australia

314-321, 3rd Floor, Plot 3, Splendor Forum, Jasola District Centre, New Delhi - 110025, India

79 Anson Road, #06-04/06, Singapore 079906

Cambridge University Press is part of the University of Cambridge.

It furthers the University's mission by disseminating knowledge in the pursuit of education, learning and research at the highest international levels of excellence.

www.cambridge.org
Information on this title: www.cambridge.org/9781107637870
DOI: 10.1017/9781107707023

First published 2017
First paperback edition 2018

A catalogue record for this publication is available from the British Library

Library of Congress Cataloging in Publication data
Names: Meulen, R. H. J. ter (Ruud H. J.), 1952- author.
Title: Solidarity and justice in health and social care / Ruud ter Meulen.
Other titles: Cambridge bioethics and law.
Description: Cambridge, United Kingdom ; New York, NY : Cambridge University
Press, 2017. | Series: Cambridge bioethics and law | Includes bibliographical references and index.
Identifiers: LCCN 2017016350 | ISBN 9781107069800 (Hardback : alk. paper)
Subjects: | MESH: Delivery of Health Care | Social Welfare | Social Justice |
Health Policy | Europe
Classification: LCC RA418 | NLM W 84 GA1 | DDC 362.1–dc23
LC record available at https://lccn.loc.gov/2017016350

ISBN 978-1-107-06980-0 Hardback
ISBN 978-1-107-63787-0 Paperback

CONTENTS

Preface   vii

1   **Solidarity: Backgrounds, Concerns and Claims**   1

1.1   An Emerging Interest in Solidarity   1

1.2   Origins of the Concept   3

1.3   Solidarity and Social Reform   10

1.4   Concerns about Solidarity   11

1.5   Solidarity as 'Interest Solidarity'   22

1.6   Five Claims about Solidarity   24

2   **The Origins of Solidarity as a Sociological Concept**   30

2.1   The Individualisation of Society in Post-Revolutionary France   31

2.2   Individualism and Enlightened Self-Interest: The Views
of Alexis De Tocqueville   37

2.3   The Call for Solidarity   40

2.4   Solidarism: The Contribution of Léon Bourgeois   43

2.5   The 'Solidarismus' of Heinrich Pesch S.J.   47

2.6   Comte and the Birth of Sociology   51

2.7   Durkheim on Solidarity   54

2.8   Marcel Mauss and the Gift Relationship   62

2.9   Solidarity in the Sociology of Max Weber   64

2.10   Conclusion   69

3   **Solidarity and Justice**   71

3.1   Introduction   71

3.2   Rawls's Theory of Justice   72

3.3   Justice and Health: The Extension by Daniels   75

3.4   The Critique from the Capabilities Approach   77

3.5   Restrictive Approaches to Justice   81

3.6   The 'Cold Side' of Justice   84

3.7   The Challenge from Libertarianism   86

3.8   Justice and Humiliation   87

3.9   The Perspective of Solidarity   91
3.10   The Communitarian Response   96
3.11   Solidarity and Recognition of Individual Differences   101
3.12   The Connection Between Solidarity and Justice   104
3.13   Conclusion   108

4   **Solidarity and Individual Responsibility in Dutch Health Care**   109
4.1   Introduction   109
4.2   Solidarity in Dutch Health Care: Backgrounds and Developments   110
4.3   Challenges to Solidarity: Trends in Costs and Income Transfer   115
4.4   Cost Control, Priority-Setting and Needs Assessment   118
4.5   Personal Responsibility in Social Care   122
4.6   Private Solutions   126
4.7   Market Competition and Individual Responsibility   128
4.8   Individual Responsibility for Health   132
4.9   The Future of Solidarity in Dutch Health Care   134
4.10   Conclusion   138

5   **Family Solidarity and Informal Care**   141
5.1   Introduction   141
5.2   Informal Care   144
5.3   A Different Type of Solidarity   148
5.4   Professional Support and Recognition in Informal Care   151
5.5   Communitarianism Revisited   154
5.6   Reflective Solidarity   158
5.7   Reflective Solidarity and Care   162
5.8   Conclusion   164

6   **Why We Need Solidarity**   167
6.1   From the Social to the Moral (Claim One)   168
6.2   Solidarity and Justice (Claim Two)   170
6.3   Solidarity and Subsidiarity (Claim Three)   173
6.4   Solidarity and Individuality (Claim Four)   176
6.5   Solidarity: An Exclusive European Value? (Claim Five)   178
6.6   Conclusion   184

References   187
Index   202

PREFACE

The idea of solidarity played an important role in many social movements in the past two centuries. Solidarity meant a preference for collaboration as a way to reach common goals as well as a justification for the subservience of one's individual interests to the collective interest of the group or of society. Solidarity was a widespread principle in various small-scale brotherhoods and associations to help the poor, but it evolved into a major principle in the build-up of welfare state arrangements in many countries in continental Europe from the 1880s onwards. Solidarity meant that the strong individuals or groups in society would set some of their direct interests aside to help the weaker groups in getting access to important societal services. It meant, for example, that individuals paid a financial contribution to collective and compulsory insurance system which enabled the weaker groups to have access to adequate health and long-term care. Solidarity became engrained in many European welfare states as the major distributive principle to enable access to health and social care, pensions and financial compensation for unemployment or lack of income due to illness. Though it has for a long time been a popular and widely supported principle, recent developments have put in doubt the sustainability of solidarity as a distributive principle for welfare and social arrangements, particularly for health and social care. The most important of these developments are the scarcity of resources, neoliberal ideologies, the introduction of market forces in health care and the emphasis on individualism and free choice.

An important problem in this context is the lack of a clear definition of the concept. This may have contributed to increasing doubts about the suitability of solidarity as a guiding principle for the organisation of health care systems, and for the rise of competitive concepts offered by the philosophy of justice. The concept of justice, particularly the accompanying language of rights, interests and obligations, benefits and burdens, pervades much of the contemporary debate on equitable access to health care. Contractual liberalism transforms the concept of solidarity in a rational decision to support societal arrangements, which should guarantee the basic rights and interests of individuals. Solidarity is then primarily conceptualised as the motivation of individuals to support the existing systems of health care and social protection. This support is balanced mainly in regard to the financial contributions by the individuals to the system, on the one hand, and on the other hand, the benefits they are expecting from the system in case they become needy themselves (so-called 'interest' solidarity).

Though the concept of solidarity has been losing its appeal in some social areas and policy domains, it has at the same time received an increasing attention in the field of bioethics like, for example, in recent reports by the *Nuffield Council on Bioethics* (2009; 2012). The importance of relationships and responsibility in health and social care as suggested in the term 'solidarity' seems to fit well with the call for social and relational approaches in bioethics and particularly to the principle of respect for autonomy. Against the predominantly liberal and libertarian views of many authors in bioethics, feminist writers and other authors emphasise that human beings are situated in networks of cooperation and dependency, and that liberal views of autonomy are disconnected with how individuals in the 'real world' perceive their relations with one another. 'Solidarity' expresses this idea of mutual dependency and is thought to function as a counterweight to the idea of the individual as an independent and abstract bearer of rights seeking his or her own individual interests.

The liberal discourse about the moral obligations between individuals in health and social care has concealed the very relational meanings of the concept of solidarity. This is particularly true for the fundamental role of human relationships in regard with the development of personal autonomy as well as recognition of the other. Continental philosophical frameworks put more emphasis on these relationships as the precondition for human flourishing and mutual recognition. Philosophers inspired by G. W. F. Hegel, like for example Axel Honneth (1995) and Rahel Jaeggi (2001), base solidarity on the mutual relatedness and fundamental interdependency of individuals. Solidarity refers to relations of support and understanding between individuals engaged in non-calculating cooperative practices based on identification with a common cause.

The focus on mutual relations and recognition of the other makes solidarity a distinctive concept in relation to justice. However, solidarity does not replace justice. As Habermas (1989) argues, liberal justice is not wrong, but it is one-sided. Its foundation in the calculations of autonomous individuals obscures the importance of an inter-subjective life-form that supports individual autonomy by keeping up relations of mutual recognition. Habermas sees justice and solidarity as two sides of a coin: justice concerns the rights and liberties of autonomous, self-interested individuals, whereas solidarity concerns the mutual recognition and well-being of the members who are connected in the life world.

However, there are concerns that the idea of solidarity is not promoting individual autonomy, but is in fact suppressing it, by emphasising the importance of the group and the subservience of individual goals to the common goals set by a group or society. This concern may have been fuelled by some communitarian philosophers who argue that the individualism of modern society presents a threat to communality and solidarity. However, this view is based on a negative moral view on the process of individualisation as leading to hedonism, consumerism, lack of social commitment and a narcissistic 'I' culture. Such an interpretation of individualism fails to appreciate that individualism also has a positive connotation in which it refers to self-realisation, individual responsibility and emancipation of traditional social ties. Individualisation can go well together with a feeling of responsibility towards the other and support for the weakest in society. Modern theories on solidarity (Dean 1995) argue for a 'reflective' approach to solidarity in which the importance of communities and the need for development and recognition of individual differences are reconciled with each other.

In the past twenty-five years I have tried to put the concept of solidarity as applied to health and social care on the bioethical and political agenda. In a range of publications I have analysed the moral significance of the concept, particularly in comparison with the concept of justice, for debates on the allocation of resources in healthcare. I have underlined the importance of 'humanitarian' solidarity which reflects the concern and responsibility for individuals who are not able any more to take care of themselves due to debilitating conditions and diseases, like dementia and psychiatric disorders.

My thinking on these issues got an important stimulus during my work as coordinator of the project *Solidarity and Care in the European Union* funded by the European Commission in the Fourth Framework Program-BIOMED 2 (Project ID BMH 4983971). This project, which lasted from 1998–2000 and which included seven European universities and research institutes combined sociological research into solidarity in health and social care with a philosophical project reflecting on the ethical and philosophical significance of solidarity (ter Meulen, Arts and Muffels 2001). I am much indebted to my colleagues Ruud Muffels and Wil Arts of the University of Tilburg who led the sociological research in this project and helped me to better understand solidarity as a sociological concept. I am incredibly indebted to Rob Houtepen of the University of Maastricht with whom I coordinated the philosophical research on solidarity in the above mentioned European project. Rob has been extremely creative and productive in regard with philosophical approaches to solidarity. He supplied many ideas which helped me to further develop my understanding of solidarity as a philosophical concept. My thinking on solidarity in health and social care arrangements was enriched by the collaboration with Hans Maarse of the University of Maastricht. Hans' thorough knowledge of health policy and market reform in health care has helped me to get a deeper understanding of solidarity as a principle in the organisation and reform of health care systems in the Netherlands and elsewhere in Europe.

I am also indebted to the Nuffield Council on Bioethics for inviting me to become member of the Working Party on *Dementia: ethical issues* led by Tony Hope. The participation in this project deepened my understanding of the ethical issues of dementia and of the contribution the concept of solidarity might make to support the care for people suffering from this horrible disease. I am thanking Tony for supporting my contributions on solidarity and dementia care, and Katherine Wright of the Nuffield Council for her collaboration on the topic of solidarity and family care for people with dementia.

Special words of thanks are for the Brocher Foundation for granting me a two-month residential fellowship at their accommodation in Hermance located near the beautiful Lake Geneva. The serenity of this idyllic place helped me to focus on my work for this book and to write its philosophical chapter. I also thank the research team and support staff at the Hastings Center in Garrison, New York, during my stay as a Visiting Scholar in the summer of 2015 and 2016. Their critical comments during the famous lunchtime presentations and other individual meetings were incredibly helpful and helped to further shape my understanding of solidarity and the role it might play in American health care. A lot of thanks to the staff at the ETHOX Centre in Oxford for their support and interest in my work during my stay in February 2016. Their comments to my presentation and discussions at other meetings were very helpful and supportive. I thank the Wellcome Trust for awarding me a small grant (WT104688MA) to relieve me from my teaching duties during my stay at the Brocher Foundation and the Hastings Center as well as to pay for my travel to Geneva and New York.

There are many other people I would like to thank for their support and interest. First of all, I want to thank Gerlof Verwey, old friend and former colleague at the Department of Philosophical Anthropology at the Catholic University of Nijmegen (now Radboud University). I have fond memories of our conversations during his holidays to the United Kingdom together with his wife Monica Meijsing. Gerlof's warm support and strong interest in my work were invaluable. His comments to Chapter 3 have greatly improved the philosophical quality and consistency of this chapter. Special thanks also to my good old friend Donna Dickenson for her great support and valuable advice. I thank Martine Annandale, my French teacher at the Alliance Française of Bristol and Bath, for her assistance with the translation of some of the French quotes in Chapter 2. There are many other people who I want to thank for their support or their input into the book by way of various conversations or collaborations. I want to thank particularly: Simone Bateman, Daniel Callahan, Michael Campbell, Ruth Chadwick, Alan Cribb, Marie Gaille, Michael Gusmano, Ruth Horn, Richard Huxtable, Bruce Jennings, Satoshi Kodama, Darian Meacham, Michael Parker, Paul Schotsmans, Mats Thorslund and Rudy Verburg.

This book is particularly dedicated to my wife Hetty Penterman and to my children Hanna and Simon. Their continuous support and interest in my work were of extreme importance and were indispensable to finish this book.

Solidarity

Backgrounds, Concerns and Claims

1.1 An Emerging Interest in Solidarity

In bioethics, there is an emerging interest in the concept of solidarity. An important milestone was the publication of the report *Solidarity: Reflections on an Emerging Concept in Bioethics*, written by Barbara Prainsack and Alena Buyx and published by the *Nuffield Council on Bioethics* in 2011. A few years earlier, the Nuffield Council on Bioethics published a report on the ethical issues in dementia which presented an ethical framework in which solidarity was included as one of its main principles (2009). This initiative was followed by the publication of a special issue in the journal *Bioethics* on the role of solidarity in bioethics with contributions on the theoretical status of the concept as well as on the role solidarity might play in ethical debates on organ donation, research with children, dementia care and global health (2012). There have also been applications of the concept of solidarity to the field of genetic databases and biobanks, particularly by Ruth Chadwick (Chadwick 1999; Chadwick & Berg 2001) and Prainsack and Buyx (2017).

The emerging interest in solidarity may be rooted in dissatisfaction with mainstream bioethics, particularly the emphasis on the principle of respect for autonomy as the main principle of the so-called Four Principles of Bioethics (Beauchamp & Childress 2012). Particularly the liberal interpretation of the principle of autonomy could be considered as the main reason for the increased attention to other, more relational, approaches of autonomy. Prainsack and Buyx (2011), for example, put solidarity forward as an alternative to an individualised concept of autonomy, in which the individual is seen as a rational decision-maker who is mainly guided by enlightened self-interest. As opposed to such a narrow view of the individual, Prainsack and Buyx (2011) argue that a solidarity-based approach considers human persons as shaped by their social relations and that social and political arrangements should take such relations into account instead of the arrangements that only look at individual interests. Further explorations of the relation between autonomy and solidarity can be found in a special issue of the journal *Theoretical Medicine and Bioethics* (2016).

Solidarity seems to be based on a different philosophical anthropology, meaning an anthropology which emphasises the importance of relationships as a condition to realise autonomy, instead of considering this autonomy as already given. This contextual approach to autonomy leads to different moral obligations, particularly a responsibility for the wellbeing of the other. The dementia report of the Nuffield Council on Bioethics, for example, states that solidarity is the idea that we are 'fellow-travellers' and 'that we have duties to support and help each other and in particular those who cannot readily support themselves' (Nuffield Council on Bioethics 2009). Solidarity, the report argues, underpins the duties of individual and society to support those with dementia and their caregivers and to reinforce our responsibility towards them. This suggests that the perspective from solidarity opens a different perspective on duties and responsibilities in health and social care than the traditional accounts in bioethics.

While the interest in bioethics in the concept of solidarity is rather recent, the concept does have a long tradition as a principle to organise access to health care and other social services in European welfare states. According to this principle the stronger groups in society are expected to make a financial contribution to a collectively organised insurance system which enables access to health and social care for the weaker groups (ter Meulen, Arts and Muffels 2001). However, welfare states have been in decline in the past decades, and it is questionable to which extent solidarity can be maintained as a principle to guide the distribution of welfare and the access to health and social care. Solidarity seems to be at odds with the increasing individualism and neoliberal reform agenda which put a strong emphasis on individual freedom and personal financial responsibility. Is solidarity with its emphasis on social cooperation not an outmoded concept that has no place in a modern society where individuality and personal differences play such an important role? Is solidarity not stifling autonomy and individuality in the interest of the common good?

Moreover, there is an important question why we should refer to solidarity if, as is usual in bioethics, there is the concept of justice which tries to find a fair balance between benefits and burdens. If we do not agree with libertarian or liberal-egalitarian accounts of justice, because of their obsession with the enlightened self-interest of individuals, is solidarity the right concept to look at? As Illingworth and Parmet (2012) argue in the Editorial to the Special Issue of Bioethics: 'what does solidarity offer that other ethical concepts, such as justice, communitarianism, egalitarianism, or even altruism, do not?'

This book will try to answer the question posed by Illingworth and Parmet: what is the specific contribution of solidarity as a moral principle to policy-making in health care? What can solidarity offer to the moral analysis of societal obligations as compared to rival accounts like liberal justice or communitarianism? Should solidarity replace justice or should it be a complimentary approach? At the same time, the book will try to answer some other important questions about the relation of solidarity and autonomy. If we think that solidarity is a valuable concept, can it be combined with the moral agenda of autonomy, individual choice and responsibility? This analysis will not only be relevant for theoretical debates in bioethics, but also for policy-making in countries where governments and policy-makers are increasingly struggling with the concept of solidarity and particularly the *limits* of solidarity as a moral principle in regard with the access to welfare state arrangements. While solidarity had a massive influence in the build-up of welfare states in Europe, what is the contribution of this concept when welfare states are in decline or retrenched as they have been in the past four decades? Finally, what can the concept offer to countries with a more individualistic culture, like, for example, the United States?

1.2 Origins of the Concept

The idea of solidarity has a long history with roots in various traditions and discourses. This rather confounded history makes it sometimes difficult to define or to pin down to a specific meaning. Solidarity means something different for example in sociology, where it is used as a descriptive concept, as compared to moral and political discourses where solidarity is used as a normative concept. To get a better understanding, of these various meanings, this section will present three main sources of the concept of solidarity: French sociology in the nineteenth century, the socialist movement and Catholic social teaching. Some of these sources, particularly the roots in sociology, will be presented in more detail in the following chapters.

Solidarity in Early French Sociology

The idea of solidarity was first introduced by philosophers and political thinkers in nineteenth century France as a response to the increasing individualisation of French society, a process which was associated by some authors with the emphasis on individual rights following the French Revolution. In the 1840s the word 'solidarity' gradually emerged in the political debate, as well as in the sociological discourse, as an alternative for what many saw as the fragmentation of French society (de Swart 1962). 'Solidarity' was increasingly seen by social critics as a solution for the social problems resulting from the lack of community, and also for the increasing industrialisation. Before the political and social discourse, the term solidarity was used in law to express the mutual indebtedness of the members of a legal enterprise. The principle of mutual assistance or unlimited liability of individuals was called 'obligation in solidum' (Bayertz 1999). 'Solidarity' designated the accountability of each member of a certain community for the debts of any other. Normally this would hold for families, but the French word *solidarité*, for instance, was originally used in the context of partnerships in law firms (Hayward 1959).

The word solidarity permeated gradually the sociopolitical discourse as an alternative to the individualism in French society on the one hand, and to anarchist, utopian, socialist positions on the other hand. In other words, solidarity became associated with a middle position between individualism and collectivism, a conciliatory type of social morality and social organisation that presented itself as a harmonious alternative to extreme positions on both sides of the political spectre (Hayward 1959). The word solidarity expressed the idea that individuals are connected with each other, not only in the contemporary society, but also with societies and individuals in the past. However, the connectedness was not seen as just an empirical, social fact: the fact that we are mutually connected implied also a *guilt* towards society and a *moral responsibility* for fellow human beings. This connection was strongly emphasised in the emerging discipline of sociology, and has remained a key feature of many interpretations of the concept in French sociological, political and economic discourse (Reisz 2007).

The idea of solidarity became entrenched in French social and political thought by the work of Léon Bourgeois, political leader and ideologue of the Radical Party which came into power in 1895. Bourgeois took up the idea of solidarity to reform the French Republic and introduce various laws to improve the situation of the poor and disadvantaged groups in French society. Bourgeois developed the ideology of 'solidarism' as a synthesis between the *laissez-faire* policies of economic liberalism and the collectivism of socialism and communism (Bourgeois 1896). The idea of solidarity, which was central in the 'solidarism' of Bourgeois, was based on the idea that individuals are connected with and dependent on each other: the isolated individual does not exist. The solidarism of Bourgeois became the official ideology for social reform by collective action in France from the late nineteenth century and early twentieth century onwards (Hayward 1961; Donzelot 1994).

As will be presented in more detail in Chapter 2, it was the French sociologist Emile Durkheim who laid the groundwork for the concept of solidarity in modern sociological thought. According to Durkheim, solidarity is a 'moral phenomenon': The goals of solidarity are moral goals, like social harmony and taking care of the needs of others. However, the implantation of social morality cannot be based on voluntary actions or cognitive processes only: the state should pay an important role in implementing moral rules. Social solidarity, according to Durkheim, is the result of an acceptance of the moral authority of the state, but this acceptance is based on a voluntary decision.

The connection between moral motives and empirical observations, which was typical for French sociology, came to an end in the first decennia of the twentieth century. This was due to the work of the German sociologist Max Weber who argued that sociology should not get involved in moral discussions or policies, but should limit itself to 'objective' and descriptive statements about social and cultural reality. In the effort to become a value-free science, solidarity became a descriptive concept to describe the degree of social cohesion in a group or society whereby individuals are willing to serve and promote the collective interest of the group or of society. An important part of sociological theory and research has been trying to find out the motivations why individuals want to serve the collective interest and how strong these motivations are.

Solidarity in the Socialist Movement

A second root of the concept of solidarity lies in the labour movement and in socialist theory. When discussing the concept of solidarity (particularly in the Anglo-American context) there is often the question whether we are talking about the Polish trade union 'Solidarnosc' which was leading the protests in the 1980s against the Polish communist regime. There is indeed a strong connection between solidarity and the struggle of the working class to improve living and work conditions by the change or overthrow of capitalist society. In socialist theory, solidarity means that the members of the working class have joint interests and should work together to reach a class-free society. Solidarity in the socialist tradition stands for social cooperation and mutual assistance whereby the members of the working class put their own individual interests aside to reach a common goal. There are two interpretations of solidarity in the works of Karl Marx (Stjernø 2004): the first one is the traditional brotherhood in capitalist society which is restricted to the working class and which has the goal to overthrow capitalist production. The second connotation of solidarity in Marx's work is solidarity in post-capitalist society or communism in which there is a genuine companion-ship and community life. Marxist theory developed into two different lines, with Leninism on the one hand and social democracy on the other hand. While Leninism limited solidarity to the working class, social democracy broadened the concept of solidarity to all those who were exploited and who could improve their living conditions by working together.

The social-democratic conception of solidarity was founded by the work of Karl Kautsky (1910) who argued that solidarity should not be embraced by the industrial proletariat only, but should include all wage earners in society (Stjernø 2004). It was Eduard Bernstein who developed the modern social-democratic version of solidarity as part of his revi-sionist version of Marxist theory. As capitalism had survived many crises and seemed not to break down in the near future, Bernstein (1899) developed the view that the working class could only improve their condition by seeking alliances with other classes and groups to establish a majority in Parliament. Instead of revolution as Marx and Lenin claimed, he argued for an evolutionary approach in which the Social-democratic party should try to achieve gradual improvements of the working class by way of parliamentary action.

An important part of Bernstein's social-democratic approach, which became influential in many European countries at the beginning of the twentieth century, was a socialist ethics which consisted of three core elements: equality, solidarity and freedom or autonomy (Stjernø 2004). The three elements needed to be balanced against each other: solidarity against autonomy, equality against individual freedom. The workers should sacrifice some of their personal autonomy and to engage in collective action to gain an improvement of their living conditions and their own freedom. But this sacrifice has its limits in personal autonomy. According to Stjernø (2004), Bernstein was the first to articulate the ethical component of socialist discourse and to emphasise the role of values, including solidarity and autonomy. However, the relation or balance between these two values remained unclear and have led to tensions in social-democratic thought.

Since the early twentieth century, social-democratic parties have been key players at the political scene in many European countries and have been largely responsible for the build-up of the welfare states in collaboration with Christian-democratic parties. Solidarity expressed the need for collaboration between individuals of all classes to work towards a better future, but it should be combined with respect for autonomy and individual freedom (Stjernø 2004). This ethical position sets the social democrats' concept of solidarity apart from Leninist theory in which the collective, and the solidarity with the collective, is overruling all other values or principles.

Catholic Teaching: Solidarity and Subsidiarity

A third root of solidarity lies in Catholic social teaching. The idea of solidarity as part of Catholic social thought was initially developed in the 'solidarism' of the Jesuit Heinrich Pesch around the turn of the nineteenth and into the twentieth century. 'Solidarism', which will be further explored in Chapter 2, was developed as an alternative to the 'collectivism' of socialism on the one hand and the 'ruthless individualism' of liberalism on the other hand. A key element of solidarism is the responsibility of all individuals for the well-being of the social community. Individual and society are fundamentally reciprocal, and because of this reciprocity individuals have an ethical duty to assist each other, which is the duty of solidarity. The individual Christian conscience is directed towards the whole and this leads to feelings of togetherness, sacrifice, self-limitation, subordination of individual interests and Christian love (Reisz 2007). This social orientation of the Christian conscience is the basis for a corporatist order of society in which not equality is the leading principle, but the creation and maintenance of an order of professions and classes where everyone should find his place and is related to others by obligations of love and justice.

Though Pesch developed solidarism into a philosophically consistent social theory, it did not receive many followers. One of the reasons was the change in Catholic philosophy from neoscholasticism towards social personalism (ter Meulen 1988). The solidarism of Pesch which was based on a scholastic ontology in which the individual was seen as an isolated ego for whom the relation with other individuals and society in general was just an instrument to develop his or her own goals. In social personalism, which became influential from the 1930s, this view was criticised: The relation with the other is not just a means for personal development, but is in itself a necessary part of this personal development (ter Meulen 2000; Verstraete 1998; Verstraete 2005; Stjernø 2004). Only by assisting the other and by taking part in the existence of the other, one can reach one's destiny. Solidarity and social engagement in social personalism were founded as ethical duties in the personal, social existence of man and no longer in an abstract ontology as was the case in Pesch's solidarism.

However, it was not just philosophical critique that was responsible for the lack of interest in solidarism in the Catholic Church. The term 'solidarity' raised suspicions because of its link with the, allegedly anti-Christian, socialist movement (Doran 1996). Instead of solidarity, 'charity' or caring for the needy was for many Catholic writers the key word to express the social commitment of the believer. It lasted until the post-war period and particularly the Second Vatican Council before solidarity was officially embraced by the Popes and the Vatican. Pius XII argued that the awareness of mutual necessity leads to the expression of solidarity which combines independence with collaboration. Pope John XXIII firmly established solidarity in Catholic social doctrine by way of his encyclical *Mater et Magistra* (1961). According to Pope John the principle of mutual solidarity is to be a guiding principle of the establishment of associations of workers and the relations between workers and employers (Doran 1996). He expanded the principle of solidarity to humanity and the needs of people in developing countries. In the Encyclical *Laborem Exercens* (1981) Pope John Paul II embraced the concept of solidarity as an action-oriented concept that is meant to support the actions of workers to improve their circumstances by creating unity and community, particularly as a reaction towards an unjust system (Dorr 1983). In *Centesimus Annus* (1991) John Paul again emphasised the role of solidarity in the struggle of individuals for improvement of their living conditions and for social justice (Verstraeten 2004).

Though solidarity is often associated with Catholic thought, the concept has never reached a firm position in Catholic social doctrine as compared to the principle of subsidiarity. This principle has to do with the help society owes to its members (*subsidium* means assistance). The best type of help society can offer is that which results in self-help (von Nell-Breuning 1978). All care or help offered by society should have the purpose to enable, to ease and to encourage the individual's development by stimulating the individual's own resources and potentials. When one tries to help and support someone else by taking the other one's place and by ignoring the possibilities of this needy other, one does not help the other. Instead, one keeps the other under tutelage and dependent by hindering the development of talents and potentials. According to the subsidiarity principle, this help is no help at all, but an obstruction of the self-development of the other (ter Meulen 2000).

The principle of subsidiarity puts limits to solidarity organised by the state: it prescribes that society should only support the ill and dependent on a supplementary basis. Social support can help a person to overcome his troubles by using his own powers and resources. Therefore the state cannot take free initiative on a lower level of society: whatever individuals can do by themselves should not be taken over by a higher level (ter Meulen 2000). However, the principle can be interpreted in a restrictive and an expansive way: the restrictive interpretations called for a limited role of the welfare state and of the principle of solidarity, while the expansive interpretation argued for a generous interpretation of solidarity and an expansion of the welfare state (Verstraeten 1998).

In the early sixties, Pope John XXIII emphasised the positive interference of the state in social life in *Mater et Magistra*. For John, the principle of subsidiarity was not an argument for limiting the role of the state, but an argument for grounding this in a positive sense, that is by formulating it as a fundamental moral duty of the government (ter Meulen 2000). The independence of the civilian should not be limited, but if civilians fail to assist one another, the government should develop initiatives together with the civilians. While John XXIII's position supported the development of the welfare state, John Paul II took a much more restrictive position in his encyclicals than the Pope of the *Aggiornamento*. According to Verstraeten (1998), John Paul II's ideas were strongly influenced by his experiences with collectivism and 'real socialism' in the Eastern European states in the post-war period. John Paul II was especially critical of the welfare state, which according to him has led to dependency and a lack of own responsibility and civil initiatives (Centesimus Annus 1991). The individualistic mentality in our current society needs to be replaced by a 'concrete commitment to solidarity and charity'. This commitment should start in the family and apart from that in intermediate communities and 'networks of solidarity'. These real communities of persons will strengthen the social fabric, preventing society from becoming an anonymous and impersonal mass. It is by personal relations on many levels that society can become more 'person-alised' (Centesimus Annus 1991).

The restrictive interpretation of solidarity argues for a retreat of the welfare state and for the fostering of concrete networks of solidarity. These arguments concur to some extent with the call for deregulation and retreat of the welfare state as advocated by neoliberal ideologues. However, the neoliberal call for markets as the guiding principle of public and private services in modern societies is difficult to reconcile with the Catholic call for social personhood. This is particularly true for health care where market-based economic principles and consumerist ideologies can have a destructive impact on care relations and personal solidarity (ter Meulen 2000).

1.3   Solidarity and Social Reform

At the time when the idea of solidarity was introduced and debated as a principle for social reform, there was already a range of local initiatives and small systems of social security and medical support. In a number of countries in the late nineteenth and early twentieth century, groups of people with a social conscience like community leaders, employers and physicians worked together to provide financial support and access to medical care for those in need (Companje et al. 2009). Sometimes initiatives for mutual support were taken by labourers and artisans themselves. One could define these initiatives as types of concrete and personal solidarity where the individuals felt personally responsible for the well-being and fate of the other and his or her family (Houtepen, ter Meulen and Widdershoven 2001). As the local and spontaneous support became increasingly difficult to maintain, these types of solidarity were gradually taken over by the state which set up a system of financing and provision of social and medical support. Solidarity became enforced by the state with compulsory payment of an insurance premium in exchange for access to medical care or financial support in case of medical need or social distress: this development meant the introduction of solidarity as a normative criterion for the operating of a system of public health care, besides or above the local spontaneous types of solidarity.

State-enforced solidarity was first developed in the early eighties of the nineteenth century by the German Chancellor Graf Otto von Bismarck, who introduced a public insurance system which was meant to compensate workers for the impact of accidents, disability and illness. Health care insurance was financed by contributions by the employers and by workers, respectively, for two-third and one-third of the costs of the premium. The health insurance system was executed by a variety of sickness funds which already existed or were erected for this special purpose (De Swaan 1989). The individuals who were insured within the Bismarck system were entitled to medical support and sick pay for a certain period. Bismarck's project was particularly developed to counteract the increasing power of the socialist movement, though it was also meant to soften the oppressive anti-socialist law (Sozialistengesetz) of 1878 (de Swaan 1989). Representatives of workers became increasingly involved in the administration of the system. Together with employers, worker organisations and their representatives are still overseeing the sickness funds which play a powerful role in contemporary Germany.

In the three decennia after Bismarck introduced his system, the principle of compulsory health care insurance was followed by several other countries including Belgium, Austria, France and Switzerland. The Netherlands followed in 1941 by force of the German occupier. Social insurance became increasingly seen as the main technology to deal with 'the social question', with 'solidarity' as the ideological legitimisation for the introduction of these insurances (Donzelot 1994). Some other European countries, particularly the United Kingdom and the Scandinavian countries, did not follow Bismarck's example, but developed a system of health care and social support based on a taxation scheme instead of a compulsory health care insurance. The leading example is the British National Health Service (NHS), founded by William Beveridge just after the Second World War. The NHS is funded by a national insurance which is collected via the national tax system and which provides access to health care for all British citizens based on need. Though solidarity is not explicitly referred in these tax-based health care systems, much of their policies have the same social goals as the solidarity-based, insurance-based systems for health care.

1.4 Concerns about Solidarity

The basic understanding of solidarity in welfare states is that everyone is assumed to make a fair financial contribution to a collectively organised insurance system that guarantees equal access to health and social care for all members of society. In fact, solidarity and equal access to care are strongly related: they can be considered the twin principles underlying insurance-based health care systems (ter Meulen, Arts and Muffels 2001).

Though prudence is a strong drive in the acceptance of compulsory solidarity, many understand this type of solidarity as a feeling of mutual responsibility and a motivation to support those who need care and who are not able to pay for care out of their own means.

In the decades after the Second World War solidarity-based policies, which were widely supported by Christian-democratic and Social-democratic parties (Stjernø 2004), led to generous systems of support for a range of social and medical needs. Solidarity became synonymous with unlimited collective responsibility leading to a universal, state provided safety net for illness and disability, as well as for unemployment, work related illness and pensioning. However, since the last decennium of the twentieth century, there is an increasing concern whether such an unlimited and generous interpretation of solidarity is sustainable. Several developments are the cause of these concerns.

Scarcity of Resources

First, there is the issue of the *scarcity of resources*, caused by the widening gap between growing demands for care on the one hand, and limited supply of care on the other hand. The rise in the demand for care is due to the ageing of the population, and particularly the increasing number of octogenarians. In 2013, life expectancy at birth in the EU-28 was estimated at 80.9 years, reaching 83.3 years for women and 77.8 years for men (Eurostat 2015). These figures mean that over the past 50 years of life expectancy at birth has increased by about 10 years for both men and women in the EU-28 (Eurostat 2015). However, as this increase in life expectancy, which is mainly due to a reduction in mortality at older ages, goes hand in hand with reduced fertility, a sharp increase is going on in the share of aged persons in the total population of the EU-28. At the moment the percentage of people over 65 years of age in the 28 EU countries is 18.5 per cent, a number that is expected to rise to nearly 28.4 per cent in 2060 (Eurostat 2015). The percentage of people over 80 years is expected to increase from 5.1 per cent of the total population to 11.8 per cent in 2060 and even 12.3 per cent in 2080. While the old-age dependency ratio was 28.1 per cent in 2014, this figure will be doubled to 51 per cent by 2080.

While the average life expectancy has risen, there are concerns about the implications of this development for the health status and the burden of disease of the older population. There are different scenarios with respect to the growing burden of disease. The pessimistic scenario argues that increased longevity has not resulted in an improvement in our health and that we will inevitably be living in decreased health for at least 18–22 years of our lives. This scenario is called the theory of expansion of disability and is coined by Gruenberg as the 'failures of success' (Gruenberg 1977). A more optimistic scenario is based on the theory of 'compression of morbidity' (Fries 1980; Fries 2005). This theory argues that an improvement in therapy and prevention will lead to increased longevity as well as a shorter period of disability. Lafortune and Balestat (2007) argue in a review of trends in disability in the ageing population of 12 OECD countries, that it is difficult to draw a conclusion about the direction of the trend in disability levels. There is clear evidence of a decline in disability among elderly people in five of the twelve countries (Denmark, Finland, Italy, the Netherlands and the United States), but three countries (Belgium, Japan and Sweden) witnessed an increasing rate of severe disability among people aged 65 and over during the past five to ten years, while two countries (Australia, Canada) report a stable rate. In France and the United Kingdom, data from different surveys show different trends in ADL (Activities of Daily Living) disability rates among elderly people. Lafortune and Balestat (2007) argue that though disability prevalence rates have declined to some extent in recent years in some countries, 'the ageing of the population and the greater longevity of individuals can be expected to lead to increasing numbers of people at older ages with a severe disability' (Lafortune and Balestat 2007: 7). The conclusion of the review is that due to the ageing of the population, 'there will be a need to expand the capacity to respond to the growing need for long-term care over the coming years in all OECD countries' (Lafortune and Balestat 2007: 7). The need for care will particularly be high in the age group of 80 years and above, who are at an increased risk of chronic and debilitating conditions like arthritis, stroke, dementia, depression and chronic heart disease.

Besides ageing, the demand for care is increased down by the rising costs of medical technology. This process is reinforced by changes in attitudes of individuals regarding quality and access to care: instead of the humble, authority-sensitive attitude of the past, modern patients have become critical and self-assertive consumers who are well informed about the possibilities of treatment and the types of services that are available. This consumerist attitude is becoming widespread under the 'baby-boom' generation and is expected to become dominant in the next elder generations. Particularly there are higher expectations regarding diagnostics, leading to increased pressures on doctors to approve access to these, often costly, services for their patients. These developments will lead to an increased pressure on the various national health care budgets.

While the demand for care is growing, national governments are under pressure to preserve or to downturn the level of public spending. In several European countries this pressure results from the creation of the European Monetary Union (EMU) which has forced national governments to comply with strict measures regarding the level of public spending and the government deficit. But also outside the EMU, for example, in the United Kingdom, governments have been taking measures in the past ten years to reduce the public deficit by cuts on public spending on health and social care. The NHS, for example, is forced to make (efficiency) savings of £20 billion by 2020, while city councils in England and Wales, which are responsible for social care, are confronted with draconian cuts of their budgets. Though the banking crisis and the resulting economic crisis are largely responsible for these 'austerity' policies, these policies are also influenced by political doctrines in regard with a limited role of the state in the development of the economy and in the organisation of society in general (see later in this chapter). Because of these policies there is a growing gap between the demand and the supply of care resulting in a shortage of care services and diminishing quality of care, particularly in long-term care for the elderly.

In the United Kingdom, a recent report by the King's Fund reported that due to cuts and grant reductions by the central government local authorities are struggling to take care of the needs of dependent older people (Humphries et al. 2016). The past six years of government austerity have brought unprecedented pressures on social care in the United Kingdom, not only by the cuts, but also by shortages of nurses and care workers, higher regulatory standards and measures to introduce the Living Wage. At the same time the number of delayed discharges from hospitals is rising rapidly due to the lack of funding for care at home (Care Quality Commission 2016). At the same time the NHS is struggling because of financial pressures as demanded by the government's policy of 'efficiency savings'. Many social care providers are surviving by relying increasingly on people who can fund their own care. However, those who are dependent on local authority contracts are in difficulty, and are at risk to lose support and care at home. Local authorities have sought to protect the most vulnerable older people with the highest needs, while at the same time encouraging others to be independent, drawing on the resources of their families and communities, and to reduce dependence on support from the state (Humphries et al. 2016).

Neoliberalist Policies

A second threat to solidarity is the growing influence of neoliberalist ideologies which emphasises the role of individual responsibility and regards the market as a superior way to organise social institutions as opposed to 'big government' exercised by the state. The term 'neoliberalism' was introduced by the economists Ludwig von Mises and Friedrich Hayek in the 1930s as a response to the New Deal policies of Franklin D. Roosevelt in the United States and the development of the welfare state in the United Kingdom. These policies were regarded by Hayek and Von Mises as the result of collectivist ideologies which were not far away from the totalitarian control by National Socialism and fascism on the far right and communism on the far left side of the political spectrum (Hayek 2012).

Neoliberalism stands for *laissez-faire* politics in economics with a limited role of governments, minimal tax and regulation and large privatisation of public services. Governments should not try to create more equality in society as that would corrupt the moral attitudes of individuals. They should instead rely on the markets as be the market ensures that everyone gets what they deserve. There is also no need for trade unions or collective bargaining as these phenomena are distortions of the market which hinder the formation of winners and losers.

Neoliberalism was waiting in the wings in the post-war period, which in many European countries was dominated by Keynesian economic policies leading to a powerful role of the government in the economy and a strong expansion of the Welfare State. However, its time came in the seventies when generous policies came to a halt due to ever growing national debts, poor quality of public services, growing unemployment rates and increasing dependency on welfare payments. Welfare states were criticised as leading to lack of creativity, increased passivity, inefficiency and spiralling costs. The call for markets and private enterprise, unregulated by governments, became louder. Despite the disasters caused by neoliberalist policies by Latin-American dictatorships, neoliberalism as advocated by Hayek and Von Mises became *salonfähig* in Europe and the United States. The call for markets, reduction of taxes and deregulation and privatisation of public services was embraced by Margaret Thatcher and Ronald Reagan. Their example was followed by other countries and political parties (including the Labour Party under Tony Blair in the United Kingdom). The dominance of the neoliberal model was unrivalled: even after the financial and economic crisis starting in 2008 there were no alternative models for government policies (Monbiot 2016).

Neoliberalism is strongly driven by conservative motives as it wants to reinforce self-reliance of individuals instead of dependency on the state and state supported institutions:

> It is one aspect of the change in moral values brought about by the advance of collectivism which provided food for thought. It is that the virtues which are held less and less in esteem in Britain and America are precise those on which Anglo-Saxons justly prided themselves and in which they were generally recognized to excel. These virtues were independence and self-reliance, individual initiative and local responsibility, the successful reliance on voluntary activity, non-interference with one's neighbor and tolerance of the different, and a healthy suspicion of power and authority.
>
> (Hayek 2012: 56)

Individuals should take more initiative in organising their life and they should turn to their families and small civic societies when they need help instead of the welfare agencies of the state. In the neoliberal view, the 'minimal state' is the best way to generate social solidarity and the flourishing of personal virtues and good character, like honesty, service, self-discipline, consideration of others self-discipline and justice (Giddens 1998). The state is destructive to such virtues, but the markets are not, as they are thriving on individual initiatives (idem). Neoliberals have a strong belief in the role of markets (Dickenson 2013). Markets should be left alone, not only at the national, but also at the global level, where they will lead to universal prosperity. According to neoliberalism, social inequalities do not exist: there are only individuals who are trying to improve their life by working hard and try to accomplish whatever lies in their capabilities: 'Inequality is recast as virtuous: a reward for utility and a generator of wealth, which trickles down to everyone' (Monbiot 2016). Individuals do not need a generous welfare state, which is destructive for individual initiative.

Neoliberal policies consider market competition a superior way of organising health care services (and other public services, like social security) than a system in which the government plays a central and active role. By enforcing competition among health care providers and insurance companies as well as between them, there will be a substantial gain in efficiency, which supposedly will lead to a reduction of costs. An example is the introduction of market competition in health insurance in the Netherlands with the Health Insurance Act of 2006, which we will further explore in Chapter 4. Market competition is expected to encourage health insurers to negotiate favourable contracts with health care providers, which is supposed to lead to better quality of care, more choice for consumers and reduction of the costs of care (Maarse and ter Meulen 2006). In the United Kingdom since the 1990s, conservative and labour governments have tried to introduce market forces in the NHS. The Health and Social Care Act of 2013 introduced local and regional Clinical Commission Groups (CCGs), which are led by General Practitioners and which have the authority to purchase health and social services. As private providers may compete for the contracts, this policy is regarded by some authors as marketisation of the NHS by stealth (Pollock 2016).

It is part of the neoliberal belief that markets will enable consumers to make their own choices regarding their own health insurance and that they will gain more influence upon the accessibility and quality of health care. The state should put aside its paternalistic role of determining what is good for the patient or the way health care should be delivered: patients are consumers who can make their own choices on health insurance and health care delivery and who can be held responsible for those choices. Though there are many promises of individual choice and personal freedom, these principles play only a limited role in the new reformed systems which usually have public constraints regarding access to care and quality of care ('regulated competition'). In the Netherlands, for example, individual responsibility is the dominant discourse in government policy on health insurance and health care delivery. However, the actual policy is, in many ways, still restrictive and paternalistic, limiting free choice and autonomous decisions (Maarse and ter Meulen 2006).

Individual responsibility is not limited to choice: it also means an increased *financial* responsibility (ter Meulen & Maarse 2008). While in the past individuals had some financial responsibility for health care, like co-payments for medical drugs and services or deductibles in insurance policies, individual responsibility has now become an explicit element in many government policies. Financial contributions by individuals are a way to cut costs and to reduce the role of collective responsibility and solidarity as embodied in the public health system. Moreover, by making the individuals aware of the costs of health care, private financial contributions could have an inhibiting effect on the use of health care services, and thus reduce costs. However, such policies will have an impact on solidarity as direct, non-income related payments to insurers or care providers mean a greater burden for lower income groups than for higher incomes (ter Meulen, Arts and Muffels 2001).

Individualisation and Reflexivity

The call for free choice and personal autonomy, consumerism and markets in health care should also be seen from the perspective of the increasing individualisation of society. The term individualisation stems from sociology and refers to the dissolution of traditional bonds and communities which tied people together. This is a process that has been going on for several centuries and has, in modern times, resulted in a disembodiment of the individual as well as instability and changeability of social and personal relations (ter Meulen, Arts and Muffels 2001). In this process traditional norms and knowledge have become less certain and have lost their status as beacons to guide individuals through institutions and the life cycle (Giddens 1991). Individuals have become the organisers and agents of their own life, but without the guidance by traditional norms and institutions. The modern individual must constantly question and revise their living conditions, a process that has been coined by Giddens as *reflexive modernity*. According to Giddens social and individual life in modern times are characterised by reflexivity, meaning that these practices are constantly examined and reformed in the light of incoming information about these practices, thus constantly changing the character of these practices (Giddens 1990). Modernity is constituted in reflexively applied knowledge in which nothing is certain and everything is in constant revision and examination.

The process of modernisation and reflexivity has important consequences for individual lives and for the constitution and formation of identities. Identities are not fixed or based any more in traditional social patterns, but are formed and redefined in a constant process of revision and reflection in the context of social and intimate practices. Identities are 'a *trajectory* across the different institutional settings of modernity over the *durée* of what was called the "life cycle". Modernity is focused on the questions "who shall I be?" and "how shall I live?"' (Giddens 1991). People are searching for their identity, sometimes called authenticity, comparing various lifestyles with each other and trying to make a choice between them. But the choices and the answers to the question of personal identity is the responsibility of the individual him or herself, using his or her reflexive capacities to revise and rewrite their personal identity.

Similar ideas about reflexive modernity are put forward by Ulrich Beck in his work on the risk society. According to Beck, the modernisation process has resulted in a society that increasingly has to deal with the risks of technological progress (Beck 2007). These risks are not just technological (like ecological risks), but also institutional, as individuals might be dealing with unpredictable and obscure institutional behaviour. To deal with risks, modern societies must become reflexive, meaning that they should reflect continuously on the hazards and insecurities of new technologies and their impact on societies. A risk society is essentially an *individualised* society as individuals have become responsible for their own risk management. These risks are not limited to the technological process only: personal development as well as intimate relations and family ties have become insecure as well. The biography of individuals has become removed from given determinations and placed into the hands of individuals themselves (Beck 2007). Individuals need to learn to become the centres of their own action and of the management of risks in their personal, physical and social environment. Individual biographies have become *self-reflexive* as they have become self-produced in a context where nothing is fixed or determined. Individuals have also become entirely responsible for the consequences of the decisions they have made (Beck 2007).

Reflexivity has resulted in a lot of freedom for individuals, but they must also feel an increasing burden: personal and social life, biographies and careers, are under constant revision and examination. There can always be a new risk and uncertainty of having made the right choice. This situation is complicated by the fact that nothing is given or fixed. Individuals, groups and institutions are replaceable in the life course of individuals: they have no fixed anchor points. Bauman (1998) has introduced the term *liquidity* to describe the process of constant change and uncertainty in modern life. Living in a liquid society means living in constant insecurity, like walking in a minefield. Everybody knows there can be an explosion at any moment and at any place, but nobody knows when the moment will come or where the place will be (Bauman and Galecki 2005).

According to Bauman, living in a reflective and liquid society means in the first place living as a consumer. In the past civilians were disciplined by the process of production. Individuals needed to cooperate and bundle their forces to collectively improve their living conditions. However, in a society where individuals have lost a role in the production process, they have become *consumers* (Bauman 1998). The balance between production and consumption in the creation of identities has tipped towards consumption. Individuals are looking for the consumption market to develop their identity and lifestyle. However, consumption is essentially an individualist activity and can, in fact, create tension between individuals, particularly when there are differences in access to the consumption market (Bauman 1998). Individuals are just interested in their own fate and believe their own solitary way of doing 'life-business' is precisely what other individuals are doing. They are led by selfish concerns and loss of control of their situation due to the continuous change of their circumstances (Bauman 2001). Komter (2005) argues that when individuals are overwhelmed by feeling of powerlessness and disorientation, there will not be much interest in the common good or belief in the effectivity of solidary action.

The individualisation of society with its emphasis on individual responsibility, personal risks, reflexivity and consumerism leads to concerns about the role of solidarity in modern society (Taylor-Gooby 2011). In the first place, there are concerns from the perspective of *sociology*: if individuals are mainly driven by their own concerns and obsessions, to which extent are they willing to support arrangements in our society which are based on solidarity? According to Durkheim, solidarity in modern societies (which he called *organic* solidarity) is a mixture of state-enforced rules on the one hand, and individual motivations and voluntary decisions to obey the rule of the state on the other hand. (Durkheim 2014). However, because of the link between individual decisions and obedience, organic solidarity can be characterised as 'weak' in comparison with the 'strong' solidarity of mechanical solidarity in premodern societies. As Lukes (2014) has pointed out, in organic solidarity there is a tension between autonomy and obedience:

> What solidarity can link individuals, who are becoming even more autonomous while living in an ever more heterogeneous society, in such a way that they willingly share the benefits and burdens of common membership: for example, to pay taxes for the common good and to care about and to support one another.
>
> (Lukes 2014: xxxv)

Lukes formulates the current problem with solidarity in our modern society, and particularly in health care: can solidarity in health care systems be sustained in view of the increased emphasis on individual autonomy and freedom to choose? If individuals are becoming more autonomous while living in an ever more heterogeneous society, there is a concern whether they stay prepared to share benefits and burdens, like paying taxes for the common good and to support the other (Lukes 2014). In a society which may drift apart due to the emphasis on individual autonomy, cultural diversity and heterogeneity of lifestyles, solidarity can become fragile and difficult to organise. In such situations, individuals need to be convinced about the importance of solidarity, not just because of a moral responsibility towards the vulnerable other, but also by appealing to their own interests. In this regard, the problems of our modern society in organising social cohesion are not so much different than the social problems in France during the nineteenth and early twentieth century which, as I will discuss in Chapter 2, led to the development of the concept of solidarity in social theory and philosophy.

In an individualised society, solidarity becomes increasingly dependent on the long-term self-interest and rational calculation of individuals (van Oorschot 1998). It will become more difficult to legitimise solidarity in situations where individuals come to the view that their interests are only partially served by the system and that they are making a larger contribution than the goods and services they receive as a return. According to Hechter (1987), individuals act as 'rational egoists': They will choose a course of action that will bring them the most utility (Hechter 1987). They will choose to belong to a group and display solidarity, when they are dependent on the members of that group to acquire their desired good. When the group does not deliver what they want, the dependency of the members on the group will diminish and their solidarity will diminish. In relation with health and social care, individuals expect a satisfactory return on solidarity with the health care system and do not accept rising premiums if, at the same time, they are faced with poor performances, such as long waiting times or poor quality due to scarce resources (ter Meulen and Houtepen 2012). If the health system is not able to deliver, the modern patient-consumer might act as a 'rational egoist' and might withdraw his support for the care system trying to find his own solutions to deal with the scarcity of available services.

However, apart from the sociological question about the legitimatisation of solidarity, individualisation raises a *normative* question about the moral acceptability of individual choice and consumerism. Many authors writing about the individualisation of society, particularly communitarian authors, complain the loss of social ties and communities which they regard as a morally doubtful process. They argue that the individualisation of society has led to an anonymisation of social life, a narcissistic occupation with the self (Lasch 1979) and lack of social or political commitment (Bellah et al. 1985; Sandel 1985). Some authors refer to the analysis of the German sociologist Ferdinand Tönnies who coined the modernisation process as the transition from *Gemeinschaft* to *Gesellschaft* (Tönnies 1887). The

'Gemeinschaft' is the state of relations between individuals characterised by strong communal bonds and social ties. This situation is typical for pre-modern societies, but can also be found in villages and small social communities and religious groups in modern times. 'Gesellschaft' is the state of society in which relations between individuals are mainly seen as instrumental to everyone's purpose. This is the situation in modern societies where individuals have reached much autonomy but are alienated from one another and chasing their personal interests only.

As we will discuss in Chapter 3 and 5, there are some communitarians who lament the modernisation process because it has resulted in the anonymisation typical of the 'Gesellschaft'. For them, solidarity is a normative concept that refers to the altruistic and supportive 'Gemeinschaft' of the premodern era (ter Meulen, Arts and Muffels 2001). They emphasise the importance of culture and religious groups which they see as constitutive of people's identity (Sandel 1990). Instead of autonomy and individual independence, a lack of communal life will result in a decrease of possibilities for personal development and a lack of autonomy instead.

Though many individuals in modern society might struggle with social alienation or indulge in private, consumerist withdrawal from social life, individualisation should not be considered as wrongful and doubtful. Individualisation does not necessarily lead to hedonism, privatism and consumerism: It could also lead to social and political commitments based on personal and autonomous choice instead of the impersonal and obligatory character of such commitments in the past. Individualisation can have a positive connotation of personal development, self-realisation and emancipation of traditional social ties of religion, small communities, family and class. Individualisation in this positive meaning can go together with and even contribute to an 'ethics of commitment', that is, a feeling of social responsibility particularly towards the weak and vulnerable in our modern society and at a global level (ter Meulen, Arts and Muffels 2001).

1.5   Solidarity as 'Interest Solidarity'

As briefly mentioned earlier in this chapter, solidarity sometimes gets the connotation of 'interest solidarity', meaning that individuals pay their premiums and taxes merely because they have an interest to do so (Hechter's 'rational egoists'). Solidarity is in this view just a matter of prudential planning and insurance against the risk of social and medical misfortune. Self-interest may have been one of the motives for the rise of welfare states and solidarity-based arrangements. Particularly the middle classes were increasingly concerned about social and medical risks and were pushing for social insurance schemes that redistributed risks. Risk could, in fact, afflict all classes, and each had an interest in burden-sharing, not just the working classes (Baldwin 1990). De Swaan analysed the rise of the welfare state as the result of increasing interdependencies of individuals: As these networks of mutual dependency are increasing, the needs of the poor and vulnerable classes were perceived as a threat by those who are less confronted with the misfortunes of industrialisation and urbanisation (De Swaan 1989). Poverty among the industrial work-force, and the risk of strikes and social unrest, came to be seen as a risk for all others in society. According to De Swaan, epidemics, like cholera, could threaten the health of everybody, which was an important reason why public health measures were supported by the middle class and higher bourgeoisie.

One could argue that in modern society solidarity still protects against risks and that individuals are solidary because they have an interest to be so. In modern solidarity regimes, the 'strong' perceive an obligation to help the 'weak' by social arrangements like social health care insurance, disability insurance or other forms of social protection. Such arrangements in which the strong support the weak may look asymmetrical at a given time, but may serve the long-term interests of the strong, too, in case they might fall ill or lose their job because of disability or redundancy.

However, the interpretation of solidarity as 'interest solidarity' is a sociological or *descriptive* statement based on empirical observations about human cooperation and societal organisation to cope with the perception of risks (like the risks of disability, illness and unemployment). It says nothing about solidarity as a *normative* concept and the moral claims that may be based on such a concept. A normative claim defends, for example, the importance of values which express and sustain the perception of mutual obligations required for a decent society. Such claims are based on normative traditions which object to the liberal individualistic interpretation of society as they do not sufficiently appreciate the need for social integration and mutual obligation. The normative approach invites us to consider individual actions in the context of personal and societal relations in which responsibility for the other plays an important role. This is particularly relevant for care practices and care arrangements in which individuals can be highly dependent on others and where the perception of mutual obligation becomes clearly visible.

However, for some philosophers, solidarity is not more than a contractual relation which is typical for the modern welfare state. Bayertz, for example, says that solidarity is another word for 'support ... legally institutionalised by the state' (Bayertz 1999: 22). He argues that this 'welfare state solidarity' is better understood with the Anglo-Saxon concept of justice:

> Since there is no (longer?) reason to assume an existing perception of common ground, from which solidarity is known spontaneously to grow, it seems reasonable to deduce obligations to help from the principle of justice. Justice requires neither group-specific common ground nor emotional attachment, but is based instead on the distanced observation and the weighing up of competing claims from a neutral position.
>
> (Bayertz 1999: 25)

One can ask whether the concept of justice as advocated by Bayertz does indeed reflect the normative inspiration of welfare state solidarity. The claim that relations between individuals and between individual and the state have become contractual does not necessarily lead us towards a liberal theory of justice based on self-interest as the one and only way to capture the normative obligations between members of a society. In fact, the transformation of the perception of solidarity in the direction of self-interest and its subsequent replacement by the concept of justice ignore the moral basis of this concept. It conceals, particularly, the relational, meanings of solidarity as advocated in bioethics publications mentioned above (Nuffield Council on Bioethics 2009; Prainsack and Buyx 2011). A relational moral understanding of solidarity argues that the commitment to support others is an important moral value, not just because we have an interest to do so, but because the other deserves our support as he or she needs it due to circumstances out of their control.

1.6   Five Claims about Solidarity

This book will try to answer whether, in view of the individualisation of society and the emphasis on autonomy and free choice, we still need the concept solidarity, particularly in health and social care. It will try to answer this question by investigating the sociological roots of the concept (Chapter 2), analysing its philosophical status as distinct from the concept of justice (Chapter 3), determining its current role in policy-making in health and social care (Chapter 4), and defining its significance in informal care giving or family care (Chapter 5). The book will conclude with a chapter (Chapter 6) which will try to define the relevance of, and the need for, the concept of solidarity by answering five claims which, implicitly and explicitly, have been made in regard with this concept in the various sociological, philosophical and political discourses.

The *first* claim is that, because individuals in modern societies are dependent on each other, they should be solidary with the needs and well-being of others and should contribute to that end. As we will discuss in Chapter 2, this claim was originally made by a number of French social theorists like Comte, Gide and Durkheim as well as political authors like Bourgeois. Their interpretation of the moral duties of solidarity, like mutual assistance and collective responsibility, was based on their view of the natural connectedness and cooperation of individuals in society. Because the accomplishments of individuals are dependent on the cooperation with others, they have a moral responsibility towards society. Many of the French theorists in the nineteenth century tried to base moral norms on factual data – in philosophical ethics called the *naturalistic fallacy*. This problem was already noted by the Jesuit author Heinrich Pesch, the founder of the theory of 'solidarism' which was supposed to be a Catholic 'middle of the road' between socialism and liberalism. Pesch argued that Bourgeois and other French sociologists formulated moral obligations based on empirical observations. In their work, he argued, the 'is' defined the 'ought'. Though Pesch's work was soon forgotten, his critique of naturalism in social philosophy and theory still stands. If we think that there is a social duty towards solidarity and mutual support, it is not enough to look at the factual interdependencies of individuals. I will argue that we need a social philosophy, and particularly a philosophical anthropology, to define human rights and mutual obligations. These definitions might be supported by empirical findings, but the philosophy leading to these definitions has an autonomous status which cannot be reduced to empirical observations.

The *second* claim is that solidarity is a superfluous concept to analyse normative obligations of modern societies regarding access to care and quality of care. This is the claim made by Bayertz, which is that justice is enough to analyse and understand such obligations. In Chapter 3 we will argue that justice and solidarity are distinct and complementary concepts, or 'two sides of coin' (Habermas 1989). While 'justice' refers to rights and duties (Kant's concept of *Moralität* or 'morality'), the concept of solidarity refers to relations of personal commitment and recognition (Hegel's concept of *Sittlichkeit* or 'ethical life'). The importance of solidarity lies in its relational aspects, particularly its emphasis on cooperation and commonality. I will support the view of Habermas that both solidarity and justice are important for the arrangement of health care practices. Solidarity can be considered as a *correction* to justice, particularly when institutions are not guided any more by common standards of decency and humanity. I will also refer to a second type of solidarity (as distinct from justice), that is the solidarity that is expressed in concrete practices to care for the needs of others. I will argue that both types of solidarity are related: solidarity as the solidarity of concrete practices can only flourish when it is supported by solidarity-based arrangements in the policy and delivery of health and social care.

The *third* claim is the neoliberal claim that the state has no role to play in the development and support of solidarity in society. Solidarity is the responsibility of individuals who should organise support for their needs in their own private life, primarily within families and small civic societies. In the neoliberal view, and in restricted interpretations of the Catholic subsidiarity principle (as for example by Pope John Paul II), the 'minimal state' is the best way to generate social solidarity and to cultivate personal virtues and justice. In Chapter 5, I will argue that this argument does not fit with the solidarity in family care, like, for example, care for people with dementia in their own homes. Family solidarity has to do with personal relations and mutual responsibilities and is based on autonomous choices to provide care for the dependent partner or family member. However, it is a type of solidarity that needs to be maintained and supported by professional help by nurses, paramedics, home help and day care centres. This professional help is a necessary condition for informal caregivers to keep caring for their partners, parents, neighbours and friends. Family care should not be regarded as a residual kind of support, but as an essential component that needs to be supported and recognised by public care agencies as a serious partner in the supply of care for dependent people.

Though professional support for family caregivers to support their solidarity, government policies are going in a different direction. In Chapter 4, I will analyse recent developments in Dutch health and social care policy, leading to a reduction of professional support for family care. Family members are increasingly expected to take care of their family members, financially and personally. In view of the ageing of the population and the growing need for long-term care, the Dutch government tries to make savings by increasing the involvement of networks of family caregivers and other volunteers in the supply of care. However, this development is not accompanied by an increase in professional support for family caregivers. At the same time, the rationing of care is accompanied by increased individual financial responsibility, which leaves many families struggling when they seek professional support for the care they give to their dependent family members. Though reports published by Advisory Boards like the RVZ Raad voor Volksgezondheid en Zorg (2013) argue that this development will strengthen solidarity at the level of personal relations, and will lead to a fair distribution of benefits and burdens (so-called *reciprocity*), the new policies will effectively shift the burden of care to families who are put under increased pressure to supply care or buy this care on the private market.

The changes in the supply of long-term care and home care in the Netherlands are part of policies to reduce the costs of care which are getting out of control. Solidarity, as it has been materialised in a generous supply of services in the health and social care system, has become unsustainable due to the rising costs of demographic change and of expensive medical technologies. Individuals are considered to take more financial responsibility instead of their dependency on public arrangements. The shift from collective to individual responsibility can be noticed in other measures, like the introduction of market forces and consumer choice. The increased emphasis on individual choice and responsibility are justified to preserve solidarity as the normative basis of a system of collectively financed health services. However, as argued in Chapter 4, there is a risk that such measures may go at the expense of solidarity with the weaker groups in our society.

The *fourth* claim is that solidarity will inevitably result in group mentality with no room for individual differences. As we will see in Chapter 3 and particularly Chapter 5, this claim can indeed be made in regard with conventional notions of solidarity. These notions tend to emphasise the unity and coherence of the group to protect the group from threats from outside. Conventional solidarity can be characterised as exclusion of others by the construction of 'us' against 'them'. However, it tends to restrict the range of individual differences and their expression in different identities by the effort to maintain the unity of the group. This 'exclusive' notion of solidarity is typical for some communitarian thinkers who argue that the conventional notion of solidarity is an important context for the development of personal identities. Instead of taking an outsider position, communitarian authors encourage individuals to further immerse themselves in practices and communal relationships to realise their own personal good.

Communitarian authors are often criticised for their tendency to emphasise the cohesiveness of the group and to reduce the importance of individual autonomy. However, in Chapter 5, I will argue that there are communitarian authors, for example, Etzioni (1998), who argue for a participatory approach to solidarity in which heterogeneity of values and differences in identities are not considered as something that needs to be erased or homogenised, but as important values in itself which should be promoted by an inclusive approach. In Chapters 3 and 5, I will present the concept of reflective solidarity as developed by Jody Dean on the basis of the concept of the 'generalised other' introduced by the social psychologist Georg Herbert Mead. According to Dean (1996), solidarity is a communicative process, which creates a community by a process of reflection on expectations regarding the generalised other. In this process, identities are affirmed and recognised as different ways of interpretation and meeting of these expectations. In Chapter 5, I will argue that solidarity and autonomy or individual difference do not necessarily exclude each other but that a reflective and participatory approach can strengthen social ties as well as open the possibility for reflection on social expectations and personal identity. This idea will be applied to practices and expectations in the field of family solidarity and care for people with dementia.

The *fifth* claim is that solidarity is a typical 'European' value which is difficult to implement in other societies and cultures. This claim is based on the idea that solidarity emphasises the relatedness of individuals and their willingness to contribute to the needs of others: it expresses a feeling of togetherness and commitment to the common good which are supposed to be typical for the old world. Illingworth and Parmet (2012), for example, refer to suggestions that in the United States there is an emphasis on the individual and autonomy, while in Europe, the orientation is towards collectives. It is true that welfare states, including universal access to health and social care, in European countries are explicitly based on the principle of solidarity. However, as I will argue in Chapter 6, the view that solidarity does not exist in the United States is rather superficial. I will refer to the observations of Alexis de Toqueville who, during his travel through the United States in the mid-nineteenth century, was impressed by the flourishing of local communities in the United States and the social and political engagement of the citizens. De Toqueville argued that individuals in local American communities were to some extent driven by enlightened self-interest. However, he also argued, as I will discuss in Chapter 2, that self-interest is not necessarily a bad thing as long as the chasing of one's own interests includes some sacrifice to help others. Such a modest sacrifice would be in the interest of both the giver as the receiver. In fact, the motive of American citizens to engage with their communities is not much different than the motive underlying solidarity of individuals in modern European societies, which is based on enlightened self-interest.

The alleged lack of solidarity in America is often associated with inequalities in access to health care and the limited willingness in American society to support government policies to improve the position of the uninsured. Americans are alleged to have more confidence in the market and to distrust the government to deliver health care. However, as Daniel Callahan (2008) argued not so long ago, the US government does play an important, and often satisfactory, role in public health care, via, for example the Medicare programme, the (semi-federal) Medicaid programmes and the Veterans Health Administration. The Affordable Care Act of President Obama has improved the access of many poor Americans to health insurance. Unfortunately, the Obama initiative has been significantly reversed by the Trump administration, leading (again) to a substantial increase of the number of uninsured as well as to higher financial insurance premiums for older people and individuals with pre-existing conditions. While the US government has taken important initiatives to improve access to care (until the Trump administration), at the other side of the Atlantic one can notice a moving away from government control and introduction of neoliberal forces in which the market is a better way to organise access and delivery of health care. While the Europeans seem to embrace more market strategies, the Americans are going in the direction of more government control (Callahan 2008).

Solidarity is a concept with many layers and meanings due to its various ideological backgrounds, moral traditions and disciplinary understandings. The best way to get a better idea of the meaning of this multi-layered concept, and particularly of its role in health and social care, is by a multi-disciplinary approach which combines ethical, philosophical, social and political perspectives. In the following chapters, I will apply this approach, presenting a range of historical, sociological, philosophical, ethical and political perspectives to the idea of solidarity. The purpose of this multi-disciplinary journey will be to answer the five claims regarding solidarity presented in this chapter. These answers, as they will be presented in Chapter 6, may help to give solidarity a solid place in the field of bioethics, particularly in regards to the ethical and philosophical reflection on access and justice in health and social care.

2

The Origins of Solidarity as a Sociological Concept

This chapter will trace the origins of solidarity as a sociological concept. The chapter will focus on how the idea of solidarity was developed by French social critics and theorists in response to the social problems and political struggles raised by the industrialisation of France in the nineteenth century. Theorists like De Bonald, De Maistre, Saint-Simon, Fourier and De Tocqueville were very concerned about the individualisation of French society and the lack of social cohesion which, in their view, would lead to a diminishment of individual welfare and social justice. These moral concerns were also driving the work of the two most important theorists in nineteenth and early twentieth century French sociology, Auguste Comte and Émile Durkheim. It was Durkheim who laid the foundations for sociological theories on solidarity, including his distinction between mechanical and organic solidarity. It was typical for a number of French social and political thinkers, like for example Léon Bourgeois, to draw moral conclusions (*solidarité-devoir*) on the basis of empirical data about the state of solidarity (*solidarité-fait*) in a certain society. The mixing of moral values and empirical observations was heavily criticised by the German social theorist Max Weber, who argued that sociology should be a 'value-free' discipline. While Durkheim was analysing the role of solidarity in the societal context, Weber focused on the meaning of solidarity in the relationships between individuals. After 1920, solidarity was established in sociology as a concept to describe the state of social cohesion and of the willingness of individuals to contribute to the greater good. The chapter concludes with an analysis of the various interpretations of solidarity, including an overview of the various reasons for individuals to support solidarity, as they were developed by sociological theorists by the early 1920s. It was in that period that the most important, and for my project most relevant, sociological interpretations regarding the concept of solidarity were made.

2.1   The Individualisation of Society in Post-Revolutionary France

To get a better understanding of solidarity as a sociological and political concept, it will be important to go back to its origins in nineteenth century France. The idea of solidarity was introduced by some philosophers and political thinkers against the background of the increasing individualisation of French society, partly under the influence of the French Revolution and its emphasis on individual rights. While brotherhood was part of the slogan *liberté, egalité, fraternité,* the policy of the Republic was to suppress the formation of spontaneous or organised groups. For example, the gilds and other professional organisations were forbidden by the decrees of 1791 (*Loi Le Chapelier*) with the argument that they would advocate their own particular interests and not the general interest of the Republic (Hayward 1959). Workers were not allowed to establish unions because of a general prohibition of coalitions or interest groups. Brotherhood meant being an individual citizen of the state, it did not mean being member of a particular community. Communities or interest groups were distrusted as they could nourish an environment of resistance against the state and its protection of individual rights against those who would like to return to the inequalities and oppression of the *ancient regime.* As communities and civic unions were suppressed, the relations between the individuals and the state lacked any intermediate level: the individuals were powerless against the government, which was in direct control of the social and political life in the Republic. There was no social cohesion within the Republic: the nation was seen as a loose collection of individual citizens without common ties or joint interests on the level of group or class. This policy was justified by Rousseau's idea of the *volonté generale,* meaning that the representatives of the citizens express the 'general will' of the people and there is no need to think or want something different than what is decided by the General Assembly of the Republic (Rousseau 1762).

Particularly after the Restoration (1814) and the Second Restoration (1815) of the monarchy under the Bourbon king Louis XVIII, there was a steady rise of reaction against the emphasis on individual rights which was seen as the cause of the 'atomisation' of society and the lack of communal life in French society (Bussemaker 1993). A leading role was played by the catholic philosopher and diplomat Joseph-Marie Count De Maistre, who was a typical representative of the so-called Counter-Enlightenment and of a conservative brand of Romanticism. These terms take together several streams of thought in France, Germany and

England which, in general, opposed the rationalism and the freedom of the individual as advocated by the philosophy of the Enlightenment. An important representative is the British political thinker Edmund Burke, who in his *Reflections on the Revolution in France* (1790) condemned the ideals of the French Revolution and particularly the idea of individual rights, which in his view destroyed the possibility of communal life in which the lives of individuals are woven into the fabric of traditions and shared values. The individualisation of society would result in a loss of traditional norms and clear guidance for the individual who, as a result, would focus on the pursuit of his own interests and utilitarian values. According to Burke, the 'commonwealth itself would, in a few generations, crumble away, be disconnected into the dust and powder of individuality, and at length dispersed to all the winds of heaven' (Burke 1988: 194; Bussemaker 1993: 262). Due to their 'irrational nature', individuals needed to be restrained by social control and by the suppression of their passions to protect them and other individuals (De Jager 1980).

Similar ideas were put forward by De Maistre who detested the rationalism of the Enlightenment and the individualism of the Revolution. These developments were responsible for the disintegration of the traditional, corporatist organisation of society. As a true disciple of the Jesuits, De Maistre distrusted the passions of individuals that, in his view, should be put under control by society. Human beings were intrinsically immoral beings who needed society and its institutions to display morally acceptable behaviour. In the spirit of the Contra-Reformation, De Maistre referred to the 'excessive fragmentation of philosophical and political doctrines' as a form of 'political protestantism carried to the most absolute individualism' (De Swart 1962: 78). It was De Maistre who might have originated the term individualism to describe, and condemn, the 'evil' consequences of the French Revolution (De Swart 1962). Like Burke, he opposed the modernism of the Revolution and what he called 'political Protestantism', which was responsible for the breakdown of traditional hierarchies and for the supremacy of the individual.

An even more radical condemnation of the idea of individual rights can be found in the work of Louis Viscount De Bonald. According to De Bonald, individuals need the state to suppress their evil tendencies and to survive as social beings. Referring to the work of Hobbes and his idea of the struggle between individuals ('*homo homini lupus est*' meaning 'a man is a wolf to another man'), De Bonald argued that the state enabled individuals to live as moral beings. As long as they obeyed the laws of the state and the customs of society, individuals had nothing to fear. But they definitely had no rights! (De Jager 1980). Human beings owe everything to society because of the way society redirects their innate evil tendencies. Christianity has taught us for many centuries that humans are sinners and that an important goal of human life is to suppress the sins. Though influenced by Hobbes, De Bonald did not agree with his idea of society as a social contract: society has not been created by man, but has existed all the time as a gift of God (De Jager 1980). Society is primary to the existence of individuals and cannot be reduced to its individual members. Society is an 'organism' of which the families and groups are members and of which individuals are only elements. And because society is an organism, one should not intervene in it or restructure it by rational or artificial means: as a 'living organism' it should be allowed to grow by fostering its main components, meaning small groups like (and foremost) the family.

A comparable critical view of the fragmentation of French society can be found in the work of Henri Saint-Simon who inspired many sociological and political thinkers in the nineteenth century (including Marx and Comte). Saint-Simon shared the concern of De Bonald and Le Maistre about the atomisation of French society which resulted in his view from the critical philosophy of the Enlightenment and the social changes brought about by the French Revolution (De Swart 1962). However, while De Bonald and Le Maistre wanted to return to the security and order of the ancient regime with its theocratic social structure, Saint-Simon was more interested in a reconstruction and reorganisation of the existing society to remedy the harmful impact of industrialisation. He was not using though the word 'individualism', but instead used the words 'anarchy' and 'egoism' to characterise the individualistic mentality which had become dominant in French society. After his death in 1825, his disciples, the Saint-Simonians, adopted the word individualism from the conservative writers to characterise the disintegration from which modern French society was suffering (De Swart 1962).

The concerns of Saint-Simon echoed in the works of Auguste Comte, who is often referred to as the founder of modern sociology. Comte took the post of secretary of Saint-Simon in 1817, but broke with him in 1824 to become his rival (though Saint-Simon died in 1825). According to Comte, individuals are fundamentally social beings, meaning they have a tendency to live in a community with others (Comte 1864; De Jager 1980). However, this social tendency, which is a higher, rational capacity, is often thrown aside by lower instincts and particularly egoistic tendencies. What is needed is a suppression of the lower egoistic tendencies by society to accomplish an ordered society. Family life could make a significant contribution to stimulate and foster the social tendencies of man. Comte opposed the contract theories of society which depicted society as the result of the negotiation by the individuals to promote their interests. In fact the interests or needs of the individuals were the product of society and not the other way around. Moreover, he argued against the liberal *laissez-faire* idea that one should not interfere in the egoistic actions of individuals as those actions would in the end serve the general interest. Instead of a natural equilibrium, the free flow and clash of the many individual actions would make society impossible (De Jager 1980).

Comte was impressed by the conservative authors and their critique of individualism, but he could not agree with a return to a theocratic order. Like Saint-Simon, he argued for a new order in society, but an order that was appropriate to the new industrial society. Society needed stability and equilibrium, but not in the traditional medieval sense (Comte 1998). To create such a new order, one needed to know the laws of human progress and their various phases and stages which needed to be followed step by step. A return to a previous stage was not possible, and neither was skipping one stage by a big jump forwards. Science could help to find these laws and help to mitigate the crisis and the social troubles of passing from one stage to another. Comte and Saint-Simon saw the merits of the old medieval order as they were advocated by De Bonald and Le Maistre. They could not agree with the way this order was rejected by Condorcet and other philosophers of the Enlightenment. Instead, they had the view that it was the philosophy of the Enlightenment which was responsible for the corrosion of the social order. However, while De Bonald and Le Maistre could only think of a static theocratic order willed by God, Comte tried to combine the idea of Order with the idea of Progress. Society should be ordered, but it went necessarily though various stages in which a new order was created. Comte saw an important role for science to help society move from one orderly situation to a new one, in order to prevent chaos and human suffering (De Jager 1980). Instead of the conflicts between individuals, and particularly between the rising social classes of industrial society, one should strive for a harmonious order in society modelled on the biological idea of an organism. The various parties in society should accept the 'organic doctrine' according to which society is composed of various elements that work together in a harmonic way in order to promote the survival of society. Such a consensus was a necessary social condition for the implementation of legal and political measures. Instead of *laissez-faire* policies and the unfettered individualism fostered by it, society needs a 'spiritual' or moral reconstruction in which the various individual goals and projects were combined in a common purpose (Jones 1998). In a comparable way Saint-Simon had argued for a transition from a feudal society to a new social order in which the various forces of industrialisation were accommodated by a new political administration. In this process, the values of the individuals played an important role, particularly their religious values, like the love of one's neighbour and a personal relation to God (Ionescu 1976). The relation of individuals with their social environment and the transformation of the individuals from within was an essential condition for social change and implementation of the new political order (Ionescu 1976). This was particularly important in an industrialised society in which the interdependence of individuals was far greater than in the feudal society (Ionescu 1976).

Comte held a moderate view on the individualisation of society and the policies on how to deal with it. He took a middle position between the conservative writing of Catholic authors like De Bonald and Le Maistre on the one hand and the radical solutions advocated by the early socialists, sometimes called pre-socialists, on the other hand. Leftist writers like Louis Blanc, Charles Fourier and Pierre Leroux were concerned about the individualisation of society, but they did not define it as self-isolation and political apathy as, for example, happened in the works of Alexis De Tocqueville. Instead, they saw individualism as a way of 'unrestrained self-assertion' which led to the exploitation of fellow human beings in their society (De Swart 1962). According to De Swart (1962), their major target was not so much the Enlightenment doctrine of the natural and inalienable rights of man as it also was the economic doctrine of *laissez-faire* according to which governments should not interfere in economic and social affairs:

> Outraged by the shocking working and living conditions of the new industrial proletariat, they did not criticize the XVIIIth-century philosophy for its equalitarian tenets (as was done by the conservative anti-individualists) but for not having coped with the increasing inequality between rich and poor.
>
> (De Swart 1962: 81)

Initially the social critics tried to implement their ideas of fraternal justice by calling for models of association which would result in greater harmony in society. One of the first thinkers to develop such ideas was

Charles Fourier, who was searching for new models of social organisation in which the gratification of individual desires would serve the general good and in which individuals would cooperate in socially useful tasks (Beecher 1986). According to Fourier, the most important social unit is not the individual but the group: the group was the place where the human passions could attain full expression (Beecher 1986). The ideal group was the so-called *Phalanx* in which the disparate interests and the destructive passions of men and women were civilised into a harmonious whole which would benefit all of its members. Within these groups differences in wealth, age, sex and social status would be transformed from sources of social conflict into instruments for the realisation of the common good (Beecher 1986). Social conflict results from repression of the passions: instead, the passions should be guided into a productive direction and harmonised in a larger social whole. The biggest issue for Fourier was social antagonism and the problem of social integration. Education was an important instrument as well as a social minimum wage. These would contribute to social harmony, but not to social equality. According to Fourier, poverty, not social inequality, was the source of social conflict (Beecher 1986). In the ideal community of the Phalanx the rich and the poor (meaning an educated selection of the poor) would co-exist harmoniously and would forget their differences in wealth and status.

The social critics and utopian writers attacked the liberal *credo* that there is a natural identity of interests between the individual and society. Instead they advocated a new order based on 'associations', 'harmony', altruism' and 'philanthropy' to curb the spirit of unfettered individualism, which in their view was responsible for the miserable conditions of the working classes (De Swart 1962). Their appeal to the 'social instincts' of France was opposed to the liberal attitude in capitalist England which had resulted in appalling social conditions. The social disruption caused by industrialisation, and particularly the unbearable conditions of the working classes, strengthened the call for brotherhood and fraternal justice to replace the dominant liberal policy of *laissez-faire* (Hayward 1959). However, they saw the solution of the social conflict mainly in the formation of associations or utopian communities instead of a reorganisation of society or a radical revolution.

The first three decennia of the nineteenth century saw a growing concern in France of an individualistic chaos as a result of the breakdown of the old social order and the rise of a new industrialist society. Saint-Simon and Comte's work reflected these concerns, but they added a new component to the mix by their call for scientific solutions. This combination of moralism and a scientific approach became an important force in the discussion and study of social change and the role of solidarity. But before turning to the concept of solidarity, and its rise in the French political and sociological discourse, we need to pay attention to the ideas of another theorist of individualisation.

2.2   Individualism and Enlightened Self-Interest: The Views of Alexis De Tocqueville

After the Revolution of 1830 (which brought Louis Philippe of the House of Orléans on the throne), a growing number of authors started to express their concerns about the harmful political and social effects of *l'odieux individualisme* ('awful individualism') as it was called (Swart 1962: 79). They included not only conservative, reconstructionist and socialist writers, but also liberal authors like the aristocrat, diplomat and political writer Alexis de Toqueville. According to De Toqueville, the weakening or disappearance of an intermediary field of institutions and social organisations had created a social vacuum which had two negative consequences. First, it enforced the power of the state which became an almighty influence in the life of individuals. As a result, instead of getting more power and autonomy, individuals became increasingly dependent on the state. Secondly, strongly related to the previous development, individuals lost their interest in political life and became only concerned about their personal interests.

According to De Tocqueville, French society democratic classes had not been aware that by destroying the power of the aristocracy, one had also destroyed local autonomy:

> We have destroyed those powers which were able single-handedly to cope with tyranny, but it is central government alone which has inherited all the prerogatives snatched from families, corporations and individuals; so that the sometimes oppressive, but often conservative strength of a small number has given way to the weakness of all.
>
> (De Tocqueville 1861; Siedentop 1994: 46)

If society is modelled on the idea of free and independent individuals, society can only be held together by laws issued and enforced by a powerful government. Without such laws, society would consist of individuals who, according to De Tocqueville, have a 'natural tendency' to chase their own interests (De Jager 1980).

Unlike other contemporary authors, De Tocqueville made a distinction between individualism and egoism or egotism.

> *Individualism* is a novel expression, to which a novel idea has given birth. Our fathers were only acquainted with *égoisme* (selfishness). Selfishness is a passionate and exaggerated love of self, which leads a man to connect everything with himself, and to prefer himself to everything in the world. Individualism is a mature and calm feeling, which disposes each member of the community to sever himself from the mass of his fellows, and to draw apart with his family and his friends; so that, after he has thus formed a little circle of his own, he willingly leaves society at large to itself ... Selfishness is a vice as old as the world, which does not belong to one form of society more than to another: individualism is of democratic origin, and it threatens to spread in the same ratio as the equality of condition. (De Toqueville 1984: 192–193)

De Toqueville's political ideal was a decentralised society based on local autonomy where individuals had the freedom to express their ideas and to create laws based on their common interests. He noticed how these local communities were flourishing in the United States, which he visited in 1831 and 1832. In his book *Democracy in America* (1835/1840), he described his fascination with the direct democracy in the United States where political and social institutions were undistorted by the conflict between the aristocracy and democratic principles (De Toqueville 1984). The background for this direct democracy was mainly because American society 'had been democratic from the outset' (Siedentop 1994: 47). French society could learn much from American society as 'that country is reaping the benefits of the democratic revolution taking place among us, without having the revolution itself' (De Tocqueville 1861; Siedentop 1994: 47). The administrative centralisation of French society and the apathy of the individual towards political life contrasted shamefully with the energetic participation of American citizens and the vitality of American society.

> What I admire most in America is not the administrative but the political effects of decentralization. In the United States the motherland's presence is felt everywhere. It is a subject of concern to the village and to the whole of the Union. The inhabitants care about each of their country's interests as if it were their own ... He has much the same feeling for his country as one has for one's family; and a sort of selfishness makes him care for the state.
>
> (De Toqueville 1861: 93-95; Siedentop 1994: 66)

In the local communities in America, individuals had to look at their own affairs *and* concern themselves with public matters. According to De

Tocqueville, the highest standard of morality then is the *enlightened self-interest*, a conception of one's own interests which takes account of the equal basic rights of others (Siedentop 1994: 68). De Tocqueville argued that one need to accept that in contemporary society individuals are led by their own self-interest. This is not necessarily a bad thing as long as the chasing of one's own interests includes a little bit of sacrifice to help others. Such a modest sacrifice would be in the interest of both the giver as the receiver. According to De Tocqueville, we do not need to appeal to noble motives to reconstruct our individualised society: it should be enough to stimulate the self-interest of individuals combined with a limited amount of self-sacrifice. Individuals have a natural tendency to chase their own interests, but if we are able to discipline them to restrain their evil and possessive tendencies it will be a solid and natural basis of a morally acceptable society. De Tocqueville did not advocate a *laissez-faire* or Social Darwinist policy (as advocated a few decades later by Herbert Spencer). Such policies were based on the view that the unfettered chasing of self-interest is inevitable in the interest of the whole society. However, such policies would in his view lead to egoism, stupid excesses and chaos. Instead, he argued for a policy that would persuade ('enlighten') citizens about the idea that giving up some of their own interests would not only be in the general interest of all but also of themselves (Bussemaker 1993). Interestingly, Spencer's Social Darwinism became highly popular in the United States in the final decades of the nineteenth century when industrialisation lead to enormous social problems. According to Spencer, these social problems, particularly the huge poverty in the slums of the big cities, would disappear with a *laissez-faire* policy which would result in the 'survival of the fittest'. However, Social Darwinism was heavily criticised and met much resistance later on from progressive social theorists like John Dewey (Hofstadter 1944).

The views of De Toqueville about the importance of enlightened self-interest as the basis for the organisation of society are still relevant, particularly regarding solidarity in modern European societies. Welfare arrangements including universal access to health care in many European countries are based on the idea of solidarity. However, the motivation to support these arrangement is often called 'interest solidarity', meaning that individuals are contributing financially to the health care system because of their 'enlightened self-interest': They can expect that when they are in need they get a return of their investment in the health system (ter Meulen and Maarse 2008). Today, enlightened self-interest is seen as an important motivation for an individual to pay a part of their income to a public insurance system (the self-sacrifice De Toqueville speaks about). The difference between the current type of solidarity and the views of De Toqueville is that in modern organisations or welfare arrangements solidarity is enforced by the state (though with the voluntary agreement of individuals), while for a liberal thinker like De Toqueville it is a matter of individual persuasion. Moreover, De Toqueville was only looking at individualism and communal interest at the level of local communities and not so much in the wider context of social policies.

2.3   The Call for Solidarity

In the 1840s the word 'solidarity' gradually emerged in the political debate, as well as in the sociological discourse, as an alternative for the individualisation of French society. 'Solidarity' was increasingly seen as a solution for the social problems resulting from the increasing industrialisation. Fourier introduced the word 'solidarity' already in 1808 to typify the ideal cooperative relations between the social classes (Reisz 2007). However, the social critics and utopians after him (like Fourier himself) used the word 'association' or 'socialism' to express the need for community and joint responsibility. Some of them were even called 'socialistes associaconnistes' (Reisz 2007: 32).

Pierre Leroux started to use the word 'solidarity' in his famous work *De l'Humanité* (1840) to express the social relations between individuals and the importance of these relations for individual life. Leroux tried to find a new basis for communal life by re-introducing spirituality and community in post-revolutionary France. Leroux argued that Christianity, and particularly the teachings of the Bible, has taught us that we are all united in one great community which he called 'la solidarité mutuelle des hommes' ('mutual solidarity between men') (Leroux 1840: 4). Christianity is grafted upon this solidarity: 'The truth is that we are all solidary, and that we live a communal life, or soon, as Jesus has said, *one* life' (Leroux 1840: 4). Solidarity goes beyond the traditional Christian obligation of charity: charity can be corrupted by egoism ('la charité, au fond c'est l'égoisme' [Leroux 1840: 47]) and can hide a fundamental contempt for the individuals who are dependent on our donations (Leroux 1840: 43–44). There is also no equality within charity: the dependent person remains inferior in relation to the rich (bourgeois) giver. We love the poor person because we *have to* love them as a Christian duty, but not because of a personal feeling of mutuality. Solidarity on the contrary is based on friendship ('amitié') and on mutual identification between individuals (Leroux 1840: 45). Individuals need to be integrated in these communities of solidarity and this can and should be done by political organisation: in the various communities, individuals find each other and recognise each other by giving and taking, by supporting and receiving assistance (Leroux 1840: 46). Leroux made a distinction between two types of solidarity. One type of solidarity rested on the similarities of individuals and unified them in order to live in a community with each other. The other type was grounded in diversity and necessitated to cooperation. It was the duty of the state to encourage and enforce such cooperation (Reisz 2007).

Before its use by utopian socialists and social critics, the term solidarity was used in law to express the mutual indebtedness of the members of a legal enterprise. Hayward (1959) traces the origins of the term in entries in Diderot's *Dictionnaire* where the words 'solidaire', 'solidairement' and 'solidarité' were meant to express the sense of collective debt in law (Hayward 1959: 270). According to Hayward, the principle of solidarity is traced by jurists to 'the co-proprietorial obligations of mutual assistance and collective responsibility within the Roma extended family' (Hayward 1959: 270): 'Each member of the family was held responsible for the payment of the whole of the debt contracted by any member, and had the right to receive payment of debts owed to the collectivity' (Hayward 1959: 270). This principle of mutual assistance or unlimited liability of individuals within families was called 'obligation in solidum' (Bayertz 1999: 3). This principle continued in voluntary associations like religious brotherhoods and workers corporations. However, these were examples of 'voluntary solidarity' as opposed to the enforced solidarity of the family association (Hayward 1959). In both cases, the interdependence of interests was regarded as 'sufficiently intense to warrant the imputation of collective responsibility, based upon the legal fiction of corporate responsibility' (Hayward 1959: 271).

The principle of collective debt was embodied in Napoléon's Code Civil of 1805 under the heading of 'Des Obligations Solidaires' (Hayward 1959: 270). However, the principle did not fit well with the essentially individualistic scope of the Code which considered the various parties in society, individual and state, employers and employed, essentially as sovereign entities who had only external relations with each other. In the Code individuals were nominally equal, but in reality this was hardly the case. Employers were far more powerful than the workers who were not allowed to negotiate for collective contracts and support measures. The 'anti-solidarist bias' (Hayward) of the Code Napoléon was increasingly criticised by legal scholars who argued that the individualist and voluntarist interpretation of the Code ignored the connectedness and mutual responsibility between individual and state, or in other words, solidarity as the 'supreme fact of social life' (Hayward 1959: 272).

While making its comeback in the legal domain, the word solidarity permeated gradually the sociopolitical discourse as, for example, in the work by Leroux mentioned earlier. Solidarity was seen as an alternative to the unfettered individualism that had become entrenched in French society. However, it was also seen as an alternative to anarchist (Proudhon), utopian and socialist (Blanc) positions on the left side of the political domain. In other words, solidarity became increasingly associated with a middle position between individualism and collectivism, a conciliatory type of social morality and social institution that presented itself as a harmonious alternative to extreme positions on both sides of the political spectre (Hayward 1959). The word solidarity expressed the idea that individuals are connected with each other, not only in the contemporary society, but also with societies and individuals in the past. However, the connectedness was not seen as just an empirical, social fact: the fact that we are mutually connected implied also a *moral responsibility* for fellow human beings. This connection was strongly emphasised in the emerging discipline of sociology, and has remained a key feature of many interpretations of the concept in the French sociological, political and economic discourse (Reisz 2007).

The combination of mutual connectedness and moral responsibility became a central feature in the work of Comte. According to Comte, individuals were connected in the contemporary society but also with the societies of the past. This connectedness created a *debt* towards the previous generations but also to other individuals in contemporary society. Comte rejected the liberal doctrine that individuals are owners of themselves and of their worldly possessions and that what they have accomplished is entirely the product of their own work (De Jager 1980). According to liberalism, individuals have only rights no obligations towards others (as nowadays is advocated by libertarian authors like Robert Nozick (1974)). Comte instead argued that individuals should become aware of the fact that the accomplishments of individuals are to a large extent the result of their dependence on the division of labour within society (Reisz 2007). This dependence creates a moral debt for individuals, not only towards contemporary society, but also to societies of the past.

Comte's ideas reflect the interpretation of solidarity as mutual assistance as well as collective responsibility and indebtedness as these were advocated in the various schools of jurisprudence in the middle of nineteenth century France. This connection between the legal and socio-logical discourse became even more visible in the works of Charles Gide (2010) who made a distinction between *solidarité-fait* and *solidarité-devoir* (solidarity 'as a matter of fact' and solidarity as a 'duty') (Reisz 2007: 36). *Solidarité-fait* means the actual mutual dependency and the cooperation resulting from it, based on (enlightened) self-interest. *Soli-darité-devoir* means the moral responsibility towards society and the redeeming of debt by the individual whose accomplishments are to a large degree dependent on the cooperation with others. *Solidarité-devoir* functions as a correction to social inequalities and social injustice which the cooperation of *solidarité-fait* cannot resolve or remove by itself. Comte and Gide argued for a cognitive process in which individuals come to insight in their social connectedness (*solidarité-fait*) which would lead to recognition of their mutual obligations (*solidarité-devoir*). This process would result in social engagement with and acceptance of a political process in which the injustices of the social cooperation were mitigated and resolved.

2.4   Solidarism: The Contribution of Léon Bourgeois

The concept of social *debt* and the distinction between *factual* and *moral* solidarity were key elements of the programmatic document *Solidarité* by the politician Léon Bourgeois which was published in 1896.[1] Bourgeois was the leader of the Radical Party which tried to develop a social policy based on the idea of *solidarism*, a political ideology which tried to create a middle position between the radical individualism of the liberal *laissez-faire* ideology on the one hand and the collectivism of socialism and communism on the other hand. The Radical Party united parts of the working class and the radical middle class in a striving for social and political reform in the eighties and nineties of the nineteenth century after a long period of unfettered liberalism and social repression during the Third Empire. After the February revolution of 1848 and the early period of the Second Republic, various measures had been taken to deal

---

[1] Please note that, to the best of the author's knowledge, the work of Léon Bourgeois has not been translated into English. The translations of fragments of the document written by Bourgeois as they have been cited in this section have been done by the author himself and have been checked by Mrs Martine Annandale, French native speaker and teacher of the Alliance Française de Bristol.

with the social and economic problems in France and to improve the situation of the working classes. Examples were the instalment of the right to work and the formation of national workshops shortly after the February Revolution. However, after the June Revolution in the same year a conservative reaction set in against the achievements of the early Second Republic. The political repression became severe during the Second Empire under Napoléon III, which started in 1852. The working classes were denied all kinds of rights, there was a limitation of free speech, and social and political gatherings (including strikes) were prohibited. Friendly societies or mutual associations were amongst the few manifestations of working-class solidarity tolerated by the government (Hayward 1959). Napoléon's defeat in the war against Prussia in 1870 and his surrender to the German chancellor Bismarck was followed by the founding of the Third Republic. Many politicians and authors who favoured the idea of solidarity returned to France after being exiled for a long time by Napoléon III. Among them was Louis Blanc who set up the Radical Movement, which tried to implement social change by political reform. The Radicals rejected the violence of the Paris Commune of 1871 and class struggle in general as a way to social justice. The Radical movement united left-wing bourgeois and reformist socialists under the banner of 'solidarism', a modest and pragmatic philosophy which wanted to create justice and social improvements by gradual legal reform.

Bourgeois was the first Prime Minister of the Radical Party which came to power in 1895. In his one-year reign as Prime Minister, Bourgeois promoted a range of social and political measures, including progressive income tax, social insurance schemes and educational reform. He was also active on the international stage, particularly after his resignation in 1896. He called for a League of Nations, the maintenance of peace through compulsory arbitration, controlled disarmament, economic sanctions and an international military force. Following World War I, he became the first President of the Council of the League of Nations and, in 1920, won the Nobel Prize for his work.

In *Solidarité* (1896) Bourgeois argued that solidarism was a synthesis between the laissez-faire policies of economic liberalism and the collectivism of socialism and communism. As a synthesis it pretended to be superior to these two ideologies. Solidarity between individuals and between generations was presented by Bourgeois as the central principle of solidarism. Individuals are connected with and dependent on each other: the isolated individual does not exist.

People live together. That is a natural fact, it precedes their consent, it goes beyond their own volition. Man cannot distract himself, factually or morally, from human association. The isolated individual does not exist.[2]

When individuals are left on their own, they will never be able to achieve any great social goal, neither can they maintain themselves in a condition of enduring prosperity and security (Bourgeois 1896: 27). They are completely dependent on solidarity which is a defining characteristic of individual life. Without solidarity, individuals cease to exist. With reference to Charles Gide, Bourgeois argued that solidarity is an essential feature of all living beings: individuals can only function in solidarity with others. And this solidarity is not a reduction of their capacities and individual life, but as a means to further develop and liberate themselves:

> Thus the law of solidarity of individual actions appears in the end between people, groups of people, human societies, in the same way as between living beings, meaning, not as a cause of diminution, but as a condition for further development; not as a necessity imposed from the outside or arbitrarily, but as a law of internal organisation which is indispensable for human life; not as a form of enslavement, but as a means of liberation.[3]

Bourgeois made a distinction between 'natural' solidarity and 'moral' solidarity. Natural solidarity is the web of social relations and interdependencies which is in principle blind, 'amoral' and unjust. This natural situation must be superseded by a 'quasi-contract' in which the injustice of the natural solidarity is redressed on the basis of reciprocal social duties. Bourgeois conceived these duties as 'debts' which are the counterpart of the benefits an advantaged individual enjoyed during various stages of the life course, especially childhood and old age. These are the stages where individuals are dependent on the support by others, before and after the time they have contributed to social activities themselves.

> For each living individual then there is a debt towards all other living individuals, in proportion with and in the degree of the favours done to

---

[2] 'Les hommes sont en société. C'est là un fait d'ordre naturel, antérieur à leur consentement, supérieur à leur volonté. L'homme ne peut se soustraire matériellement ou moralement à l'association humaine. L'homme isolé n'existe pas' (Bourgeois 1896: 53).

[3] 'Ainsi la loi de solidarité des actions individuelles finit par apparaître, entre les hommes, les groupes d'hommes, les sociétés humaines, avec le même caractère qu'entre les êtres vivants, c'est-à-dire, non comme une cause de diminution, mais comme une condition de développement; non comme une nécessité extérieurement et arbitrairement imposée, mais comme une loi d'organisation intérieure indispensable à la vie; non comme une servitude, mais comme un moyen de libération' (Bourgeois 1896: 27).

them by the efforts of all. This exchange of favours is the matter of the quasi-contract of association which ties all individuals, and it is the just evaluation of the exchanged favours, that is the just distribution of benefits and burdens, of the social and passive activity which is the legitimate object of the social law.[4]

Each generation has a debt towards the previous generation, and this was paid again to the future generations. This temporal solidarity between the generations supplements the spatial solidarity between individuals in contemporary society. Social duties are then not just a matter of conscience or voluntary decisions: they have legal force as they are grounded in the quasi-contract which regulates the mutual obligations between individuals. The quasi-contract allows the state to interfere to enforce the acquittal of the debts. Bourgeois makes clear that such interference and enforcement has only to do with the relations in the natural solidarity, not about relations in the private sphere: the quasi-contract and the obligations resulting from it are only about the social relations between people ('rapports communs entre chacun'), that is the 'payment for renting the services and utilities that represent the communal toolkit of humanity' (Bourgeois 1896: 57).

In return for the advantages which individuals enjoy as a result of solidarity, they should agree to guarantee all others to help and support them against the injustices, risks and evils which might affect their lives. This insurance to share the benefits and burdens of mutual assistance is for Bourgeois the necessary condition for social peace: it is the basis for the planning of society of a range of social measures to which all should give their consent (Hayward 1961).

Bourgeois claimed that society was responsible for the good as well as the evil conditions in which individuals are born and within which they lived as a result of spatial and temporal interdependencies (Hayward 1961). This social duty was 'wider than the traditional conception of justice but more precise, rigorous and obligatory than charity' (Hayward 1961: 26). Instead of the laissez-faire policies advocated by liberal economists and Social Darwinists, Bourgeois argued that association and solidarity (and not economic competition or a Darwinist 'struggle for existence') are the defining features of social life.

---

[4] 'Il y a donc pour chaque homme vivant, dette envers tous les hommes vivants, à raison et dans la mesure des services à lui rendus par l'effort de tous. Cet échange de services est la matière du quasi-contrat d'association qui lie tous les hommes, et c'est l'équitable évaluation des services échangés, c'est-à-dire l'équitable répartition des profits et des charges, de l'actif et du passif social qui est l'objet légitime de la loi sociale' (Bourgeois 1896: 54).

Like Comte, Gide, Durkheim and many other French social theorists, Bourgeois based the moral duties of solidarity on the natural connectedness of individuals in society. In the same way as Comte and Gide, Bourgeois assumed that insight in the natural solidarity would stimulate individuals to come to insight in the existence of a quasi-contract and acceptance of the moral obligations deriving from this contract and their enforcement by the state. However, the quasi-contract and the mutual debt between individuals and generations was based on a certain, rather liberal interpretation of the factual interdependencies of individuals, not on a moral theory. According to Hayward, the solidarism of Bourgeois 'favoured calculated appeals to enlightened self-interest rather than impassioned appeals for self-sacrifice and invocations of universal fraternity [and] charity of love' (Hayward 1959: 279). This liberal spirit of Bourgeois' solidarism, combined with its strong plea for social reform, expressed the interests of the liberal-socialist coalition represented in the Radical Party. The call for solidarity had become loud in the nineties of the nineteenth century: 'it had become a truism and a tautology to stress the need for social solidarity: to champion social legislation and governmental intervention; to promote voluntary association' (Hayward 1959: 278). However, this was not the solidarity of utopian socialism or communist class struggle.

Late nineteenth century 'bourgeois' solidarism was appreciably more restrained in its criticisms and timid in its proposed reforms of the status quo and generally more moderate in tone than its mid-century 'proletarian' predecessor. It stressed the rational and realistic elements in the solidaristic message rather than its utopian and idealistic aspects' (Hayward 1959: 278–279). Though attacked from one side by laissez-faire liberals and from another side by socialists and communists, solidarism succeeded in becoming the official ideology for social reform by collective action in France from the late nineteenth century and early twentieth century onwards. Solidarity became an extremely popular word which became entrenched in French political and social thought and has guided the establishment of the welfare state in France.

2.5   The 'Solidarismus' of Heinrich Pesch S.J.

The ideas of Bourgeois were inspirational to some theorists at the other side of the French-German border. In particular, the German Jesuit Heinrich Pesch (1902) developed his own version of solidarism called *Solidarismus* as an alternative to *Sozialismus* (socialism) and

Individualismus (Individualism). According to Pesch, the principle of solidarity expressed 'first and foremost the social interdependence and actual reciprocal dependence of human beings on one another' (Ederer 1991: 598). The principle of solidarity was opposed to the atomisation of modern society where social harmony was expected to arrive as the automatic result of the competition between individuals in the free market. Solidarity was also opposed to the collectivism which was underlying socialism where social justice was expected as the eventual outcome of class struggle (Ederer 1991). Pesch felt strongly connected with the political and national economic writings of Adolf Wagner, the leading economic thinker in late nineteenth century imperial Germany (Große Kracht 2007: 70).

The version of solidarism by Pesch was different from the solidarism of Bourgeois. While Bourgeois called for moral and political action ('solidarité-devoir') on the basis of empirical insights ('solidarité-fait'), Pesch argued that the grounding of moral obligations in factual data was indefensible. He criticised the 'short cut' from factual interdependency to moral mutual dependency by writing that 'the obvious deficiency of the "solidarism" of Bourgeois is, that it remains totally unable to bridge the gap from *factual* to *moral* solidarity'.[5] In philosophy, the grounding of moral claims on factual statements was later called a 'naturalistic fallacy', a term introduced by G.E. Moore (1903) to describe efforts to explain what is 'good' or what one 'ought' to do on the basis of statements of what 'is'.[6]

Pesch criticised the way Bourgeois made moral claims on the basis of factual statements. Instead, Pesch argued that the moral obligation to solidarity should be based on a philosophical theory. For the Jesuit Pesch, this meant Aristotelian-Thomistic philosophy which was recommended by Pope Leo XIII in his Encyclical *Aeterni Patris* (1879) as a safe philosophical method for catholic philosophers (Harris 1946). The Encyclical gave rise to a revival of Aristotelian-Thomistic philosophy, also called *neo-scholasticism*, among catholic philosophers (ter Meulen 1988). Neo-scholasticism can be characterised by a *teleological* interpretation of the social and natural reality, which is seen as developing according to God's will.

---

[5] '[Es sei] eben der große, aber selbtverständliche Mangel des "Solidarismus" eines Bourgeois, daß er völlig außer Stande bleibt, von der *thatsächlichen* Solidarität die Brücke zu schlagen zur *sittlichen* Solidarität!' (Pesch 1902: 308 quoted by Große Kracht 2007: 77–78)

[6] The 'is-ought' problem was for the first time discussed by Hume (1978) who in his *Treatise on Human Nature* (1739–1740) argued that normative statements are different then empirical observations, and that you cannot move from descriptive to prescriptive statements.

The factual solidarity and the increased dependence of human individuals on each other are anchored by God in their social nature which is essentially directed towards other human beings and via them towards God:

> the factual and with advanced division of labour increased mutual dependency as a teleological relationship willed by God and controlled by the goal to benefit all participants, [appears] as a situation in which individuals come together not as isolated, purely egoistic beings without obligations toward each other, but as individuals who by the duties towards mutual assistance and help are connected with each other.[7]

The mutual connectedness or solidarity in the social reality is on the one hand an empirical finding, but is also an ontological principle of God's Creation (Große Kracht 2007). It is only as an ontological principle, and not by the empirical findings alone, that we can postulate a moral duty to mutual assistance as a social-legal principle ('soziale Rechtspflicht') (idem). The de facto solidarity, which is described and analysed by the discipline of sociology, is for Pesch just the starting point of his philosophy and the political doctrine of Solidarismus.

A key element of the Solidarismus is the responsibility of the individual, meaning the person, the group, the profession, etc. All individuals are jointly responsible for the well-being of the social community as a whole. The individual Christian conscience can be characterised as being directed towards the whole which leads to a strengthening of the feelings of togetherness, sacrifice, self-limitation, subordination of individual interests and Christian love (Reisz 2007). These are qualities which need to be implanted within individuals by moral education. It will contribute to a society in which equality is not the leading principle, but the creation and maintenance of an order of professions and classes where each individual should find his place and is related to others by obligations of love and justice (Reisz 2007).

In the solidarism of Bourgeois, the only way to bridge the gap between the factual and the moral, and to create a moral basis for solidarity, is the voluntary consent of individuals acting out of their own self-interest.

---

[7] 'die thatsächliche und mit fortgeschrittener Arbeitsteilung intensiver sich gestaltende, wechselseitige Abhängigkeit als ein von Gott gewolltes, teleologisches, durch den Zweck des Wohles aller Beteiligten beherrschtes Verhältnis, als ein Zustand, innerhalb dessen die Individuen nicht als isolierte, rein auf ihr Ich gestellte Wesen sich einander pflichtlos gegenüber treten dürfen, sondern durch Pflichten gegenseitiger Rücksichtnahme und Hilfe miteinander verbunden sind' (Pesch 1902: 320 quoted by Große Kracht 2007: 67).

Pesch argued that such a basis for moral obligations is weak as it does not express an absolute duty, but in fact is dependent on arbitrariness. According to Pesch (1902), the solidarism of Bourgeois was in fact based on a liberal idea of the social contract in which individuals voluntarily agreed to the terms and obligations of the supposed solidarity which needed to be enforced by the state (Große Kracht 2007).

Pesch tried to limit the freedom of the individual by emphasising the responsibility of individuals for the moral and social order. He criticised the liberal ideology, which paid only attention to individual interests, as well as collectivism and communism as they denied the responsibility of the individual. The individual is responsible for the well-being of others and of society as a whole, but can never be totally subordinated to the will of the state. He increasingly distanced himself from Bourgeois, who was initially criticised by him because of his alleged liberalism. In later stages he argued not only against the 'lay morality' of Bourgeois (and French society), but also against the tendency of Bourgeois' solidarism 'towards a destruction of social peace, a proclamation of class-struggle, paving the way for collective solutions'.[8]

The solidarism of Pesch never had the impact on political life like Bourgeois had with his brand of solidarism. While the solidarism of Bourgeois became the leading ideology of the French Third Republic (Hayward 1961), the solidarism of Pesch got hardly any followers and was soon forgotten (Große Kracht 2007). Solidarity became a leading principle in the German Christian social teachings however, but not because of the solidarism of Pesch. Solidarity was embraced by Christian politicians and Christian-democratic parties, because it became a basic concept in catholic social teaching as formulated in papal encyclicals. Though there is some influence of Pesch ideas and his followers in the encyclical *Quadragesimo Anno* (1931), these ideas hardly played a role in later social encyclicals in the 1960s and later on (Große Kracht 2007). There were not many followers in the Jesuit order either. Gustav Gundlach who was supposed to further develop the work of Pesch, took a different path by going into the direction of speculative social metaphysics, ignoring both empirical sociology as well as the solidarism of Bourgeois (Große Kracht 2007). Oswald von Nell-Breuning, who became the leading catholic moral theologian in twentieth-century Germany, hardly referred to the solidarism of Pesch.

---

[8] 'den sozialen Frieden zu stören, den Klassenkamf zu proklamieren, dem Kollektivismus die Wege zu ebenen' (Pesch 1902: 396 quoted by Große Kracht 2007: 79).

He argued that the solidarism was often misunderstood as a sort of social ethics, a teaching of societal obligations, while in fact it is 'a teaching of societal *being* ('eine Lehre vom gesellschaftlichen *Sein*') (Große Kracht 2007: 83). Another important reason for the lack of following was the gradual change in catholic philosophical thinking from rational and teleological neo-scholasticism, towards social personalism. The metaphysical ideas of Pesch (and Gundlach after him) were increasingly seen by catholic philosophers and theologians as too abstract and too distanced from social reality (ter Meulen 1988). Instead the human *relationship* and the human *encounter* became the leading term in the catholic social philosophical discourse instead of the teleological order and the duties based on natural law (ter Meulen 1988).

However, Pesch did raise an important point in his critique of the way Bourgeois and other French sociologists formulated moral obligations on the basis of empirical observations. In their work, he argued, the 'is' defined the 'ought'. The fact that we are connected does not mean that we do have a moral duty towards each other. Pesch's work was an effort to limit the impact of naturalistic thinking by emphasising the independent role of moral concepts as formulated by moral and social philosophy. The fact that the philosophy he used became increasingly outmoded, does not mean that the link between philosophy and sociology should be seen as irrelevant. If we think that there is a social duty towards solidarity and mutual support, it is not enough to look at the interdependencies alone. We also need a social philosophy, and particularly a philosophical anthropology, to define human rights and obligations. These definitions might be supported by empirical findings, but the philosophy leading to these definitions has an autonomous status which cannot be reduced to knowledge of the facts. We will return to this issue in Chapter 6.

2.6   Comte and the Birth of Sociology

The fight against individualisation and the urge towards social integration and solidarity were important factors in the genesis of sociology as an empirical science. The development of sociology into a modern science was to a large extent the work of August Comte, though some credit must also go to his master Henri de Saint-Simon. The primary task of sociology according to Comte was the discovery of the laws of the development of societies by empirical investigation of social facts.

There were three stages of human development which Comte called the law of human progress (Thompson 1976). The first stage was the *theological* stage, in which the nature of beings is seen as developed by supernatural powers. This stage is followed by a second, intermediate stage called the *metaphysical* stage which is a modification of the first as supernatural powers are replaced by abstract forces to explain the nature and order of beings. The third and definite stage is the *positive* stage in which the 'mind has given over the vain search after absolute notions, the origin and destination of the universe, and the causes of phenomena, and applies itself to the study of their laws' (Comte 1976: 40). The positive stage is characterised by reasoning and observing in order to reach an explanation of facts and the establishment of a connection between single phenomena and general facts. Comte called the science of the third stage *positive philosophy* as it regards all phenomena as subjected to invariable natural laws. Its primary task is to find causes for social developments which will result in the discovery of the laws that are guiding these developments. The purpose is to reduce these laws to the smallest possible number and then to use these laws to explain and predict future developments (Comte 1976). Comte envisaged an important role for positive philosophy in the restructuring of society: by knowing the laws of progress one could reduce and mitigate the crises which were inevitably connected with the progressive development of society. One cannot change the course of social development, but one can influence its impact on individuals.

According to Comte the development of positive knowledge is the only way to reach *spiritual unity* in society which is the precondition for the establishment of political unity (Jones 1998). Comte used the terms *spiritual* power and *temporal* power as a way to accomplish social unity. 'Spiritual power' is the power of religion or what we nowadays would call moral values. It needs to be distinguished from what Comte called 'temporal power' that is the political power of the government backed by military power. In the course of history, societies have known a different balance between the two types of power. Comte argued that in the past three centuries we have seen a 'spiritual disintegration' and 'mental anarchy' as a result of which 'it has gradually become absolutely impossible, in the mass, to obtain any real and durable agreement between just two minds' (Comte 1998: 196). According to Comte this has resulted in a 'blooming of individual ambitions' which are no longer contained by anything.

[As a result] each individual is gradually led to make himself the centre of the great social relationships, and as the notion of private interest alone remains wholly clear amidst all this moral chaos, pure egoism naturally becomes the only motive with enough energy to direct active existence.

(Comte 1998: 197)

According to Comte, spiritual power and the establishment of spiritual unity is more important than unity on the basis of temporal (political) power alone. In each political system the formation of spiritual power has preceded the development of the temporal power:

Generally, indeed, spiritual association founded on communion of doctrines and the homogeneity of sentiments that results from it must in the nature of things precede temporal association, which is founded on conformity of interests ... Temporal association cannot wholly maintain itself on its own without the cooperation of spiritual power, whereas the spiritual association logically can exist to a certain extent without the aid of the temporal power.

(Comte 1998: 213)

A 'truly complete and stable society' can exist only when the two conditions (spiritual and political unity) are to a certain extent satisfied simultaneously (Comte 1998: 213). Because of its contribution to spiritual unity (and social harmony) Comte regarded positivism as a new secular religion in which the worship of humanity replaced the worship of the Christian God (Jones 1998). Comte had a detailed vision of his religion of humanity including a hierarchy of priests with himself as the head. It included 'a calendar of positive saints; social sacraments; and quasi-religious festivals celebrating social relations' (Jones 1998: xi).

The emphasis on the importance of spiritual reconstruction as a necessary condition for political reorganisation meant a break with the dominant ideology of laissez-faire politics. Instead of the leading liberal principle of non-interference, Comte advocated a policy of planning to implement unity at the spiritual level. Liberalism led to individual anarchy, while planning on the basis of positive science would lead to consensus and therewith to a harmonic and orderly society in which individuals would be included in social groups and communities. In this process, an important role should be played by *education* of individuals in the laws of social progress. What individuals should learn by way of education is that living in a society means making a *sacrifice* without which society would not be possible. The progress of civilisation does not mean a continual state of individual satisfaction, but rather a continual giving up by the individuals of some of their pleasures and tendencies. Some of these tendencies might be opposed to each other and might lead to antagonisms between the individuals which may threaten social harmony and may lead to the destruction of society.

> In more precise terms, in any particular act there is for each individual a certain degree of satisfaction without which society could not be possible, and a certain degree of sacrifice without which it could not be maintained, given the opposite tendencies of individuals, which are to some degree inevitable.
>
> (Comte 1998: 216)

The 'greatest imaginable social perfection' would in the end be reached when individuals fulfil in the overall system the particular functions to which they are best suited (Comte 1998: 216). But even in this (perfect) situation, individuals still need a 'moral government', because 'no one could spontaneously contain his personal propensities within limits consistent with his own condition' (idem). 'Moral government' means in fact self-restraint and government of the individual passions and impulses which may be rather divergent and diverse in intensity.

> Whence, therefore, the need for special action to develop the natural morality in man, to reduce as far as possible the impulses of each individual to the scale required by the harmony of the whole, by making people accustomed from childhood *to the voluntary subordination of private interest to the common interest*, and by never ceasing to reproduce consideration of the social point of view in active life, with all the necessary emphasis.
>
> (Comte 1998: 216–217; italics added)

Comte wrote these words in his essay *Considerations on the spiritual power* which was published in 1825/1826 (Comte 1998). He formulated here the essence of the idea of solidarity which was to be further developed in the work of Émile Durkheim 70 years later, in the 1890s. Essentially, solidarity in Comte's, and later Durkheim's, view means that individuals need to give up some of their tendencies to make society possible. This includes giving up aspirations that do not fit with individuals' abilities and role in society. On the basis of this moral (or 'spiritual') reform, and not by revolution, order would be created within society.

2.7   Durkheim on Solidarity

In sociology, the concept of solidarity has become strongly associated with the work of Émile Durkheim. In his analysis of previous and modern societies, Durkheim emphasised the importance of collective values and moral consensus, or what he called collective consciousness (*conscience collective*), to retain order in society. The breakdown of traditional society has resulted in an increasing individualisation of society, but that did not mean that society could be reduced to an 'aggregate of individuals each pursuing their particular 'best interests'' (Giddens 1972: 4). He attacked utilitarianism which gave prominence to the emergence of individualism in nineteenth century society by formulating a theory of society 'composed of egoistic, or self-seeking, individuals' which 'would not be society at all' (Giddens 1972: 2). According to Durkheim, it was unacceptable that the 'narrow utilitarianism and utilitarian egoism' of Spencer and (*laissez-faire*) economists, 'should be presented as the only one that there is, or even could be' (Durkheim 1972: 147). The Social Darwinist philosophy of Spencer (which by the end of the nineteenth century attracted crowds of supporters, particularly in the United States; Hofstadter 1944), was 'of such a moral poverty that it now has hardly any supporters' (Durkheim 1972: 147). In Social Darwinism, economic liberalism and utilitarianism, the individual 'becomes the object of a sort of religion' (Durkheim 1972: 146): 'We have a cult of personal dignity which, as with every strong cult, already has its superstitions' (Durkheim 1972: 146).

The problem with utilitarianism (and related ideologies) is that, although they express a common sentiment in society, they do not look further than the wills and wishes of individuals. They lack the idea of the social that goes beyond the individual wills or the sum of the individual wills. The 'individuation' of society is an inevitable fact of society, but it does not mean that there is no need any more for a moral order. Though individuals have become more aware of themselves as distinct personalities, and of their moral responsibilities, it is of crucial importance that there should be a set of moral rules which specify the rights and obligations of individuals (Giddens 1972: 11). It is only by the development of a moral structure which makes possible the freedoms of thought and action in association with the increasing 'individuation' of society (Giddens 1972: 43). Individuals can only reach freedom in their lives when they agree to accept a moral order which set limits on the one hand, but which gives them opportunities on the other hand. According to Giddens (1972), the 'key to Durkheim's whole life's work is to be found in his attempt to resolve the apparent paradox that the liberty of the individual is only achieved through his dependency upon society' (Giddens 1972: 45).

Durkheim's paradox of freedom and order can be explained by his analysis of suicide and its relation with *anomie*. This term means the absence of moral order and moral laws to rule the behaviour and passions of individuals. In such a situation, the 'floodgates' are opened for individuals for a completely free pursuit of their passions without any limitations. This may look like a positive situation for individuals, but the opposite is true. If the individuals lose the capacity to restrain their own desires, these desires become insatiable, and this leads inevitably to morbidity (suicide) as the desires of individuals will never be satisfied, which leads to perpetual unhappiness (Durkheim 1972).

> Being unlimited, they constantly and infinitely surpass the means at their command; they cannot be quenched. Inextinguishable thirst is constantly renewed torture ... However, one does not advance when one proceeds towards no goal ... when the goal is in infinity. Since the distance between us and it is always the same, whatever road we take, it is just as if we have not moved. Even our feeling of pride looking back at the distance covered can only give a deceptive satisfaction, since the remaining distance is not proportionately reduced.
>
> (Durkheim 1972: 175)

Durkheim argued that 'the more one has, the more one wants', and 'satisfactions received only stimulate instead of filling needs' (Durkheim 1972: 176). Only by social order and moral restriction of the passions, individuals will experience happiness and satisfaction with their performances.

> To achieve any other result, the passions first must be limited. Only then can they be harmonised with capacities and satisfied. But since the individual has no way of limiting them, this must necessarily be accomplished by some force outside him. A regulative force must play the same role for moral needs which the organism plays for physical needs. This means that the force can only be moral.
>
> (Durkheim 1972: 176)

It is important that there should be moral rules within the professions which specify the rights and obligations of individuals who are in some occupation towards those who are in another occupation. However, the division of labour becomes anomic when there are great inequalities in the distribution of occupational opportunities. Moral regulation of the division of labour and the implementation of moral rules within the professions can only be developed when it is 'spontaneous', that is when individuals are not forced into certain positions, but are allowed to take on occupational positions which accord to their talents and capabilities

(Giddens 1972: 11). Professional organisations, occupations and other civil strata need to play an important role in society as they can help to define the various positions in society and to guide individuals to those positions according to their talents. In this way the empty space between the state and the individuals (which, for example, was criticised by De Tocqueville because of its destructive impact on social and political life) could be filled by an active civil society.

Durkheim argued that for the cooperation and cohesion in a society, there is more needed than just a powerful state. In a review of the book *Gemeinschaft und Gesellschaft* by Ferdinand Tönnies (1887), Durkheim criticised the views of Tönnies regarding the transition of 'Gemeinschaft', meaning the strong communal life typical for example for communities in the Middle Ages, to 'Gesellschaft' a term with which Tönnies typified the individualised anonymous relations of modern society. According to Durkheim, Tönnies could only see artificial means to prevent the harmful effects of individualism (Durkheim 1889). In the 'Gesellschaft' the remains of a collective life are not the result of an 'internal spontaneity' but from the 'wholly external stimulus of the state' (Durkheim 1889: 421). This is the situation 'as Bentham conceived it', that is, a full and limitless pursuit of individual passions and desires which would in the end only be limited to some extent by the state.

Though we have passed from a traditional society towards a modern society, 'just as in old times', there is still a collective activity or conscience collective which keeps society together and stimulates individuals to cooperative activities without the use of force (Lukes 2014: xxviii). However, collective consciousness in the modern era is different than the collective consciousness of primitive societies as it needs to give room to individuality: it is less strong and self-evident with respect to social obligations. This collective consciousness still expresses social obligations in society and the need to take care of the needs of others, but it is more individualised, reflecting the changing social structure and division of labour. These ideas were further elaborated in *La Division du Travail* (1893) in which Durkheim presented his theory of the two main types of solidarity, mechanical solidarity, which is typical of social relations in traditional societies, and organic solidarity which is the type of relations in modern societies with a highly developed division of labour (Durkheim 2014).

Traditional societies typically have simple structures which consist mainly of family groups or clans. There is only a rudimentary division of labour as each family unit has its own production and is independent of the other units. Society is formed of similar segments and these in their turn enclose only homogeneous elements. For segmental organisation to be possible, the segments must resemble one another: without that they would not be united (Durkheim 1972). Durkheim called this cooperation mechanical in comparison with the molecules of inorganic bodies. The social molecules in a traditional society can act together only in so far as they have no action of their own (Durkheim 1972). Each cell is comparable to another and can be replaced without destroying the unity of the social organism (Giddens 1972: 6). He emphasised that this is just analogy: the term mechanical does not mean that the cooperation is achieved by mechanical or artificial means. The term is used to express the link between the individual and society as comparable 'to that which unites a thing to a person' (Durkheim 1972: 139). The collective consciousness in this situation of mechanical solidarity is characterised by a strong intensity and rigidity: there exists a strictly defined set of values and beliefs which ensures that the actions of all individuals conform to common norms (Giddens 1972):

> The individual consciousness [in mechanical solidarity] is a simple appendage of the collective type and follows all of its actions, as the possessed object follows those of its owner. In societies where this type of solidarity is highly developed, the individual is not his own master . . . solidarity is, literally something society possesses.
>
> (Durkheim 1972: 139)

This situation changes with the increasing division of labour and the development of organic solidarity of modern societies. The division of labour results in an increasing individualisation of the social structure due to the differentiation of tasks. Individuals are not grouped according to family ties or clan membership, but according to the function they fulfil. The social elements have become different from each other and are distributed in different ways. Durkheim called this type of solidarity 'organic' solidarity as he compared the relations between individuals with the organs within an organism:

> Each organ, in effect, has its special character and autonomy; and yet the unity of the organism is as great as the individuation of the parts is more marked. Because of this analogy, we propose to call the solidarity which is due to the division of labour, 'organic'.
>
> (Durkheim 1972: 140)

The collective conscience in a state of organic solidarity is different than in a state of mechanical solidarity, as it expresses the differentiation of tasks within society. In organic solidarity, collective consciousness becomes more diffuse and ill-defined. While in mechanical solidarity the collective conscience completely envelopes the individual consciousness; in the collective consciousness of organic solidarity there is more room for individual differences. The personal sphere has become more important in the collective conscience and the differences between individuals become more pronounced (Durkheim 1972). Durkheim emphasises that this does not mean that it is to disappear completely. Instead it increasingly comes to consist of very general and indeterminate ways of thought and sentiment, which leaves room open for a growing variety of individual differences.

> The situation is entirely different in the case of solidarity that brings about the division of labour. Whereas the other solidarity implies that individuals resemble one another, the latter assumes that they are different from one another. The former type is possible only in so far as the individual personality is absorbed into the collective personality; the latter is possible only if each one of us has a sphere of action that is peculiar our own, and consequently a personality. Thus the collective consciousness must leave uncovered a part of the individual consciousness, so that there may be established in it those special functions that it cannot regulate. The more extensive this free area is, the stronger the cohesion that arises from this solidarity.
>
> (Durkheim 2014: 102)

According to Durkheim, in a state of developed division of labour it is necessary that the collective consciousness leaves room for the individual consciousness in order that special functions may be established, functions 'which the collective consciousness cannot regulate' (Durkheim 1972: 140). The more this individual region is extended, the stronger the social cohesion, which results from the solidarity:

> In fact, on the one hand, every individual depends more directly on society as labour becomes more divided; and, on the other, the activity of every individual becomes more personalised to the degree that it is more specialised. No doubt . . . it is never completely original; even in the exercise of our occupation we conform to conventions and practices which are common to our whole occupational group. But, in this instance, the yoke that we submit to is much less heavy than when society completely controls us, and it leaves much more place open for the free play of our initiative . . . Society becomes more capable of collective action, at the same time that each of its elements has more freedom of action.
>
> (Durkheim 1972: 140)

Durkheim tried to combine 'obligation' with 'spontaneity': they are not opposites, but are fused together in human conduct (Giddens 1972: 43). Obligations are not restrictions which place limits on individual actions: they are boundaries to human action but they also shape these actions, leaving room for individual expression. Social cohesion in a state of organic solidarity can become quite strong as it is linked to social boundaries on the hand and individual tasks and positions on the other hand.

Durkheim argued that the division of labour is not just an economic phenomenon, but also a moral phenomenon (Durkheim 2014). Though he did not use the term 'debt' (like Comte, Gide and Bourgeois were doing), he argued that the goals of solidarity are moral goals and that social solidarity itself is a 'wholly moral phenomenon' (Durkheim 2014: 52). The moral goals are harmony, order and taking care of the needs of others. Durkheim left it open whether the increased collaboration and mutual attraction of individuals was responsible for social solidarity or the other way around (Durkheim 2014). Morality is not just something external to individuals, which has to be implanted in them. It is not a mere 'juxtaposition of individuals' who upon entering social cooperation bring some intrinsic morality to it. Man is a moral being only because he lives in society with the group, and varies according to that solidarity (Durkheim 2014). Morality at all levels, individual and collective, is always a social morality. But this morality must be adjusted to the changing social realities of the division of labour, and not reflect the old social ties and conformity of the mechanical solidarity, otherwise it will lose hold of the individuals:

> Thus if the only ties that were forged were based on similarities, the disappearance of the segmentary type of society would be accompanied by a steady decline in morality. Man would do no longer be adequately controlled. He would no longer feel around him and above him that salutary pressure of society that moderates his egoism, making of him a moral creature. This is that constitutes the moral value of the division of labor. This is because through it the individual is once more made aware of his dependent state vis-à-vis society. It is from society that the forces holding him in check proceed, keeping him within bounds. In short, since the division of labour becomes the predominant source of social solidarity, it becomes at the same time the foundation of the moral order.
>
> (Durkheim 2014: 312)

The state plays an important role in the implementation of the ideals embodied in moral individualism. The primary function of the state is to articulate the collective attitudes in a society but also to initiate policies to canalise these attitudes into practice. However, the state should not become too powerful or tyrannical. Its powers should be balanced by other agencies in order to foster individual freedom (Giddens 1972). An important role should be played by education which should be responsive to the ideals of moral individualism. The educator should take into account the individuality of every child instead of applying inflexible rules.

The fact that morality is based on obligations and voluntariness does not mean that there is no authority which individuals need to follow. In fact, morality constitutes a category of rules where the idea of authority plays an 'absolutely preponderant' role (Durkheim 1972: 98). As Durkheim argued in his discussion of anomie, individuals need rules and limits to tame their insatiable desires. Individuals will only be prepared to moderate their desires 'when the limitations are issued by an authority he respects and for whom he bows only society is in a position to play that mediating role … because she is the only moral force which stands above the individuals and which superiority is accepted by the individual. Society is the only instance that has the authority that is necessary to issue laws and to show the passions the point she are not allowed to pass' (Durkheim 1897; De Jager 1980: 222). We act in a prescribed way, 'not because the required conduct is attractive to us, not because we are so inclined by some innate or learned predisposition, but because there is a certain compelling influence in the authority dictating it' (Durkheim 1972: 98). However, individuals should not conform to rules out of deference to the authority that is the source of these rules. Durkheim speaks here of voluntary obedience which is the result of acquiescence to a moral authority.

Social solidarity is the result of an acceptance of its moral authority, but this acceptance is based on a voluntary decision. Durkheim argued that the acceptance of moral authority should not be guided by selfish utilitarian motives. In *L'Éducation morale* (1925) he compared the acceptance of moral rules with advice on hygiene or doctor's orders in case of illness (Durkheim 1972). We follow the prescriptions of the doctor, not only because of his authority, but also because we expect to become cured of the illness. In such cases, the respect of authority is combined with 'utilitarian considerations' (Durkheim 1972: 98–99). According to Durkheim, 'it is quite otherwise with moral rules': 'But it is a certain and incontestable fact that an act is not moral, even when it is in substantial agreement with the rule, if the consideration of the consequences has determined it' (idem). The rules should be obeyed because of the rules themselves. We need to obey them not in order to avoid 'disagreeable' results or some moral or material punishment, or to obtain a certain reward, 'but very simply because we must, regardless of the consequences our conduct may have for us' (idem).

As social solidarity is equated by Durkheim with morality, some interpretations in the sociological literature of organic solidarity as based on self-interest or personal utility do not seem to reflect Durkheim's intentions. For example, Van Oorschot and Komter (1998) define organic solidarity in Durkheim's theory as 'shared utility' (as opposed to the 'shared identity' of mechanical solidarity). This interpretation does not accord with the argument by Durkheim that morality, and thus social solidarity, should not be based on utilitarian motives. The views of Durkheim are in this respect not much different than the vision of Comte who also argued that individuals need to give up their direct interests and restrain their passions as society requires it. However, it was De Toqueville who argued that self-interest can be the basis for (partially) giving up one's desires and interests as this might be in the interest of the individual themselves. His views seem more in accord with the current (liberal) interpretation of solidarity (called interest solidarity) than the views of Durkheim and Comte.

2.8   Marcel Mauss and the Gift Relationship

As we have seen, Durkheim rejected the idea that social solidarity was based on self-interest or personal utility: solidarity is meant to contain the desires and passions of the individual by a voluntary obedience to a moral authority. This is needed to create harmony and order in society, and also to promote happiness and prevent pathology (suicide) in the lives of individuals. His disciple (and nephew) Marcel Mauss took a different approach by clearly linking solidarity with self-interest and utilitarian calculations. Mauss wrote a small monograph called *The Gift* (1925) in which he analysed the role of the gift in primitive societies. Gifts in these societies look generous, but according to Mauss are in fact *moral* transactions which serve the interest of both the giver and the receiver of the goods. In *The Gift*, Mauss analysed the system of the 'kula' among the Trobrianders, a primitive society in Melanesia. The 'kula' resembles the system of the 'potlatch' which is a ceremonial feast of American Indians of the northwest coast marked by a lavish distribution by the host of the feast. The potlatch is meant to demonstrate wealth and generosity in order to determine the positon of the host in the hierarchy inside a tribe or between tribes. The potlatch has a strong antagonistic character and often includes severe rivalry (Mauss 2011). The potlatch is a system that existed in many other cultures and societies and is guided by various ideas and principles. According to Mauss, the most important mechanism or obligation of the potlatch is the obligation to give, the obligation to receive, and, what Mauss called the essence of the potlatch, the obligation of individuals to repay for a gift received.

The 'kula' in Melanesia like the American potlatch consists in giving and receiving with the donors on one occasion being the receivers on the next occasion (Mauss 2011). Mauss analysed the observations by Malinowski who made a detailed study of the giving and receiving, presentations and counter-presentations as part of the 'kula', which seemed to embrace the whole social life of the Trobrianders. Social life of the Trobrianders is a constant give-and-take; gifts are rendered, received and repaid as an obligation and out of self-interest, magnanimity, for repayment of services, or as challenges or pledges (Mauss 2011).

The system of gifts and returns is not spontaneous or without self-interest. Gifts are not 'pure gifts' but are means not just to pay for goods or services, but also to maintain a profitable alliance which it would be unwise to reject (Maus 2011). This can be a partnership between fishing tribes or tribes of hunters and potters. It is a way to create social cohesion by binding the clans together as well as to keep them separate. Even in our contemporary culture gifts are never purely free and gratuitous presentations, and neither are they purely interested and guided by utilitarian motives: 'it is kind of a hybrid' (Mauss 2011: 70). The gift creates a range of obligations resulting in a system of dependencies and hierarchies which binds the members of a tribe with another tribe.

In our modern society there are many remnants of the gift relationship. Our Western societies have 'recently turned man into an economic animal' or a 'calculating machine' (Mauss 2011: 74). But we are 'far from frigid utilitarian calculation', as there are many desires that cannot be fulfilled by wealth alone. For this reason it is important that there exists means of expenditure and exchange other than economic ones: 'The mere pursuit of individual ends is harmful to the ends and peace of the whole, to the rhythm of its work and pleasures, and hence in the end to the individual' (Mauss 2011: 75). Such comments echo the concerns of social theorists and political philosophers in nineteenth century France about the social disintegration and individualism fostered by *laissez-fair* policies at the economic level. Mauss argues that the struggles between capital and labour 'are starting to rise to this "social" level' as there is an increasing insight that to motivate the labour force one should recompense them fairly for their gift.

According to Mauss the gift relationship is a powerful way to pacify relations between individuals and social groups: the exchange of goods satisfies mutual interests, promotes negotiation instead of aggression and helps to build up mutual respect:

> In order to trade, man must first lay down his spear. When that is done he can succeed in exchanging goods and persons not only between clan and clan but between tribe and tribe and nation and nation, and above all between individuals. It is only then that people can create, can satisfy their interests mutually and define them without recourse to arms. It is in this way that the clan, the tribe and nation have learnt – just as in the future the classes and nations and individuals will learn – how to oppose one another without slaughter and to give without sacrificing themselves to others. That is one of the secrets of their wisdom and solidarity.
>
> (Mauss 2011: 80)

The vast knowledge and subtle appraisal of the anthropological literature led Mauss to the discovery of the gift relationship as a key element in social solidarity: the mutual obligations created by the gift resulted not only in a pacification between individuals and groups, but also in a stable order which benefits the individual and the society which they are part of. The gift is never pure: it is driven by personal interests and utilitarian calculations which benefits both parties and creates a bond between them. This type of solidarity is indeed driven by 'shared utility'. However, it is not Durkheim's idea of organic solidarity, but the gift as analysed by Mauss which can be regarded as based on individual calculations of utility. In fact, Mauss explains very well one of the modern interpretations of solidarity: individuals agree to make financial contributions ('gift') to the health care system because they expect to be treated when they are themselves in need in the near or far away future ('return'). Modern solidarity is to an important extent based on the self-interest and utilitarian calculation of the gift which, as Mauss demonstrated, has in fact very ancient roots in human societies.

2.9   Solidarity in the Sociology of Max Weber

The idea of solidarity was analysed in a different way in the work of Max Weber. While Durkheim was concerned about the disintegration of society and argued that solidarity was needed to create social cohesion,

Weber was more interested in the role of solidarity in human relationships. As Van Oorschot and Komter (1998) argue, Durkheim analysed the concept and role of solidarity on the macro level, but it was Weber who explored the significance of solidarity on the micro level, meaning the level of interactions and mutual obligations between individuals.

In his book *Wirtschaft und Gesellschaft*, published posthumously in 1925 and translated into English by Talcott Parsons as *The Theory of Social and Economic Organisation* (1947), Weber made a distinction between two types of 'solidary' social relationships: the communal and the associative relationships. Relationships are *communal* 'if and so far as the orientation of social action ... is based on subjective feeling of the parties, whether affectual or traditional, that they belong together' (Weber 1947: 136). Relationships will be called *associative*, 'if and so far as the orientation of social action within it rests on a rationally motivated adjustment of interests or a similarly motivated agreement' (idem). According to Weber, it is common, but not inevitable, for the associative relationships to rest on a 'rational agreement by mutual consent' (idem). The corresponding action is oriented to a rational belief 'in the binding validity of the obligation to adhere to it, or to a rational expectation that the other party will live up to it' (idem).

Weber distinguished a few different examples of associative relationships, like the market exchange ('a compromise of opposed but complementary interests'), the pure voluntary association based on self-interest and the voluntary association of individuals motivated by an adherence to common values. An example of the latter is the 'rational sect', in so far as it does not cultivate emotional and affective interests, but only seeks to serve a cause.

Communal relationships may rest on various types of affectual, emotional or traditional bases (Weber 1947: 137). Weber mentions the examples of the religious brotherhood, an erotic relationship, a relation of personal loyalty, a national community and an 'esprit de corps' of a military unit. But the most typical case of a communal relationship is the family. Weber argued that many social relationships which are primarily based on calculating and associative relationships also include communal ties and emotional values 'which transcend the utilitarian significance':]

> Every social relationship which goes beyond the pursuit of immediate common ends, which hence lasts for long periods, involves relatively permanent social relationships between the same persons, and these cannot be exclusively confined to the technically necessary activities.

> (Weber 1947: 137)

Conversely, communal relationships, like, for example, a family, may be used or exploited by some of its members for their own ends. Though the communal relationship is the 'antithesis of conflict', there can be various degrees of coercion within such relationships, particularly 'if one party is weaker in character than the other' (Weber, 1947: 137). Associative relationships on the other hand, often consist of 'compromises between rival interests'. Outside the area of compromise, the conflict between rival interests remains unchanged.

In Weber's theory the associative relationship is a type of solidarity based on self-interest. These relationships are typical for the market, in which individuals are encouraged to acts of exchange and competition. They must mutually orient their actions to each other and agree to certain rules to regulate their transactions. According to Weber, the market and the competitive economy resting on it form 'the most important type of reciprocal determination of action in terms of pure self-interest, a type which is characteristic of modern economic life' (Weber 1947: 139).

As Parsons argues in a footnote in the translation of Weber's monumental work, the two types of relationships, which Weber called in German *Vergemeinschaftung* and *Vergesellschaftung*, are adaptations of the terms *Gemeinschaft* and *Gesellschaft* introduced by Ferdinand Tönnies in 1887. The distinction by Tönnies, part of which was heavily criticised by Durkheim (see earlier in this chapter), became highly influential in German sociology as a way to characterise the change in individual relationships due to the rise of capitalism and the rationalisation of social life. A considerable part of Weber's work was dedicated to the analysis of the role of rationalisation and its impact on the social and economic life of Western societies. He did not conceptualise the process of rationalisation as a mere reflection of economic processes, as for example in the historic materialism of Karl Marx, but as the result of a change in mind and worldview in connection with the rise of Protestantism and the Protestant work ethic (Weber 1920). An essential element of the coming of capitalism is the rational reorganisation of production directed towards maximising productive efficiency (Giddens 1971). According to Weber (1920), this cannot be explained by the sudden influx of capital in the modes of production: it is rather the result of 'a new spirit of entrepreneurial enterprise – the capitalist spirit' (Giddens idem) which combines rigorous calculation, foresight and caution, as well as an ascetic attitude towards the accumulation of wealth.

Weber made a distinction between two kinds of rationality: goal rationality and value rationality. Goal rationality (or *Zweckrationalität*) is the behaviour of an individual who makes use of his expectations of the behaviour of other individuals or of objects as means to reach his own rationally chosen ends. Goal rationality is a *formal* rationality as it has only to do with considerations and calculations about the choice of means to reach certain ends, but not with the choice of these ends. Value rationality is a *substantive* rationality, and involves 'a conscious belief in the absolute value of some ethical, aesthetic or religious beliefs, or other forms of behaviour, entirely for its own sake and independently of any prospects of external successes' (Weber 1947: 115).

According to Weber, social life in Western societies has become dominated by goal rationality, by the increased emphasis on calculation, prediction, effectiveness, bureaucracy and control as the basic principles of social life. Though goal rationality has resulted in a greater control and improvement of our economic and social circumstances, it has also resulted in a disappearing of the sense of meaning in our natural and social world. He called this the *Entzauberung der Welt* ('disenchantment of the world'). The behaviour of individuals is increasingly motivated by the calculations of goal rationality at the expense of the value rationality which reflects on the goals of our existence, the meaning of life and what kind of acts are better in terms of these goals. Individuals have become deprived of the capacities to experience meaning in the world, but also to share moral values with each other. Individuals are more and more able to control their material and social circumstances, but this development has been accompanied by a loss of the capacity to determine which values should guide our lives. The rationalisation of modern life has produced a 'cage' in which we are confined and which hinders us to develop a life according to our own autonomously chosen values and to develop meaningful relations with others.

Weber's views on the role of values in relation to solidarity were different from the views of Durkheim. According to Durkheim, values are needed to combat insatiable hedonism and to create order and cohesion in society. Weber saw values as inspirations to the good life, as orientations to meaningful activities and relationships, and not as technical means to create order. He was afraid that the associative solidarity and the emphasis on economic calculations would lead to the suffocating of individual autonomy and the diminishing of social and individual life (Gouldner 1970). There is another difference between Weber, on the one hand, and Durkheim and other French sociologists, on the other hand. Both Durkheim and Comte had a strong moral motivation to argue for solidarity as a way to combat individualism and to create order in society. According to Durkheim, the individualisation and the insatiable hedonistic motivations of individuals would lead to anomie and social disintegration. For Durkheim, solidarity was for this reason a 'wholly moral phenomenon'. Comte also warned against the 'blooming of individual ambitions' and the egoism which resulted in 'moral chaos'. According to Comte, individuals must learn to make sacrifices without which society would not be possible. Weber, however, argued that sociology should not get involved in moral discussions or policies, but should limit itself to 'objective' and descriptive statements about social and cultural reality. Though he was concerned about the impact of the rationalist and instrumentalist worldview on the life of individuals, he insisted that science, including sociological science, cannot prescribe which action policy-makers or politicians should take. Influenced by Kantian philosophy, Weber argued that there is a logical discontinuity between the factual and the normative: it is not possible to define by empirical methods what 'ought to be' (Giddens 1971: 135). The argument by Comte and other French sociologists like Gide that individuals have a moral debt towards society because they are histor- ically and synchronically connected with each other, meant an unacceptable short cut from the factual to the normative. Similarly the connection by Gide, and later by Bourgeois, between 'solidarité de fait' and 'solidarité-devoir' were illogical as far as Weber was concerned. Scientists can be guided by moral values, but they should never use factual statements as an argument for moral propositions or social policies. Science cannot tell policy-makers which decisions they should make: they can only present the 'facts' which the decision-makers can use to develop their policies (Giddens 1971). It was Pesch who made a comparable observation and critique of some of the French sociologists and of Léon Bourgeois. Nonetheless Weber sharply attacked Pesch because of the way Pesch tried to understand social phenomena from a metaphysical perspective instead of empirical, 'value-free' observation.

Though Weber supported a 'value-free' sociology, it does not mean that he was not concerned about certain developments in society. Par- ticularly the disenchantment of the world and the suffocation of indi- viduality by way of rationality and bureaucracy, did not leave him indifferent (Weber 1919). However, he argued that it is not the task of sociology to promote a certain policy or moral intervention in society.

2.10 Conclusion

By the early 1920s, sociologists increasingly refrained from expressing moral commitments in their writings. In an effort to become a 'value-free' science, sociology stripped the concept of solidarity from any moral connotations: solidarity became a descriptive concept to describe the degree of social cohesion in a group or society whereby individuals are willing to serve and promote the collective interest of the group or of society. In this chapter we have come across a range of motivations why individuals would support solidarity. We can order them under the following five main motivations:

1) *Enlightened self-interest*: this motive was observed by De Toqueville in the small communities in the United States. It is also a motivation in the gift relationship of Mauss and the associative relationships of Weber.
2) *Mutual affection and identification*: this motive can be linked with the communal relationships of Weber.
3) *Acceptance of moral authority*: this motive is typical for both the mechanical and organic solidarity as presented by Durkheim (though there are important differences between these two types).
4) *Reciprocity*: this motivation can be found in the work of Comte and Bourgeois (and to some extent in the work of Mauss) when they speak of the moral debt of individuals towards each other and towards society.
5) *Moral responsibility*: this is a central motivation in the work of Pesch who argued that individuals are responsible for the well-being of others and of society as a whole and that this responsibility puts limits to their freedom.

Each of the five motivations can be a reason for individuals to serve the general interest by subordinating their own (direct) goals and interests. The presence and strength of these motivations may vary according to the context in which solidarity is at stake. For example, the solidarity which is typical for many contemporary health and welfare arrangements, is the so-called 'interest solidarity' which is an example of solidarity based on *enlightened self-interest* (Motivation One). As will be discussed in Chapters 3 and 4, individuals contribute to contemporary health and welfare arrangements because they expect something in return when they are becoming ill or dependent. They have in other words an interest in such arrangements and are willing (to some extent!)

to make a (financial) sacrifice for it. *Mutual affection and identification* (Motivation Two) is a type of solidarity which plays an important role in families and family caregiving which I will discuss in Chapter 5. Individuals are willing to help and support their dependent family members (for example who are suffering from dementia) not because of self-interest, but because they have an affective relation with them. *Acceptance of moral authority* (Motivation Three) plays a role in social or national health and welfare state arrangements and is another reason for individuals to contribute financially to these arrangements. National governments force individuals to make a financial contribution to state organised health and welfare arrangements by obligatory insurance schemes which individuals accept because of the state's authority. *Reciprocity* (Motivation Four) is the background for discussions on life-style solidarity in the discussions on the limits of solidarity: should we be solidarity with individuals who are neglecting their health by unhealthy lifestyles and should we expect something in return for our contributions to their health care. Solidarity as reciprocity is also often referred to in recent reports of Dutch Advisory Councils as a new way to limit solidarity and to put more emphasis on individual responsibility. *Moral responsibility* (Motivation Five) is also typical for health and welfare state arrangements as they try to support vulnerable individuals and individuals who are in difficult circumstances which they could not control. This is a type of solidarity that puts emphasis on the responsibility of society for the needs of vulnerable people; it is also an important motivation at the micro level of caring relationships as we will discuss in Chapters 3 and 5.

These five motivations (interest, affection, authority, duty and responsibility) provide an important sociological and psychological framework which may help to better understand the moral and political discussions on the role of solidarity in health and social care arrangements within contemporary welfare states. They can particularly help to clarify *which type of solidarity* is being discussed or referred to in the ethical and political debates. However, these motivations are just *descriptive* categories: they do not say anything about the moral significance of solidarity or the *ethical importance* of solidarity as compared to other moral or philosophical concepts. This philosophical discussion will be the topic of the next chapter.

Solidarity and Justice

3.1 Introduction

Though solidarity is often referred to in debates on health care reform and reform of the Welfare State, justice is the key term in the ethical and philosophical vocabulary to discuss the normative aspects of developments in (health) care and the welfare state. Why should we bother with the concept of solidarity since issues of fair distribution of resources and access to health care have been analysed and debated much more thoroughly by the philosophy of justice? This is particularly true for the Anglo-Saxon world, where solidarity is seen by many as an outlandish concept that refers to a Polish trade union or a socialist ideology. What, then, is the added value of solidarity as compared to justice?

To answer this question, we will first present Rawls's *Theory of Justice*, which is the main theoretical framework for liberal justice. I will continue with the extension of Rawls's theory to health and health care by Daniels. After discussing some of the main theoretical critiques of the approach by Rawls, like the capabilities approach by Nussbaum and Sen, I will deal with more recent directions in liberal and liberal-egalitarian theories, particularly the more restrictive versions in opportunity-based egalitarianism. These restrictive approaches are leading to what I call the 'cold side of justice', criticised by Margalit and Wolff because of the way it humiliates individuals. The criticisms of liberal justice are an 'overture' to the discussion of solidarity as non-instrumental cooperation in the life world. This chapter discusses the contributions by authors working in the tradition of the *Critical Theory* which is rooted in the former *Frankfurt Schule*. It will present the views of Habermas, Honneth and Jaeggi who are departing from the distinction between *Moralität* (ethics as defined by rights) which is typical for the work of Kant and *Sittlichkeit* (ethical life) which goes back to the work of Hegel. While 'justice' refers to rights and duties (*Moralität*), the concept of solidarity refers to relations of personal commitment and recognition (*Sittlichkeit*). The importance of solidarity lies in its relational aspects, particularly its emphasis on cooperation and commonality. The paper argues that both solidarity and justice are important for the arrangement of health care practices and that like Habermas argues they must be seen as 'two sides of a coin'. This section is followed by a discussion of communitarianism and the critique of this approach in regard with the recognition of individual differences. The final section of the chapter will give an idea how solidarity and justice can be connected to enable health care policies and practices in which individuals are not humiliated and are connected on the basis of *humanitarian solidarity* or *shared humanity* (Margalit).

3.2   Rawls's Theory of Justice

The philosophy of justice interprets society and the problem of just distribution of resources in terms of a social contract: does everyone involved get a fair share of the fruits of the deal? The liberal approach is based on the concept of autonomous individuals negotiating their interests. From this perspective, liberal debates tend to focus on the normative evaluation of the performance of the system in terms of the distribution of services. This model is most outspoken in the influential book *A Theory of Justice* by John Rawls (1972) in which he proposed two principles of justice to evaluate the distribution of social and economic advantages in a society. According to Rawls, these principles would be accepted by individuals when they would deliberate about a just distribution behind a 'veil of ignorance' that is without knowing their own particular circumstances or social position. The First Principle of Justice is that 'each person is to have an equal right to the most extensive basic liberty compatible with a similar liberty for others'. The Second Principle is that 'social and economic inequalities are to be arranged so that they are both a) reasonably expected to be to one's advantage, and b) attached to positions and offices open to all' (Rawls 1989: 60).

Rawls developed his theory in response to utilitarianism and particularly the utility principle which advocates that we should strive towards a distribution of social goods that would result in the greatest possible benefit of the greatest possible number. According to Rawls, utilitarianism cannot avoid the fact that the greater gains of the largest group in society can only be established at the expense of the preferences and rights of some other individuals. For utilitarianism, it does not matter how the sum of satisfactions is distributed among individuals any more than it matters how one man distributes his satisfactions over time

(Rawls 1989: 26). The correct distribution of benefits or satisfactions in either case is the one that yields the maximum fulfilment of these satisfactions, but in itself no distribution is better than another. However, utilitarianism cannot explain why the greater gains of some should not compensate for the lesser losses of others, or why the violation of liberty of a few might not be made right by the greater good shared by many (idem). In fact, the most natural way of utilitarianism to reach its aims is to adopt for society as a whole the principle of rational choice for one man (Rawls 1989: 26–27). Rawls argues that, in view of the diverse wishes and preferences of individuals, utilitarianism has to embrace the perspective of the impartial spectator as the perfect rational individual who identifies with and experiences the desires of others as his own (Rawls 1989: 27). In the end such a perspective conflates all persons into one through the imaginative acts of the impartial sympathetic spectator: 'Utilitarianism does not take seriously the distinction between persons' (Rawls 1989: 27).

As a deontological philosopher Rawls argues that each member of society has an inviolability founded on justice, which the welfare of society cannot override: 'Justice denies that the loss of freedom for some is made right by a greater good shared by others ... in a just society the basic liberties are taken for granted and the rights secured by justice are not subject to political bargaining or to the calculus of social interests' (Rawls 1989: 28). For Rawls justice is fairness, meaning that each individual has basic liberties and rights which cannot be overruled by a utilitarian calculus or other social interest. The principles as agreed in the original position are based on a fair procedure: they require equal liberties for all and permit only those economic and social inequalities which are to each person's interests (Rawls 1989: 33). The difference between justice as fairness and utilitarianism is described by Rawls as follows:

> In the one we think of a well-ordered society as a scheme of cooperation for reciprocal advantage regulated by the principles which persons would choose in an initial situation that is fair, in the other as the efficient administration of social resources to maximize the satisfaction of the system of desire constructed by the impartial spectator from the many individual systems of desires accepted as given.
>
> (Rawls 1989: 33)

The principles of justice put limits on individual satisfactions and conceptions of the good as they specify the boundaries of what individuals and society need to respect. This perspective then leads to Rawls's famous words that in justice as fairness *the concept of right is prior to that of the good* (Rawls 1989: 31; italics added). A just social system provides the framework of rights and opportunities in which the individuals develop their aims and satisfactions. This principle, the priority of the right over the good, is a central feature in Rawls's conception of justice, but it is also the principle which has been heavily criticised, particularly by communitarian authors.[1]

An important element of Rawls's Theory of Justice is the development of an index of primary goods which can serve as a yardstick for assessing to which extent inequalities can be justified or not. According to Rawls, primary goods are things a rational man would like to have for himself, they are things that 'he would prefer more or less' (Rawls 1989: 92). With these primary goods a rational man can be assured of greater success in carrying out certain intentions and life plans. Primary social goods are 'rights and liberties, opportunities and powers, income and wealth' (idem). The assumption of Rawls is that, while all individuals might have different final ends and plans, they all require for their execution certain primary goods, which can be natural or social. Intelligence, wealth and opportunity are examples of primary goods that will enable individuals to reach ends they would not reach otherwise. Individuals in the original position would want more of those goods as it is in their interest to have them. Liberty is a primary good shared equally by individuals, while the share in other primary goods is dependent on the principle that 'some can have more if they are acquired in ways which improve the situation of those who have less' (Rawls 1989: 94). An index of primary goods then is the total of expectations a reasonable man would prefer and look forward to in order to achieve a successful life. As individuals are born with different and arbitrary starting places in terms of natural contingencies and social fortune, justice tries to mitigate the impact of these differences on the life plans of individuals by guaranteeing equal citizenship and redistribution of income and wealth. Institutions are then ranked by how effectively they guarantee equal liberty and fair equality of opportunity. Rawls's theory is called liberal egalitarianism or even egalitarianism, because of the egalitarian implications of his theory for redistributive policies. In spite of the egalitarian implications, it does not leave out the possibility for differences in access to certain social goods or

---

[1] See Section 3.9 of this chapter.

services like, for example, in health care, provided that there is a basic level of services which is equally accessible for all.

The precise content of the index of primary goods is defined by what Rawls calls the 'thin theory of the good' (Rawls 1989: 397). It is thin as it includes only minimal assumptions which are shared by individuals about what kinds of goods are useful to all individual conceptions of the good. The thin theory of the good is distinct from the 'full theory of the good' as the thin theory is only giving the kinds of things that can be agreed upon at a minimal level, while the full theory includes particular conceptions of the good based on the values and ends of individuals. According to Rawls, we need the thin theory of the good to explain the rational preferences for primary goods and to explicate the notion of rationality underlying the choice of principles in the original positon. The thin theory of the good which the parties are assumed to accept shows 'that they should try to secure liberty and self-respect, and that, in order to advance their aims, whatever these are, they normally require more rather than less of the other primary goods' (Rawls 1989: 397).

3.3   Justice and Health: The Extension by Daniels

Rawls did not apply his principles of justice to health care and never answered the question whether health could be considered a primary good. According to Daniels (2007), health should not be added as a primary good: adding health to the list of goods would not only lengthen the list of primary goods (which would then lose its normative significance), but we might likely lose 'our shared political conception of the needs of citizens' (Daniels 2007: 56). Moreover, Daniels argues that adding health to the index of primary goods would force Rawls into comparisons of well-being or utility, which his philosophy (including the list of primary goods) wants to avoid. In view of the many different needs and preferences regarding health, we would end up in the utilitarian approach of the impartial spectator who would decide which needs are more important than other, ignoring the needs of minorities and the rights of individuals.[2]

However, not including health in the index of goods does not mean that health is not important for a just society. In his books *Just Health Care* (1985) and *Just Health* (2007) Daniels argues that health is

---

[2] See Section 3.2.

important because it underlies normal functioning which in turn protects people's fair share of the normal opportunity range in a society. In *Just Health Care* Daniels explains the concept of normal functioning by way of the bio-statistical theory of health as developed by Christopher Boorse (1977). According to Boorse, health can be defined as 'normal species function' which he narrows down to survival and reproduction. A biological function can be defined as a causal contribution to normal species function, while a departure from such a biological function is a statistical deviation from the normal causal contribution. Daniels argues that such a view of health as normal species function will help us to ascribe health and departures from it 'as objective and value-free as the biomedical sciences themselves' (Daniels 2007: 38). Such a perspective is needed to generate objective claims for support in case of departures of normal functioning, which then elicits a response from society which is agreed by the public as being based in objective needs instead of subjective preferences. This does not mean, Daniels argues, that we have eliminated all normative judgements: while the claim for medical support might be based in objective processes, our response to it, and particularly how to rank the various needs, remains a normative task. Daniels acknowledges that there are critiques on Boorse's model, like the critique that it ignores the social construction of health and disease and that by consequence definitions of health and disease may change over time (Engelhardt 1974; 1986). However, these criticisms only confirm that we should get away from subjective definitions of health and base such a theory of health on the biomedical sciences as the only way to reach public agreement on support for health needs. Nonetheless, some disabilities and mental health issues do not fit with Boorse's bio-statistical model and would not be able to count on publicly funded health care if one would follow Daniels's approach.

Daniels argues that individuals have a share in what he calls the normal opportunity range in society according to their individual talents and skills. Pathology, such as a serious disease, injury or disability, are a significant impairment of normal functioning and impair the range of opportunities open to that individual. The moral significance of health care is based in the fact that it restores the access to the share of individuals to the normal opportunity range. Just as we must use resources to counter the opportunity advantages that some get in the social lottery, we must also use resources to counter the disadvantages induced by pathology (Daniels 2007: 58). The purpose is not to eliminate or level individual differences in the share of the normal opportunity range but only to protect their fair share in it. These fair shares will not be equal shares as individuals differ in relation to their talents and skills.

Meeting health needs is important to promote normal functioning of individuals in order to assure them access to the normal opportunity range which they would normally have in the absence of disease or disability. But 'health' should not be included in the index of primary goods. Instead health care *institutions* should be part of the basic institutions involved in providing for fair equality of opportunity: 'The special importance and unequal distribution of health-care needs, like educational needs, are acknowledged by connecting the needs to institutions that provide for fair equality of opportunity. But opportunity, not health care or education, remains the primary social good' (Daniels 2007: 57).

The principle of fair equality of opportunity does not stand on its own: it needs to be combined with the difference principle. The principle of fair equality of opportunity (which supports access to health care institutions) does not correct all individual differences in talents and skills. This principle accepts the differences between individuals as a 'baseline' and leaves it to the difference principle 'to mitigate the effects on opportunity of being born with less marketable talents and skills' (Daniels 2007: 58).

3.4   The Critique from the Capabilities Approach

Rawls tried to develop a theory of justice based on rights independent of conceptions of the good: rights are primary to the good. A just society is one that helps individuals to realise their life plans as they see fit by promoting access to primary goods and providing fair equality of opportunity, for example by adequate access to health care institutions. This is what Rawls calls the 'thin theory of the good', meaning the ordering of society is led by some ideas of the good as they are agreed behind the veil of ignorance. Society should not further interfere in the life plans of individuals and their conceptions of the good that guide these plans. Nor should these 'thick' conceptions of the good be the starting point of the social structure of society or of the principles which promote social justice.

However, this approach is criticised as too narrow as it is limiting support to social arrangements that assure only *negative* freedom, meaning non-interference in the lives of individuals (Ram Tiktin 2012). Instead Amartya Sen and Martha Nussbaum argue that *actual* freedom should be the starting point of distributive justice. According to Sen

(1990) a fair distribution of primary goods does not say anything about the extent of the freedom of individuals to choose a way of living according to their values. According to Sen, individual claims must not be assessed by the resources or primary goods (Rawls) these individuals hold, but by the actual freedom they enjoy to achieve what they would like to do or to be in their lives. This actual freedom is represented by what Sen calls *capabilities*: while Rawls focuses on the *means* to enjoy a good life, it is more important to assess to which extent individuals are *capable* to actually make use of these means. Persons with disabilities might have more primary goods (liberty, income, wealth and so on) than many other people, but they have less capability to use these resources due to their disability (Sen 1990). Another example are people in wealthy countries who are poor in terms of income and other primary goods also have characteristics, like age, disabilities and proneness to disease, that make it more difficult to convert primary goods into basic capabilities, like leading a healthy life (Sen 1990). According to Sen, neither primary goods nor resources can represent the capability a person actually enjoys to lead the life he or she wants. There are many variations between individuals related to sex, age, genetic endowments, which give them unequal powers to convert resources (or primary goods) into actual freedoms. Regarding distributive justice, then, we should not look at the distribution of means but examine the capabilities we actually enjoy (Sen 1990).

A similar argument has been made by Martha Nussbaum (1992). From an Aristotelian point of view, she argues that wealth and income are not good in their own right and that they are only good as they promote human functioning (Nussbaum 1992). For Rawls, on the other hand, primary goods like income and wealth are just things of which more is always better, independently of the 'concrete conception of the good'. 'Better off' and 'worse off' are defined by Rawls in terms of the quantities individuals have of these resources instead of their functioning or capability to make use of them. According to Nussbaum (2011), the capabilities approach is sensitive to the complexity and the qualitative diversity of the goals that people pursue and that people may need different quantities of resources if they are to come up to the same level of ability to choose and act, particularly if they begin from different social positions. Like Sen, Nussbaum gives various examples of how the possession of resources does not say much about the needs of individuals and of their capacity to live a life according to their own values.

> A pregnant woman has nutritional needs that are different from those of a
> nonpregnant woman and a child from those of an adult. The child who has
> exactly the same amount of protein in her diet as an adult is less well off,
> given her greater needs. A person whose mobility is impaired will need a
> significantly greater amount of resources than will a person of average
> mobility in order to achieve the same level of capability to move about.
>
> (Nussbaum 1992: 233)

According to Nussbaum, by defining well off only in terms of wealth, liberal philosophers fail to recognise the importance of impediments to functioning in many people's lives. This is an 'important defect' in liberal theory: though liberty is indeed an important primary good, we need to go further than that by making a list of primary goods 'not a list of resources and commodities at all. but a list of basic capabilities of the person' (Nussbaum 1992: 234).

Nussbaum's views are strongly linked to her Aristotelian approach which tries to define essential elements or features that make human life flourishing. Such an account includes a list of basic needs and capabilities that is necessary for human functioning and human flourishing. According to Nussbaum, this position is challenged by anthropologists and economists as being 'essentialist': it leaves no room for relative accounts of human functioning including the importance of historical and cultural values. This 'anti-essentialism' is supported by the liberal conception of autonomy as negative liberty or non-interference. The liberal philosopher would argue that drawing a list of capabilities would mean a 'neglect of autonomy' (Nussbaum 1992: 225) and would remove from the citizens the chance to make their own choices about the good life. Nussbaum argues, however, that the list is a list of capabilities, not actually functions, because such a list would enable individuals to make a choice about their lives. Governments using such lists would not push citizens in any direction or to act in any prescribed ways. Instead, such a list is directed to make sure all human beings have the necessary resources and conditions to act in ways they find important, 'it leaves the choice up to them' (Nussbaum 1992: 225).

> A person with plenty of good can always choose to fast; a person who has
> access to subsidized university education can always decide to do some-
> thing else instead. By making opportunities available, government
> enhances, and does not remove, choice.
>
> (Nussbaum 1992: 225)

Daniels (2007) answers the critique by Sen and Nussbaum by saying that, in fact, there is much convergence between their capabilities approach and Rawls's theory of justice. This is particularly true after extension by Daniels of Rawls's theory to health and health care, including the broadening of the normal opportunity range to include access to health care services. According to Daniels, there is not a real difference between his concept of the normal opportunity range and Sen's capabilities approach. The normal opportunity range is the same as the capability space Sen defines with a different terminology. This concept of the capability space 'seems only to differ in terminology' from the Rawlsian language of having a fair share in the normal opportunity range and the idea of a set of life plans people can reasonably adopt given their talents and skills. People can reasonably adopt a plan for life 'if they have the capabilities to do and be what that plan calls for' (Daniels 2007: 66).

However, there is a difference between the two approaches. This difference has to do with the limits set by society in assisting individuals to have an adequate set of capabilities. Though capabilities are important for human functioning, Daniels argues that Sen does not pursue an equal set of capabilities for all. The individual sets of capabilities are ranked differently by the individuals, but it does not mean that they should be supported equally by society (Daniels 2007: 68–69). If that was the case society would be obliged to improve or develop every capability individuals would want for themselves. We would then make the principle of equality of opportunity 'hostage to expensive and demanding preferences for certain capabilities' (Daniels 2007: 69):

> Just as we are not obliged to use our resources to make others happy when they are unhappy because of extravagant tastes, so too we are not obliged to improve any and every capability that they judge to be disadvantageous, given their plans of life.
>
> (Daniels 2007: 69)

Daniels argues, that Sen does not offer a real account of what a sufficient or adequate set of capabilities should look like and that his (Daniels's) own goal of preserving normal functioning, and the significance of the impact of significant disease and disability on normal opportunities or disabilities, 'might provide what is missing' (Daniels 2007: 70).

While Daniels tries to neutralise the critique of Sen and Nussbaum on Rawls's theory of justice and his own extension of Rawls's theory to health care, he fails to see the point Sen, and certainly Nussbaum, are making of the essential link between justice and the question of how to lead a good life. Liberalism is interested in rights, not in the good, as this is subject to individual preferences and disagreements. Liberalism, including Rawls's and Daniels's theory, focuses on the resources to live a good life, not on the good life itself. An answer to the question of whether individuals can live a decent life under conditions of justice, or how justice can promote, or *prevent,* a decent life, beyond supplying the means to do so, is not part of the liberal *discourse.* While liberal philosophy, including the impressive work of Rawls on justice and its extension by Daniels to health care, pays only attention to negative liberty, Sen and Nussbaum explore the relation between justice and *positive* freedom, that is the way justice can (or cannot) contribute to a good and flourishing life. This is an important step away from the one-sidedness of the justice discourse, though it is not enough: what we are interested in is not the impact of justice on the positive freedom of individuals, but on the way justice promotes *solidarity* meaning relations of recognition and identity which are the basis of freedom, seen as freedom-in-relation-to-others. We will return to the relation between justice and the good life, and more particularly between justice and solidarity further down in this chapter.

3.5 Restrictive Approaches to Justice

According to Daniels, the principle of fair equality of opportunity leaves the differences in capabilities in place, and focuses on keeping functioning as normally as possible. Capabilities will not be equalised, but supported by access to the normal opportunity range. The differences in capabilities will of course generate differences in access to social goods. Rawls mitigates the effects of this basic inequality by requiring that inequalities in primary goods like wealth and income be constrained so that they work to the advantage of the worst-off. 'In this way, those with more marketable talents and skill must harness their advantages to maximize the prospects of those who have the least marketable talents and skills' (Daniels 2007: 67). The two principles, the principle of difference and the principle of fair equality, must work together to mitigate the effects of differences in capabilities in order to create a more just society.

Rawls argues that the difference principle gives weight to considerations based on the principle of *redress.* This is the principle 'that undeserved inequalities call for redress; and since inequalities of birth and natural endowment are undeserved, these inequalities are to be somehow compensated for' (Rawls 1989: 100). Rawls continues that to treat all persons equally and to provide equality of opportunity, 'society must give more attention to those with fewer native assets and to those born into the less favorable social positions' (Rawls 1989: 100).

According to Rawls, the difference principle is not the same as the principle of redress, but it achieves some of the intent of the latter. No one should gain or lose from his arbitrary place in the distribution of natural access or initial position in society without giving or receiving compensating advantages. The task of institutions is to redress these differences and inequalities:

> The natural distribution is neither just nor unjust; nor is it unjust that men are born into society at some particular position. These are simply natural facts. What is just and unjust is the way that institutions deal with these facts ... The social system is not an unchangeable order beyond human control but a pattern of human action. In justice as fairness men agree to share one another's fate. In designing institutions they undertake to avail themselves of the accidents of nature and social circumstance only when doing so is for the common benefit. The two principles are a fair way of meeting the arbitrariness of fortune; and while no doubt imperfect in other ways, the institutions which satisfy these principles are just.
>
> (Rawls 1989: 102)

However, Rawls does not clarify to which extent social circumstances are fully the result of social structures or forces beyond the control of the individual or whether there is an element of choice or personal responsibility which make some persons worse off than others. Should we compensate for the disadvantages of individuals when these disadvantages are (partly) the result of their own choices? Kymlicka (2002) gives the example of the tennis player and the gardener to illustrate this point. Two people with equal talents and social backgrounds are given the same amount of money, one uses the money to buy a tennis court because he likes playing tennis, the other one spends the money to buy a piece of land to grow vegetables. While the tennis player enjoys tennis, the gardener is working long hours to grow vegetables on the land. She makes a profit by selling the vegetables on the market, while the tennis player gradually has no income and gets poorer in the course of time. The question is then whether the gardener should support the tennis player or, alternatively, the government should transfer income from the gardener to the tennis player in order to equalise income (Kymlicka 2002: 74).

According to Kymlicka, one could argue that it is unjust if people are disadvantaged by inequalities in their circumstances, but that it is equally unjust to demand that someone has to pay for the costs of the choices of somebody else. He argues that Rawls would not wish to make the gardener subsidise the tennis player. Rawls theory of justice is supposed to be concerned with inequalities related to people's life chances, not with inequalities that arise from people's life choices which are the individual's own responsibility. However, the difference principle 'does not make a distinction between chosen and unchosen inequalities' (Kymlicka 2002: 74). One possible result of the difference principle is then to make some people pay for the choices of others, should it be the case that these others have the least income and that they are in that position, like the tennis player, by their own choice. According to Kymlicka, Rawls wants to mitigate the unjust effects of natural and social disadvantage, 'but it also mitigates the legitimate effects of personal choice and effort' (Kymlicka 2002: 74).

In liberal philosophy the distinction between choice and circumstance has become more important, like, for example, in the work of Ronald Dworkin. Dworkin (1981) makes a distinction between 'ambition-sensitive' and 'endowment-sensitive' approaches to distributive justice, meaning that people's fate should not depend on their circumstances only, but also on their ambitions in terms of life plans and projects. With this distinction, Dworkin tried to emphasise that the welfare state can be made more choice sensitive by enabling those with resources to have more choices (for example, allowing supplementary private health insurance), while at the same time ensuring that the lazy or imprudent do not impose the costs of their choices on others (for example by requiring people on welfare benefits to perform some work, also called workfare) (Kymlicka 2002: 93). Dworkin's work is also called the *opportunity* approach to equality: both the gardener and the tennis player in Kymlicka's example have the opportunity to increase their resources. If they fail to do so, any redistribution is not a matter of justice but of personal responsibility. Opportunity-based egalitarianism has important implications for welfare policies. It will justify, for example, that, in case there is work available, individuals who refuse to work should not receive benefits. Such people do not lack the opportunities as the employed have, and there is no reason or argument from justice to transfer benefits from the employed to the voluntary unemployed, also called the *undeserving poor* (Wolff 1998).

Emphasising the role of choice and opportunity in regard with distributive justice reinforced the agenda of the New Right which is 'obsessed with identifying and punishing the irresponsible and indolent' (Kymlicka 2002: 93). According to the New Right, the welfare state wrongly limits the choices and ambitions of the well off in order to subsidise the irresponsible behaviour of welfare dependants (Kymlicka 2002: 93). Focusing on personal choice and opportunity as some liberal theorists like Dworkin do, did nothing to mitigate the effects of unequal circumstances. Though it was Dworkin's intention to emphasise *both* choice sensitivity and circumstance sensitivity, the New Right exploited the idea of choice sensitivity to make welfare more conditional to individual responsibility and to stigmatise the needy whose plight is pictured as the result of their own fault ('blaming the victim') (Kymlicka 2002: 94). Liberal egalitarians, on the other hand, insist that 'society can only legitimately hold people responsible if their preferences and capacities have been formed under condition of justice' (Kymlicka 2002: 93). To hold people responsible for their choices without providing adequate education is an example of 'bad faith' (idem). This argument could be raised in the debate about limiting access to treatments for individuals because of their unhealthy food and drink habits. In many cases, these individuals are living in poor neighbourhoods and have not had adequate education about healthy lifestyles. Holding them responsible for their lifestyle and arguing that the problems resulting from their choices are their own fault can be seen as stigmatisation of the needy and 'blaming the victim' (Kymlicka 2002: 94).

3.6   The 'Cold Side' of Justice

While Rawls argues that the deliberations behind the veil of ignorance are led by rational and impartial motivations, one can also argue that these deliberations can only take place if there is some sense of benevolence among the individuals towards the less well off in society. The obligations and principles which the individuals are supposed to agree with are in the end rooted in contingent and empirical conceptions of our obligations to the other. One can argue then that benevolence precedes justice and is more fundamental than justice. According to Sandel (1998), justice has a 'remedial function' towards the circumstances of benevolence and fraternity. When fraternity fades, justice may help to redeem the loss of benevolence that is typical for the pre-existing relationship (Sandel 1998: 32–33). But the replacement by justice does not necessarily lead to a moral improvement. There is a risk that justice can become so dominant and restricting that it may destroy the relations of benevolence in which it is rooted. Sandel gives the example of the (ideal) family where relations are governed by spontaneous affection and circumstances of justice prevail to a small degree (Sandel 1998: 33). Individual rights are seldom invoked due to a spirit of generosity in which the members of the family do not have any inclination to claim a fair share. However, when the family is wrought with dissension and individual interests grow divergent, the circumstances of justice become more acute. The affection and spontaneity of previous days give way to demands for fairness and observance of rights. Even when the parents and children abide conscientiously by the rights and duties which they agreed, something has been lost compared to the circumstances of the previous situation.

However, a more worrying situation arises when from a misplaced sense of justice individuals take on a calculating attitude and claim a precise share of the expenditures or income. According to Sandel, in such a situation individuals may lose the spontaneous mutual benevolence which may be typical for the previous situation. There may be no injustice, but the exercise of justice in such an inappropriate way may have brought about an overall decline in the moral character of the association: 'justice in this case will have been not a virtue but a vice' (Sandel 1998: 35).

Rawls's idea of justice can certainly not be characterised as a vice and lacking benevolence towards those in unfortunate circumstances. His idea of social order can be justified to everyone and particularly to those who are less favoured (Rawls 1989: 102). It is an egalitarian scheme which is supposed to benefit all. However, in opportunity based egalitarianism, and particularly in New Right approaches, elements of commonality and reciprocity are exchanged or narrowed down to individual choice and rational calculation of opportunity. Apart from problems of individualism and rationalism, the practical weakness of this picture lies in the lack of reciprocity and negative identification with the 'receiver' of goods. As soon as others are perceived as making extravagant claims or are otherwise undeserving (because they do not take the opportunities offered to them), there are less reasons for a high standard of goods to be distributed. People need very few examples of others making ill use of the system to reduce their support (as can be illustrated by the example of unhealthy behaviour as a reason to limit access to health care services).

While Rawls may have endorsed fairly high standards for collective distribution of basic goods to mitigate natural and social inequalities, there is a stimulus in opportunity-based liberalism to restrict standards of provisions and obligations for support to a minimum. As a result, public (middle class) support for policies that would try to mitigate this injustice have eroded and have resulted in less generous levels of support for the needy. Political liberalism, particularly opportunity egalitarianism and its interpretation by the New Right, has for this reason been accused of an attitude of 'coldness', concealed as rationality: social support is conceptually limited to the ascription of rights and based on a scrutiny of people's needs and the opportunities that have been open to them (Houtepen and ter Meulen 2000b; Pasini and Reichlin 2001).

3.7   The Challenge from Libertarianism

A more radical emphasis on personal choice and personal responsibility can be found in libertarianism. This approach rejects the outcome-based approach as proposed by Rawls and Daniels. For example, Nozick (1974), argues for a freedom-based concept of justice in which distributions of goods are made in accordance with the consent of the individuals. In libertarianism, justice is defined as beneficence constrained by the principle of autonomy. In bioethics, libertarianism is represented by Engelhardt (1986) who argues that justice means first and foremost giving to each the right to be respected as a free individual in the disposition of personal services and private goods. Applied to health care this means that health care systems should have two tiers, one tier allowing private choices, and another basic tier supporting a 'general social sympathy' for those in need (Engelhardt 1986: 361). However, such a 'compromise' between communal provisions and individual choices should not be based on outcome-oriented criteria (like fair equality of opportunity), but on the consent of individuals and societal choices. What constitutes a communally provided level of care can only be created in a process of negotiation between individuals.

Libertarianism does not deny that unequal circumstances can create unfairness, but it argues that there is no clear line between choice and circumstance. As a result it denies that undeserved inequalities in circumstances give rise to moral claims on societal welfare policies (Kymlicka 2002). It does not deny that individuals could support each other but this can only happen on the basis of free consent or as a personal virtuous commitment. When the state takes over individual decisions and personal moral commitments, we are on 'the slippery slope to oppressive social intervention, centralised planning, and even human engineering' which would lead down the road to serfdom (Kymlicka 2002: 154).

Kymlicka points to the fact that libertarianism should not be seen as synonymous with the ideology and policies of the New Right (Kymlicka 2002: 156). While libertarianism excludes and rejects any redistribution by the state to mitigate unequal circumstances, the New Right does believe in such redistribution policies, albeit to a more minimal extent as compared to Rawls's approach. The New Right, which became dominant in the Thatcher-Reagan area, argues that the state is asking too much (taxing) from hard-working citizens in order to subsidise the lazy and indolent. Moreover, the state has failed to remedy the disadvantages facing the poor and has created a culture of passivity and dependency. But this does not mean that the state has no role to play in promoting social justice: the New Right wants the poor to take up the opportunities that are open in society and to earn their living. This means that benefits are reduced and welfare recipients are forced to take up work (so-called 'workfare' programmes). But these policies are not an embrace of libertarianism and the radical individualism it represents. If there is support for the New Right among the population, particularly the middle classes, it is because there is lack of trust in policies by the state to implement distributive policies based on the principles of liberal egalitarianism (Kymlicka 2002). It is not because there is no support for such principles, but, instead, because there is a different interpretation who *deserves* to be supported.

3.8 Justice and Humiliation

In his book *The Decent Society* (1996) Avishai Margalit makes a distinction between a just society and a decent society. According to Margalit, a decent society is one in which institutions are designed to prevent the humiliation of people by other people. Humiliation is defined by Margalit as 'any behavior or condition that constitutes a sound reason for a person to consider his or her self-respect injured' (Margalit 1996: 9). Institutions have an inherent tendency to humiliate people, for example by rejection, exclusion, paternalism and denial of rights. Margalit notes that many institutions of the welfare state put their beneficiaries through humiliating procedures in order to obtain their rightful provisions. In contrast, a decent society is one that cares that the institutions themselves do not operate in a humiliating way:

> A decent society is one that fights conditions which constitute a justification for its dependents to consider themselves humiliated. A society is decent if its institutions do not act in ways that give the people under their authority sound reasons to consider themselves humiliated.
>
> (Margalit 1996: 10–11)

According to Margalit a *just* society is not necessarily a *decent* society. There is no doubt that the spirit of a just society, based on Rawls's principles of liberty and justified difference, conflicts essentially with a non-decent society (Margalit 1996: 272). However, Margalit argues, a Rawls-style just society and the just distribution of primary goods, can still contain humiliating institutions. According to Rawls, part of the primary goods is the sense people have of themselves as having a value, and the sense that their life plans are worthy of realisation as well as the confidence to be able to carry out these plans. Self-respect is in fact the most basic primary good, as without it there is no point in doing anything whatsoever:

> When we feel that our plans are of little value, we cannot pursue them with pleasure or take delight in their execution. Nor plagued by failure and self-doubt can we continue in our endeavors. It is clear then why self-respect is a primary good. Without it nothing may seem worth doing, or if some things have value for us, we lack the will to strive for them. All desire and activity becomes empty and vain, and we sink into apathy and cynicism.
>
> (Rawls 1998: 440)

Rawls argues that the parties in the original position would wish to avoid at almost any costs the social conditions that undermine self-respect. Rational people wanting to establish a just society will do everything to avoid creating humiliating institutions or conditions, since these would diminish the most basic primary social good. One can accept differences in the distributions of some of the primary goods, but there is no room for any inequality in the distribution of self-respect (Margalit 1996: 273). If humiliating means damaging people's self-respect, it should be clear that a necessary condition for a just society is that it should be a society that does not humiliate its members.

In order to evaluate whether a just society is also a decent society, it is important to make a distinction between the *pattern* of distribution and the *procedure* to obtain the just distribution (Margalit 1996). The distribution may be just and efficient, but it may still be humiliating. Margalit reminds us of the old fear 'that justice may lack compassion and might even be an expression of vindictiveness' (Margalit 1996: 280). In practice, justice may become very calculating about what is just, instead of being humane and gentle. Margalit argues that the just society as defined by Rawls is, in spirit, a decidedly decent society. However, Rawls cannot avoid that, in practice, the just society may be an indecent society, particularly in the *procedures* of how goods are distributed to needy individuals. The distribution of services may be efficient and just, but can still reflect a lack of compassion and an expression of vindictiveness.

> There is a suspicion that the just society may become mired in rigid calculations of what is just, which may replace gentleness and humane consideration in simple human relations. The requirement that a just society should also be a decent one means that it is not enough for goods to be distributed justly and efficiently – the style of their distribution must also be taken into account.
>
> (Margalit 1996: 280–281)

Similar comments are made by Jonathan Wolff (1998) in regard to opportunity egalitarians like Dworkin and others. As described in the previous section, opportunity egalitarians argue that those who are able to work at a time when work is available, should receive no benefits if they do not work. The reason why is that if there is an opportunity to work, there is no reason why the employed should transfer resources to the voluntary unemployed or the so-called 'undeserving poor'. The example given by Kymlicka of the tennis player and the gardener illustrates this argument. Wolff argues that this argument results in disrespect and humiliating practices, 'subjecting the poor to a level of scrutiny and control not experienced by the better off' (Wolff 1998: 121–122). According to Wolff, the poor are not only confronted with lack of trust and common courtesy, they are also subjected to what he calls 'shameful revelation': this is the practice in which people are required to demean themselves by behaving or revealing things about themselves which can 'rationally be expected to reduce their respect-standing' (Wolff 1998: 109). The purpose of such practices is to verify to which extent the fortune of individuals is the result of their choices and how much can be contributed to their circumstances. This means that the authorities or institutions want to collect various forms of data from individuals and want to make the welfare or benefit payments entirely conditional on the information collected. As a result, 'welfare claimants are often treated with great rudeness and in some cases are routinely humiliated' (Wolff 1998: 110–111).

If there is no lack of opportunity, the failure of individuals is assumed to be the result of their own lack of abilities or talents. To press a claim, Wolff argues, is not only to admit, but also 'to make out a convincing case that one is a failure, unable to admit to gain employment even when there is no difficulty for others' (Wolff 1998: 114). This 'removes any last shred of dignity from those already in a very unfortunate position' (Wolff 1998: 114). The unemployed are required to give humiliating answers to humiliating questions in order to qualify for welfare benefits. This leads not only to scrutiny by the institutions, but also to self-scrutiny and diminishing self-respect:

> In this case one is required to reveal facts that one finds demeaning or shameful, even humiliating. Surely it is very difficult to retain any sense of oneself as an equal under such circumstances.
>
> (Wolff 1998: 114)

According to Wolff, fairness as proposed by the opportunity egalitarians leads to diminishing respect, humiliation and loss of feelings of equality. Egalitarian legislators should try to keep justice and respect in a balance.

While Wolff discusses humiliation in the context of unemployment and welfare practices, the argument can be extended to health and social care. As discussed earlier, in a situation of diminishing resources for health care, there is decreasing support for individuals who do not behave responsibly because of unhealthy lifestyles. From the perspective of opportunity egalitarianism, such individuals are abusing the access to health services and do not 'deserve' to get their health care costs paid by the public health care system. Justice in this context means that the contributions by the 'givers' must be matched by the 'right' behaviour by the 'recipients' of health care.

A comparable development can be noted in regard with the funding of long-term care, home care and social care. In view of the lack of resources, home care services are reduced to short-term visits of 15 minutes per visit, while families must prove that they are not able to support their family members at home. Applications for home care support are scrutinised by city councils or central agencies, in order to determine whether families (particularly spouses) have the capacity to take care of their loved ones themselves and whether they are not abusing the system. An example of such a procedure are the 'kitchen table discussions' which were recently introduced in The Netherlands to assess the capacity of spouses and other family members to support their dependent family members and to determine the eligibility for home care support.[3] Similarly, access to long-term care facilities in institutions like nursing homes is becoming severely restricted, as admissions are based on a scrutiny of

---

[3] See Chapter 4.

the potential within families to deliver care at home. However, humiliation can also take place because of discrimination of people with disabilities or negative stereotypes of vulnerable individuals like the frail elderly who have become dependent on our care. Though care for dependent individuals may be just from the perspective of distributive justice (meaning a compensation for the debilitating circumstances of old age or disability), it can still be *indecent*, because of the humiliating way this care is provided (ter Meulen 2011).

3.9 The Perspective of Solidarity

The *Theory of Justice* by Rawls, and the philosophy of justice in general, are often criticised for its individualistic bias and for ruling out communitarian sentiments or mutual recognition between individuals. Liberal (and libertarian) discourses tend to define issues of justice as the result of negotiations between rational individuals who share no element of commonality and mutuality. In the liberal tradition, justice is interpreted as a matter of universal duties between individuals which can be justified on the basis of rational deliberations in the original position (Verburg and ter Meulen 2005). According to Nagel, the original position, as proposed by Rawls, 'seems to presuppose not just a neutral theory of the good, but a liberal, individualistic conception according to which the best that can be wished for is the unimpeded pursuit of his own path, provided it does not interfere with the rights of others' (Nagel 1989: 10). Rawls does discuss justice in the context of social cooperation: however, he analyses such relations between individuals from the perspective of individual self-interest and rational decision-making.

One can ask whether the idea of the rational independent decision maker, which underpins liberal theories of justice, does reflect the social reality in which it is rooted. In fact, the idea of the rational decision maker can be regarded as an ideological construct: it is a correct *and* incorrect reflection of social reality (Lorrain 1979). It is *correct* in the sense that individuals are expected to deal with each other as self-conscious, rational beings with mutual respect. It is *incorrect* as it ignores the underlying, social processes which can be characterised as moving towards increasing social dependencies by which individuals are connected to each other. According to the sociologist Norbert Elias, the modern individual is seeing himself as a closed 'ego', a *homo clausus*, who regards him or herself as distinct and independent of fellow human beings. This idea of human beings as independent decision makers is a

fiction, it is 'an artefact of human thinking that is characteristic for a
certain level in the development of human self-understanding' (Elias
1971: 113). Instead of seeing man as a 'closed' personality' we should
see man as an 'open' personality 'who in his relation with fellow human
beings can reach a higher or lower level of autonomy, but never absolute
or full autonomy, who during his life is continuously relying on and
dependent on other human beings' (Elias 1971: 115). The social interdependencies and the need to cooperate for one's own and society's interests are widely ignored by Rawls and other liberal and libertarian authors
as they focus on individualistic values and fail to see the social processes
which are responsible for the process of individualisation.

Liberal theories of justice are criticised for ignoring the moral, and
particularly relational, commitments between individuals (ter Meulen and
Houtepen 2012). Instead of rational calculation, the support of others can
also be understood because such a support and commitment is an important
value *in itself*, not just because we have an interest to do so. The concept of
solidarity expresses this commitment for the other, who deserves our
support as he or she is in need of it due to circumstances out of their control.
Solidarity at a concrete, personal level has more fundamental moral meaning than the political and ideological meaning of solidarity as a value for the
arrangements of the welfare state. According to Jaeggi, solidarity should not
be equated with the 'shallower common interest of a coalition' (Jaeggi 2001:
289) which is typical for the 'interest solidarity' or 'shared utility' which are
seen as important motivations to support the welfare state.[4] On the one
hand, solidarity may be based on common interest, a common fate and
certain interdependencies. On the other hand, solidarity seems to express a
deeper commitment than is necessary for a coalition, which is only formed
to achieve a certain goal (Jaeggi 2001). One does not change these commitments the way one changes sides in coalitions for strategic reasons. Moreover, Jaeggi argues, many attitudes of solidarity do not seem to be directed
by simple self-interest or 'shared utility': they are not strategic relations as
they try to transcend a narrow conception of individual interests.

Jaeggi conceptualises solidarity as a relational concept: it refers to
relations of support and understanding between individuals engaged in
cooperative practices. Acting out of solidarity means 'standing up for
each other because one recognises "one's own fate in the fate of the
other"' (Jaeggi 2001: 291). As a moral concept, solidarity implies a sense

---

[4] See Chapter 2.

of non-calculating cooperation based on identification with a common cause. This interpretation of solidarity as non-instrumental cooperation connects this concept to Hegel's idea of *Sittlichkeit* or 'ethical life'. Jaeggi refers to Theunissen (1981) who defines ethical life as 'those conditions in which the individual first and foremost finds his own self' (Jaeggi 2001: 295). According to Jaeggi individuals realise themselves by connecting to those kinds of relations that are intersubjective conditions of self-realisation. The 'Other' is not the limitation but the precondition of my freedom. Human beings are socially constituted on a fundamental level:

> Embedded in a certain culture, acting within an already present structure of social cooperation, it would be mistaken to see [human beings] as 'using' these relations in order to promote their own good. Rather it is only the very background conditions that provide him with the possibility to articulate his own good. To share a common life form ... in this perspective is essential – not only with regard to the problem of social integration but also with regard to the individual's possibility for self-realization.

> (Jaeggi 2001: 295)

Solidarity is firmly established by Honneth (1995) as one of the three 'patterns of recognition' which are essential to self-realisation: love, rights and solidarity. *Love* is the relationship in which individuals build up trust and self-confidence, starting with the relationship between mother and child. *Rights* express the recognition of and respect for persons as agents capable of acting on the basis of reasons, as morally responsible persons. *Solidarity* is the experience of recognition of oneself as a person with a particular identity in the intersubjective context of mutual recognition. Inspired by Hegel's idea of *Sittlichkeit* or ethical life (see earlier), this approach is based on a relational and contextual view of individual development. Solidarity is an essential part of the 'ethical life' as it is a necessary precondition for individual self-esteem.

> The only way in which individuals are constituted as persons is by learning to refer to themselves, from the perspective of an approving or encouraging other, as beings with certain positive traits and abilities. The scope of such traits – and hence the extent of one's positive relation-to-self – increases with each new form of recognition that individuals are able to apply to themselves as subjects.

> (Honneth 1995: 173)

The forms of recognition associated with love, rights and solidarity provide the intersubjective conditions for the process of articulating and recognising individual identity based on a positive relation to oneself.

According to Honneth, solidarity creates a climate in which self-esteem becomes possible. A good society is one in which individuals have a real opportunity for full self-realisation. This would be a society 'in which the common values would match the concerns of individuals in such a way that no member of society would be denied the opportunity to earn esteem for his or her contribution to the common good' (Anderson 1995: xvii). According to Honneth, one can speak of a state of societal solidarity to 'the extent to which every member of a society is in a position to esteem himself or herself' (Honneth 1995: 129). This does not mean that the Kantian concept of *Moralität* (morality) is not important for Honneth. While Kant's concept of the dignity of persons respects and protects human rights, solidarity promotes self-esteem under the condition of mutual relatedness and fundamental interdependency of individuals.

A relational understanding of solidarity is put forward by Habermas, particularly in his concept of the life world (Habermas 1989). In Habermas' theory, the life world denotes the sphere of interaction guided by communicative processes. Such processes thrive on the mutual preparedness to accept criticism and to search for common understanding. Communication involves cognitive, social and expressive dimensions, with truth, solidarity and identity as their respective regulative ideals. According to Habermas, these ideals are neither idealistic nor subjective. Communicative processes simply cannot be sustained without a basis of mutual orientation towards agreement on facts, norms and identities. On the other hand, such agreement does not need to empirically exist at all times and at all levels. For the sustainment of the communication process, it is sufficient that we credit others that their claims make sense from some perspective and thence negotiate which differences to accept and which to address.

The life world does not imply total social harmony or homogeneity, nor does it imply a general and genuine propensity for altruism. It does imply a sufficient level of 'connectedness', mutual recognition and mutual tolerance to be able to deal reasonably with differences of interest and opinion. Solidarity denotes the level of mutuality required to sustain communicative processes. Substantially, it encompasses a minimal sense of equality, reciprocity and mutuality. While the life world is the virtual ensemble of the meaningful 'worlds' that are referred to in everyday interaction, the system world is made up by the economic and political systems. In the industrialised world these are the market and the state. Within these systems, the communicative logic of mutual recognition and agreement is replaced by the logic of interests and the trade-off of interests. The legitimacy of strategic operations within the systems, however, is dependent upon sufficient agreement in the life world on the basic principles of economic, political and bureaucratic action. Democratic institutions and the legal system are the prime hinges between the life world and the world of systems.

The framework of life world and system world enables Habermas to make a political analysis of solidarity that is critical of both liberal and communitarian 'solutions'. Habermas agrees with communitarians that liberals tend to reduce such problems to problems of the system: do the distribution mechanisms of the welfare state work properly and does everyone get a fair share? He criticises attempts to offer solutions in terms of more market mechanisms or reorganisation of bureaucratic procedures, which do not address the cultural issues at stake. Against communitarianism, however, he claims that it is empirically proven that the cultural values of the welfare state are insufficient to withstand the onslaught of system-problems and neoliberal solutions.

Like Jaeggi and Honneth, Habermas argues that because of its relational aspect solidarity is a distinctive concept in relation to justice. Habermas argues that liberal justice is not wrong, but *one-sided*. Its foundation in the calculations of autonomous individuals obscures the importance of an intersubjective life form that supports individual autonomy by keeping up relations of mutual recognition (Habermas 1989). Habermas sees justice and solidarity as 'two sides of a coin': justice concerns the rights and liberties of autonomous, self-interested individuals, whereas solidarity concerns the mutual recognition and well-being of the members who are connected in the life world (Habermas 1989: 101; Houtepen and ter Meulen 2000b).

The *ethic of care* (Tronto, 1993) is one of the ethical theories that tries to respond to the one-sidedness of the ethic of justice. The ethic of care argues that caring relationships are not contractual relationships between equals as presumed in liberal concepts of justice (Held 2006). In many cases, care involves a relationship between people who are not equal, between a care giver and a patient suffering from a chronic illness like a patient suffering from dementia, stroke or a heart attack. The ethic of justice and the contract perspective ought to play an important role in health care, as they give rights and protect the autonomy of individuals. However, a contractual ethic needs to be balanced by a *substantial* ethic by way of an increased emphasis on responsibility, involvement and recognition.

In a comparable way, Honneth emphasises that his views on solidarity and recognition do not mean a departure from the Kantian concept of morality. On the basis of a Kantian concept of morality, individuals should be accorded the same respect as anybody else or to have their interests taken into consideration in the same fair way. Universal respect for others as advocated by Kant is one of the several protective measures that serve the general purpose of enabling a good life. At the same time, he emphasises the importance of solidarity and mutual recognition in the 'ethical life' as the basis for the development of identities and as the condition for self-esteem. Self-respect (rights) and self-esteem (solidarity) are analytically distinct, but they are complimentary in regard with the recognition of individuals.

3.10   The Communitarian Response

The connection of solidarity with the recognition of identities, as emphasised by Honneth and Habermas, seems to resonate to some extent with the communitarian critique on liberalism. In this critique, liberalism presents the individual as an autonomous, independent entity before it engages with others in social practices. According to liberalism, individuals are not defined by their membership of communities or practices, but are free to decide or reject to be part of any such community whether they are religious, political, sexual, or something else. Rawls expresses this view in his statement that 'the self is prior to the ends which are affirmed by it' (Rawls 1989: 560). According to Rawls, 'even a dominant end must be chosen from among numerous possibilities' (idem). Rawls follows Kant who defended the view that the self is prior to given roles and relationships and is free to distance him or herself by using reason.

The problem of liberalism according to the communitarians then is not its 'universalism', but its 'individualism' (Kymlicka 2002: 212): it presents individuals as disconnected from social practices and communities and refuses to see that their identity of individuals, their well-being and their values are constituted by and in their participation in these communities. Self-determination and individual freedom can only be exerted within social practices and with reference to the common good. The language of rights separates individuals in an artificial way from the social practices in which they are embedded.

Communitarian critics of modern liberalism, like Charles Taylor and Michael Sandel refer to the distinction between *Moralität* and *Sittlichkeit* to claim an important role of the community in shaping the moral life of individuals. According to Taylor the doctrine of *Sittlichkeit* is 'that morality reaches its completion in a community' (Taylor 1984: 178). Kant's morals remain an 'ethics of the individual' because it does not accept the 'only valid content, which comes from the society to which we belong' (idem). The fulfilment of morality 'comes in a realized *Sittlichkeit* ... [this] is the point where Hegel runs counter to the moral instinct of liberalism then and now' (Taylor 1984: 178). As an individual, a man depends on his society in a host of ways, 'and if it is unregenerate, then he cannot realize the good' (Taylor 1984: 179). The doctrine of *Sittlichkeit* 'requires a notion of society as a larger community life ... in which man participates as a member' (Taylor 1984: 180). This notion 'displaces the centre of gravity ... from the individual on to the community, which is seen as the locus of a life or subjectivity of which the individuals are phases' (Taylor 1984: 180).

Communitarian authors question the claim of Rawls about the priority of the right over the good, and 'the picture of the freely-choosing individual it embodies' (Sandel 1984: 5). We cannot conceive our personhood without reference to our role as citizens, and as participants in a common life (Sandel 1984: 5). According to Sandel, the problem of rights-based liberalism is that we cannot conceive ourselves as independent in this way 'as bearers of selves wholly detached from our aims and attachments' (Sandel 1984: 5):

> Open-ended though it be, the story of my life is always embedded in the story of those communities from which I derive my identity – whether family or city, tribe or nation, party or cause. On the communitarian view, these stories make a moral difference, not only a psychological one. They situate us in the world, and give our lives their moral particularity.
>
> (Sandel 1984: 6)

Communitarianism is often accused that it would lead to a 'slippery slope of totalitarian temptations' (Sandel 1984: 7) meaning that individuals are not only immersed within communities but are also forced to live and act according to the values of these communities without any political influence.[5] Sandel rejects this argument by saying that instead 'intolerance flourishes most where forms of life are dislocated, roots unsettled, traditions undone' (Sandel 1984: 7). When common involvement in the political life has withered due to the individualisation and atomisation

---

[5] See the discussion in Section 5.5.

of society, we will be vulnerable to political domination and, possibly, totalitarian regimes. Communitarianism, as the 'party of the common good' (Sandel 1984: 7) wants to end political apathy by supporting and cherishing civic republican commitments. Some communitarian writers, particularly Sandel and Taylor, are driven by a civic and republican ethos of involvement in the political life of communities. As our roles in society, and in the various communities we inhabit, are constitutive of our personhood and identity, we should also be involved in the purposes and aims of these communities.

One of the main concerns of communitarianism is the individualism and individual choice in our contemporary society and that, as a result, communities have fallen apart. This critique of modern life is directed, amongst others, towards the excessive individualism of the market in which individuals are alleged to be interested in their own claims and interests only and not to feel responsible for the needs of others. In the view of communitarian thinkers, excessive individualisation is a morally doubtful process that tends to undermine the organic ties in society and therewith the social responsibilities of individuals. Communitarians blame liberal individualism for the fragmentation of modern society and for the feelings of disorientation of the modern individual. Referring to the individualism of American society, Robert Bellah et al. (1985) argue that the individualistic achievement and the ideal of self-fulfilment make it often difficult for people to sustain their commitment to others, either in intimate relationships or in the public sphere.

Daniel Callahan is an important representative of communitarian thinking in health care ethics, particularly regarding the allocation of scarce health care resources and care for the elderly. Callahan underlines the importance of shared values within the health care system. Health, for example, is nowadays seen as an important value, and for some people health is even the most important value in their life. By consequence, much energy and a lot of financial resources are spent to reach a better health, a phenomenon that is also known as medicalisation or 'healthisation'. According to Callahan, health is only an instrumental value and can never be an absolute or intrinsic value: we are healthy in order to achieve other things in our life. We do not live in order to be healthy. In making health an absolute value, individuals make ever rising demands on the quality and the possibilities of the health system, up to the point that medical technology threatens to dominate our lives. These claims are putting an increasing strain on the societal resources for health care.

Callahan argues that, instead of being the slaves of the health care system, we should ask ourselves what kind of life we want to live. Only on the basis of such an orientation can we determine what kind of health care we need to fulfil our life plans and expectations. However, the determination of these orientations should not be left to the individuals. If every individual was allowed to determine the kind of care he needs on the basis of his own life plans, society would be ruined very soon. Individualism and moral pluralism are in great part responsible for the unbridled claims on the health system and by consequence for the scarcity of resources. These are questions about the common good which cannot be left to individuals. It takes a community to discuss these fundamental questions and to provide mutual help and enlightenment to find the answers (Callahan 1988).

According to Callahan, liberal individualism is 'poorly equipped' to help us as human communities to deal with the complexities of biomedical progress and the impact on our lives. The greatest weakness of liberal individualism is often seen as its greatest strength, which is 'eschewing a public pursuit of comprehensive ways of understanding the human good and its fortune' (Callahan 2003: 500). However, the impact of technology and biomedical developments may affect our lives and institutions in ways that go beyond individual choice and the principle of autonomy:

> As an individual, I need to make choices about how I will respond to those changes. But more important, *we* have to make political and social decisions about which choices will, and will not, be good for us as a community, and about the moral principles, rules, and virtues that ought to superintend the introduction of new technologies into the societal mainstream. Only if we believe that there will be no socially coercive or inadvertent culture-shaping consequences of present and forthcoming medical technologies can we deny the need to take common, and not just individual, responsibility for the deployment of a biomedicine that can change just about everything in our lives.
>
> (Callahan 2003: 500)

The emphasis on the perspective of the community when discussing health needs and priorities can also be found in the work of Michael Walzer. According to Walzer (1984), distributive justice in health care has a two-fold meaning: it refers to the recognition of need and to the recognition of membership: 'Goods must be provided to needy members because of their neediness, but they must also be provided in such a way as to sustain their membership' (Walzer 1984: 204). When we are discussing individual needs, we should not look at individual rights, but on the character of a political community and the sustaining of a political community life. This community is 'more than a mutual benefit club' of rational agents who agree to participate on the basis of their personal interests. The agreement of the rational contractors says nothing about the sort of redistribution of benefits and burdens, the amount of redistribution and the purposes of it. This leaves the redistribution of health care open to conflicts and particular interests. Instead, the ultimate appeal should be 'not to the particular interests, not even to a public interest conceived as their sum, but to collective values, shared understandings of membership, health, food and shelter, work and leisure' (Walzer 1984: 207). Redistribution in health care is more than just a social contract: it is an agreement in accordance with a shared understanding of the needs of the members of a community:

> The contract is a moral bond. It connects the strong and the weak, the lucky and the unlucky, the rich and the poor, creating a union that transcends all differences of interest, drawing its strength from history, culture, religion, language, and so on.

> (Walzer 1984: 208)

According to Walzer, arguments about redistribution of health care are interpretations of this moral bond. The closer and more inclusive it is, the wider the recognition of needs and the greater the number of social goods drawn into it.

An important problem for communitarianism is how to reach a general consensus on how to live our life and, in the example of Callahan's and Walzer's work, how to value health care and its services on a societal level. Even when the communitarian diagnosis of the problem (a lack of common values) would be right, it is unclear where their solution (shared values) should come from. Liberal critics also fear that the search for commonality as the basis for public policy will result in infringements upon the liberties of individuals. Historically, the call for community has been associated with oppressive policies. Moreover, communitarianism is unable to detach itself from the nostalgic and moralistic atmosphere that pervades much of the discourse on values and social ties.[6]

However, according to some communitarians, society has gone too far with acknowledging and honouring individual preferences at the cost of fulfilling our communal responsibilities (Kymlicka 2002). Feminism, gay rights, and multiculturalism together with consumerism and materialism

---

[6] See Section 5.5.

(Kymlicka 2002) have resulted in an 'anything goes' culture in which individuals have lost the connection with moral and spiritual frameworks of the communities and religions. Some communitarians then lament about the decline of traditional societies in which individuals could find moral orientation in the values of family, school, church, cultural and political associations. This longing for the past can be characterised by the word '*Gemeinschaft*' of Tönnies to describe the strong communal ties of society in the Middle Ages and other pre-modern societies (Tönnies 1887)[7]. The strong social cohesion of the *Gemeinschaft* is opposed to the emphasis on the individual and the lack of communal ties in the modern *Gesellschaft*. While the *Gemeinschaft* can be typified by strong mutual bonds and feelings of togetherness, the individuals in the *Gesellschaft* see society merely as instrumental to their own personal ends. However, while some communitarian authors display a nostalgia for the communal ties of past societies, there are some others who accept the fact that we live in a multicultural, multireligious and multiracial society, and who support the role of individual choice.[8] For example, Charles Taylor emphasised the importance of the idea of authenticity in our modern culture, even though the idea is often misunderstood (Taylor 1991).

The fear of communitarians for excessive individualisation might be justified when individualisation is taken in its negative moral connotation. In this negative meaning, individualism refers to hedonism, privatism, consumerism and the 'I' culture and stands opposite to solidarity as normative concept (in the meaning of companionship, altruism and defence of the weakest). However, such an interpretation of individualism fails to appreciate that individualism also has a positive connotation in which it refers to self-realisation, individual responsibility and emancipation of the traditional social ties of family, class or religion. Individualisation in this positive meaning can go together with, and can even contribute to, an 'ethics of commitment', that is, a feeling of responsibility towards the weakest in society.

3.11   Solidarity and Recognition of Individual Differences

Though many communitarian authors are influenced by Hegel and the politics of recognition, they have a tendency to put too much emphasis on the cohesiveness of the group or cultural community. Pasini and

---

[7] See Section 2.7.   [8] See Section 5.5.

Reichlin emphasise that solidarity as the 'other side of justice' (Habermas) is different than advocating a communitarian sense of brotherhood of a closed community (Pasini and Reichlin 2001: 324). Unlike solidarity as recognition (Honneth), solidarity in some forms of communitarianism is based on the construction of 'us' against 'them'. In such notions, the range of individual differences and of their expression in different identities is restricted by the effort to maintain the unity of the group (Bellah et al. 1985). However, solidarity in the sense of mutual recognition is not the solidarity of the 'us' against 'them': it is a sense of brotherhood but one that connects a concern for the well-being of the other with the universality of human rights and of protection of dignity. It is not an *exclusive* solidarity of the group or class, but an *inclusive* solidarity which promotes self-esteem by way of solidarity and self-respect by protection of rights (Honneth).

Modern theories of solidarity try to reconcile the recognition of individual differences with an inclusive interpretation of solidarity. Dean (1996), for example, argues for an interpretation of solidarity as a communicative practice in which the individuals create a 'we' by reflecting on expectations regarding the generalised other.[9] In this process, identities are affirmed and recognised as different ways to meet those expectations. Dean introduces the concept of the 'hypothetical third' as part of this continuous reflection. The perspective of the 'third' helps to break open the homogeneity and isolation of the social group and to redefine solidarity as something else than a group mentality with insiders and outsiders. According to Dean, once we take a reflective attitude towards this shared understanding, we realise that citizenship in a pluralist society requires support of the other in her or his difference (Dean 1996).

Honneth comes to a comparable understanding of solidarity and the recognition of difference. While legal recognition of individual rights, which promote self-respect, expresses the universal features of human subjects, solidarity as the promotion of self-esteem emphasises the particular qualities that characterise individuals in their difference. Where modern law provides a medium for the recognition of universal rights, solidarity requires also a medium to express the characteristic differences between individuals. Honneth (like Dean) refers to the work of the social psychologist G.H. Mead when he argues for a symbolic articulation at a societal level of a 'framework of orientation' (Honneth 1995: 122), in

---

[9] See Section 5.6 for more detail.

which 'those ethical values and goals are articulated that, taken together, comprise the cultural self-understanding of a society' (Honneth 1995: 122). Such a framework can serve as a 'system of reference' for the appraisal of individual personality features, 'because their social "worth" is measured by the degree to which they appear to be in a position to contribute to the realization of societal goods' (idem). According to Honneth, the cultural self-understanding of a society provides the criteria for the social esteem of persons, because their abilities and achievements are judged intersubjectively according to the degree they help to realise culturally defined values:

> For self and other can mutually esteem each other as individualized persons only on the condition that they share an orientation to those values and goals that indicate to each other the significance or contribution of their qualities for the life of the other.
>
> (Honneth 1995: 121)

Solidarity in Honneth's work then means an interactive relationship in which individuals mutually sympathise with each other's different ways of life because they esteem each other in reference to a shared value horizon. While the group is the first instance for such recognition of individual differences, and for the self-esteem resulting from it, such solidarity can be extended to other members of society (Honneth 1995). One can speak of *societal* solidarity to the extent that every member in society is in a position to esteem himself or herself in relation with a shared value horizon.

> In this sense, to esteem one another symmetrically means to view one another in light of values that allow the abilities and traits of the other to appear significant for shared praxis. Relationships of this sort can be said to be cases of 'solidarity', because they inspire not just passive tolerance but felt concern for what is individual and particular about the other person. For only to the degree to which I actively care about the development of the other's characteristics (which seem foreign to me) can our shared goals be realized.
>
> (Honneth 1995:129)

Honneth and Dean distance themselves from the traditional accounts of solidarity as put forward by some communitarian authors in which the values of the group leave little room for personal development and individual differences in relation to lifestyle, sexual orientation, religion or race (Sandel 1990). In a modern version of solidarity, as proposed by Honneth and Dean, individual differences are recognised, but not just

because of the differences only: the value horizon (Honneth) or 'hypothetical third' (Dean) provides a social context for the development of
self-esteem. This idea goes beyond the liberal idea of the unencumbered
individual who is free to make any choices he or she sees as important,
and for whom society is a hindrance, not a condition for personal
development and self-esteem.

3.12   The Connection Between Solidarity and Justice

The presentation of the principles of justice as universal theory rights and
obligations has contributed to the obliteration of the normative basis of
these commitments, which can be identified as solidarity. The crucial
element that distinguishes solidarity from justice is the attention to the
practical and communicative aspects of reciprocal recognition as
members of a shared life world. A practical theory of solidarity then does
not focus on the moral rights and duties of individuals only, but also
wants to engage with the question of how to promote relations of
responsibility and recognition at an institutional level. The delivery of
health and social care, including the rights and duties of individuals,
should be arranged in such a way that it promotes the reciprocal recognition of identities and responsibilities. Though justice has become a
dominant value in health care policy, solidarity as recognition of the
other can be considered the corresponding fundamental value. As Habermas argues, justice and solidarity are two sides of a coin: justice concerns
the rights and liberties of autonomous, self-interested individuals,
whereas solidarity concerns the mutual recognition and well-being of
the members who are connected in the life world.

The different perspective between Kant's morality and Hegel's ethical
life is also at the background of the distinction by Benhabib (1992)
between the 'generalised other' and the 'concrete other'. The generalised
other represents the standpoint of 'the universalistic commitment to the
consideration of every human individual as being worthy of universal
moral respect' (Benhabib 1992: 10). This standpoint can be linked with
the liberal tradition of human rights and is institutionalised in various
explicit legal and other policies to protect these rights. The standpoint of
the concrete other is implicit in ethical relationships 'in which we are
already immersed in the lifeworld' (idem). The ethical relationships with
the concrete other, which are in the first place family members like being a
father, mother or child, spouse, brother or sister, means that we as concrete
individuals 'know what is expected from us in virtue of the kind of social

bonds which tie us to the other' (idem). The generalised other and the concrete other are thought of as existing along a continuum, 'extending from universal respect for all as moral persons at one end to the care, solidarity, and solicitation demanded of us and shown to us by those to whom we stand in the closest relationship at the other' (idem). Benhabib then tries to find out how the universalistic point of view of the generalised other can be situated in the ethical life of the ethical community.

Liberal theories of justice are generally not interested in promoting the good life or 'ethical life' ('Sittlichkeit') including relations of recognition and solidarity. They present themselves as universal theories of rights and duties ('Moralität') by abstracting from the particular conceptions of the good life and personal relationships. Liberal theorists do not regard values of personal commitment and recognition as unimportant, but they do not see it as the task of society to promote such values or to interfere in personal plans or life forms. The task of society is to enable individuals to facilitate their personal plans on the basis of a principle of equality or fair equality of opportunity (Daniels 1985; Daniels 2007). Modern society should not be founded on a particular conception of the good life as that would discriminate against individuals with a minority view. The central ethic of procedural liberalism is the ethics of the *right* rather than the ethic of the *good* (Taylor 1997: 186; Rawls 1989). There are, of course, areas in society where individuals bond and share a conception of the good life, like families, friendship, social clubs and neighbourhoods, but on an institutional level such ties and bonds are irrelevant: institutions like health care or education are collective instruments to help individuals reach their individual goals and fulfil their life plans.

According to Taylor, one can ask whether such abstract and atomist models of social life can be viable. Taylor argues that in republican societies freedom can only flourish by a shared understanding of the common good or identification with common values (Taylor 1997). Taylor makes the distinction here between the self-interest of individuals to maintain certain public services and commitment to the welfare of others. The bond of solidarity with compatriots in a functioning republic is based on a 'shared fate, where the sharing itself is of value' (Taylor 1997: 192). A society is more than just an instrumentality for individual life plans. It is also a place for common action and common identification with values. Identification with a common cause, or a shared vision of the common good, will help to promote self-discipline and to ask from the members of a community or nation to do things 'that they normally would try to avoid' (Taylor 1997: 193). A neutral state undermines the shared sense of the common good which is required for citizens to accept the sacrifices of the welfare state (Kymlicka 2002). When citizens are distancing themselves from a shared communal life, they are less inclined to support the welfare arrangements that are based on these common views. In fact, this can lead to a legitimation crisis in which citizens are asked to make increasing sacrifices in the name of justice, while they share less and less with those for whom they are making sacrifices (Kymlicka 2002: 253).

In his books *The Ethics of Memory* (2002) and *On Compromise and Rotten Compromises* (2010), Margalit makes a distinction between *ethics* and *morality*: while ethics is concerned with *thick* relations between individuals, that is, relations that call for actions, morality regulates our *thin* relations, which express our concerns for humanity.[10] A society can be ethical but immoral (like Nazi Germany where there were strong tribal ties but where there was a lack of humanity), or it can be moral, where people are very concerned about rights but are not interested in relations of compassion. The former leads to a society that is *immoral*, the latter to a society that is *indifferent* (Margalit 2010: 127). A society that is dominated by liberal principles and rights only risks to become an indifferent society which is hardly interested in the well-being of fellow citizens. Such a society is particularly dangerous in respect with the responsibility for those who cannot help themselves, like people with dementia, learning disabilities, psychiatric problems and other vulnerable people who are struggling with a loss of autonomy, failing health and a lack of security. Care for these vulnerable individuals will not only support their health and social needs, but will also keep them included in our society. Care for them can be regarded as an expression of what Margalit calls 'shared humanity' (Margalit 2010: 122). Failing to provide decent care for vulnerable people does not only express a lack of ethical concern, but is also a violation of the rules of humanity in which respect of human dignity is central.

For example, Alzheimer's patients or people with severe intellectual disabilities can be ignored at hospital wards because of a lack of interest or understanding among health care personnel. They can be treated with diminished respect as they seem to lack the rational capacities of the 'normal' members of our society. They can be treated with a lack of respect and can suffer humiliation because they may display 'strange' behaviour, which is often wrongly understood. This is particularly true

---

[10] This distinction by Margalit reflects in many ways the distinction between *Moralität* and *Sittlichkeit* mentioned earlier in this chapter.

for people with dementia (Nuffield Council on Bioethics 2009). Even when individuals with dementia or intellectual disabilities receive care that should be provided according to so-called quality frameworks, the care may be delivered in a paternalistic and humiliating way, denying them dignity, respect and understanding. Another example is leaving a woman with dementia partially clothed in a communal room of a nursing home, or spooning food quickly into a the mouth of a person unable to feed herself, or leaving her alone all day in complete passivity or in a state of anger, shouting and swearing without any attempt by the staff to understand her behaviour or to give personal attention.

In previous publications (ter Meulen 1995; 2008; 2011; 2016) I have called the solidarity with the vulnerable groups in society *humanitarian* solidarity: this is not a solidarity based on personal interest but a solidarity based on identification with the values of humanity and responsibility for the other. Humanitarian solidarity combines the principles of morality (Kant's *Moralität*) by respecting rights and preventing humiliation, and the concerns of ethics (Hegel's *Sittlichkeit*). Humanitarian solidarity is based on the personhood of the other whose existence is threatened by circumstances beyond their control. It leads to the decision to take part in the existence of the other and to protect and take over the care of the other when he or she is not able to take care of him or herself anymore (Van der Wal 1988). Humanitarian solidarity could be a candidate for the common value or common cause as discussed by Taylor: it is a value that goes beyond the self-interest and the indifference which are typical for a society which is based on liberal rights only. Humanitarian solidarity is a commitment that can define a particular society and should never be abandoned in favour of the rational self-interest of the liberal discourse.

The concept of solidarity tries to capture the commitment to the well-being of the other by emphasising the importance of recognition of identities and the promotion of dignity in the context of personal relationships (ter Meulen 2016). This is not to say that justice should be discarded in the arrangement of health care policies and practices in favour of solidarity: solidarity does not attempt to offer an alternative for distributive justice, but must be regarded as an important corrective to arrangements of health care practices that are based on a just distribution of goods only. Health care policies and arrangements should go beyond merely meeting needs and rights, by exploring how people's personal dignity and sense of belonging can be sustained within relations of recognition, reciprocity and support.

3.13   Conclusion

In this chapter, I have come to distinguish between two types of solidarity. In the first place I distinguished a type of solidarity that is not related to a specific practice, but refers to a general attitude among the population. It is the solidarity that is the common basis for certain collectivist welfare arrangements in Europe (which Taylor and some communitarians might call the 'common good'). Solidarity in this sense is a shared value within a national community, and is the basis for building just institutions in health care and accepting these institutions as an expression of this commitment. It acts as a *corrective force* for justice, particularly when these institutions are not guided any more 'by the experience of a shared life world, a common cause and common standards of decency and humanity' (Houtepen and ter Meulen 2000a). Solidarity in this role helps to create an ethical society, in which individuals are not humiliated and are connected with society on the basis of humanitarian solidarity or 'shared humanity' (Margalit).

The second type of solidarity is expressed in concrete practices particularly of care for the needs of others. This is the solidarity which is theorised by Honneth (and Jaeggi and Habermas) and which is an important basis for the building of self-esteem by way of recognition of the other. It is not the solidarity of the strong communal bonds as promoted by some communitarian authors: such a type of solidarity is not acceptable any more in a society which emphasises the importance of individuality and the recognition of difference. The second type is the solidarity of practices in which both self-respect (rights) and self-esteem (solidarity) are the main ethical principles, and where recognition of individual difference in relation to a horizon of shared values (reflective solidarity) is the basis for inclusive practices.

Both types of solidarity are of course related: solidarity as the solidarity of concrete practices can only flourish when it is supported by specific arrangements in the policy and delivery of health and social care. This means that policies in the (public) health system must not be based on rational interests of individual contributors solely, but should also express the general willingness to contribute to the common goal of humanitarian solidarity (or shared humanity) by specific support of certain care policies and health and social care arrangements.

In the following chapters we will follow this distinction by analysing the role of solidarity as a value in health and social care policies (Chapter 4) and the role of solidarity at the level of health and social care practices (Chapter 5).

Solidarity and Individual Responsibility in Dutch Health Care

4.1 Introduction

Solidarity is a basic principle underlying public health insurance in many countries throughout continental Europe. The origin of this type of solidarity can be found in local initiatives in the nineteenth and early twentieth century to arrange small systems of social security and medical support. As the local and spontaneous support became increasingly difficult to maintain, these types of solidarity were gradually taken over by the state which set up a system of financing and provision of social and medical support. Solidarity became enforced by the state with compulsory payment of an insurance premium in exchange for access to medical care or financial support in case of medical need or social distress. State-enforced solidarity in health care came about in the 1880s as part of the public insurance system set up by the German Chancellor Graf Otto von Bismarck to compensate workers for the impact of accidents, disability and illness.[1] The principle of compulsory health care insurance based on solidarity was followed by other countries like Belgium, France, Austria and Switzerland.

While solidarity has been a leading principle in the design of public health systems in many European countries, the rising costs of care have resulted in a discussion about the limits of this principle (ter Meulen 1995). Another development is the increasing influence of neoliberalism with its emphasis on individual responsibility and the role of markets as an allegedly superior way to organise and distribute health care than state-controlled systems.[2] As a result of these developments, many European health systems have begun replacing the collective responsibilities for health care with more individual responsibility and individual financial contributions for the delivery of health and social care services (Maarse 2004a). What do such debates and policies to increase individual

---

[1] See Section 1.3. [2] Idem.

responsibility mean for the role of solidarity? We will try to answer this question with an analysis of the policies in the health care system of the Netherlands, where privatisation and the introduction of market forces have had a significant impact on the role of individual consumers and patients. There is currently an intense debate in the Netherlands about the limits of solidarity in contemporary health care and the contribution of individuals to the health care system. This debate is to some extent influenced by policies towards an active engagement and participation of citizens in society which should lead to an emancipation of the individual from the support and control by the state. These ideas to limit collective support in favour of individual responsibility and reciprocity (RVZ 2013) may help to redefine the meaning of solidarity as a principle in health and social care not only in the Netherlands but also in other countries struggling with the limits of solidarity.

4.2   Solidarity in Dutch Health Care: Backgrounds and Developments

The system of solidarity-based compulsory health insurance took off in the Netherlands in the years after the Second World War. Before that time, many individuals, particularly in the lower income groups, were insured by way of a *ziekenfonds* (sickness fund). These small-scale and often local initiatives came into existence by the end of the eighteenth and early nineteenth centuries, mostly in the larger towns and cities (Companje et al. 2009). During the nineteenth century these associations came to include not only the costs of medical care, but also of burial and loss of income due to illness. There were many types of sickness funds, like philanthropic funds, commercial funds, funds which were enacted by medical doctors, and so-called mutualities which were very popular among socialists and Catholics (and are still the main type of sickness fund in Belgium). The legal regulation of sickness funds and social health insurance lagged behind development in the neighbouring countries and this situation lasted until the sickness funds decree by the German occupier in 1941. This decree was maintained after the Second World War and transferred into the *Ziekenfondsbesluit* (Sickness Fund Decision) of 1965, later called the *Ziekenfondswet ZFW* (Sickness Fund Law). Much earlier, in 1913, a law had come into force which protected individuals against the loss of income due to disability or sickness. This insurance for sick pay was kept out of the Sickness fund decree of 1941 and the Sickness fund decision of 1965. The social health insurance in the Netherlands was different in this respect than the Bismarck model which kept these types of protection in one insurance.

The strong position of solidarity in the field of health care was partly the result of the leading role of Catholic and Social-democratic parties after the Second World War. Both parties converged in their ideas about the social and political organisation of society where cooperation, and not class struggle, was seen as the way forward in dealing with social relationships. Political life at that time was strongly influenced by corporatism, which is the view that society should be seen as a 'body' with various organs which are working together in matters of common interest. Capital and labour are the primary examples of such organs or 'corporate groups', to which also belong agricultural groups, the military or scientific associations. However, it was mainly tripartite corporatism, in which capital, labour and the state are seen as the main parties, which dominated political thinking of these two main political parties. Corporatism reinforced the idea of social collaboration in the social health insurance which was operated at a lower level by independent organisations (sickness funds) and was overseen by both workers and employers, and to some extent by the state.

Corporatism was also dominant in the provision of health care arrangements which were not organised by the state but relegated to private institutions like Catholic and Protestant hospitals and home care organisations. These arrangements were typical examples of the so-called 'pillorisation' of Dutch society in which each confessional or secular grouping ('pillars') operated their own care institution in the field of heath care (Houtepen, ter Meulen and Widdershoven 2001). The state was the 'roof' that sheltered the Catholic, Protestant, liberal and socialist pillars (Lijphart 1975). Though solidarity referred to an obligation by society to take care of the sick and needy, the provision of this care is still highly privatised in the Dutch system (Maarse and Okma 2004).

A second principle in Dutch health care, next to and strongly related to solidarity, is the principle of equality in the delivery of health care services. In fact, solidarity and equality are twin principles in the organisation of Dutch health care: an important goal of solidarity is to promote equal access to health care for all (ter Meulen and Van der Made 2000). Every citizen should be able to use health care services, irrespective of the person's health condition or geographical or financial position. The principle of equality is laid down in Article 1 of the Dutch constitution: 'All who are in the Netherlands will be treated equally in equal conditions'. The right to health care is anchored in Article 22: 'The government will take measures to promote public health'. This is interpreted as a governmental responsibility for the geographical, functional and financial accessibility of health care. This so-called social right to health care expresses involvement and solidarity with the weaker members of society. It does not constitute absolute claims because the right is limited by the availability of resources. It is the responsibility of the government to set limits and determine the range of the right to health care (ter Meulen and van der Made 2000).

The health care insurance system in the Netherlands has a dual character consisting of a public and a private system (Maarse and Okma 2004). This public–private mix existed for a long time in the 60 years after the Second World War and was maintained in the new system that started with the *Zorgverzekeringswet Zvw* (Health Care Insurance Law) of 2006 and the new *Wet langetermijn zorg Wlz* (Long-Term Care Law) of 2015. In the old system, the public part included two social health insurance schemes: a sickness fund insurance and a national scheme for exceptional medical expenses. In addition to these compulsory insurance schemes, there were two types of private insurance: one for those who could not enrol in the sickness fund insurance and one for those who come under the sickness fund scheme and opt for extras. These four insurance programmes show various mixes of public and private responsibilities and contained different rights to health care services (idem).

The *sickness fund insurance* and the *private health care insurance* covered access to all curative medical services such as hospital care, services of GPs and pharmaceuticals. The sickness fund insurance was compulsory for employees with an annual income below a fixed income level (in 2005: € 33,000 Euro), their dependants and for some other groups. Premiums for the sickness fund insurance were partly income related and partly flat-rate. Both the employer and the employee payed the income-related premium, while the flat-rate premium was paid fully by the employee. The government decided on the benefits package and the income-related premium whereas the flat-rate premium was determined by the insurer (idem). The premium for the sickness fund insurance was generally modest while it gave access to a wide range of health care services. It was the duty of the insurer to provide the insured with the health care services to which they were entitled. Insurers were (and still are) not allowed to deliver health care services themselves: they had to contract private health care providers or to reimburse their subscribers.

The sickness fund regulations were based on two types of solidarity: *income solidarity* and *risk solidarity* (ter Meulen and van der Made 2000).

Income solidarity means the contribution by the higher income groups to the health care of the lower income groups, while risk solidarity means the contribution by the 'better' risks to the care of the 'bad risks' (persons with high health needs). While these two types of solidarity were (and still are) essential in the sickness fund, they were non-existent in the private insurance. Individuals with incomes above the income limit were expected to take such a private insurance which gave access to an approximately similar range of services as the sickness fund insurance. In the private insurance, premiums were not income related, but related to risk, especially as it was affected by age resulting in the young paying a lower premium than the elderly. Those insured could opt for deductibles or elect not to be covered for specific services, in return for premium reduction. The sickness fund insured were not offered these options.

The sickness fund insurance included 65 per cent of the population, while 35 per cent had private insurance. Solidarity only partly existed in the Dutch health care system: it only existed within the sickness fund system (ter Meulen and van der Made 2000). There was also no solidarity between the sickness fund insurance system and the private insurance system (idem). In Belgium, almost the entire population is insured by a *mutualiteit* (type of sickness fund), while in Germany about 90 per cent of the population is member of one of the *Krankenkassen*. The new health insurance legislation Zvw (Health Care Insurance Law) of 1 January 2006 replaced the traditional divide between a private and a public health insurance by introducing one publicly funded basic national health insurance for the whole population with a possibility for privately funded complimentary insurances for specific services not included in the basic insurance (Bartholomee and Maarse 2006). Similar to the sickness fund premiums of the previous period, the premium for the national insurance is composed of a flat nominal premium and an income-dependent part. The income-related part is shared by the employee and the employer. Lower income groups (including pensioners) can apply for a compensation (*zorgtoeslag*) via the tax system. In the new system, solidarity, including income and risk solidarity, was extended to the whole population instead being limited to the 65 per cent of the population who were insured under the sickness fund regulations. However, this extension of solidarity only regards the insurance for the basic package, not the complimentary insurances which can exclude individuals because of their higher risks or can charge higher premiums for this reason.

The health insurance system presented in this chapter was meant to ensure the access of individuals to curative care services. Access to special or long-term care, like care for people with disabilities and psychiatric patients, was covered by the *Algemene Wet Bijzondere Ziektekosten AWBZ* (Exceptional Medical Expenses Law) which came into force in 1968. The AWBZ was a compulsory scheme based on national insurance collected via the tax service and covering the entire population. Although the AWBZ insurance was originally intended as insurance for heavy risks such as chronic mental illness and physical handicaps, it gradually developed into insurance for long-term care and home care (ter Meulen and van der Made 2000). The central government had a prominent regulatory role in determining premium levels and the content of the package of this insurance. However, due to financial and organisational reasons, the AWBZ was replaced in 2015 by *Wet langetermijnzorg Wlz* (Long-Term Care Law). As the AWBZ was an open-ended scheme, providing universal access to an ever growing large package of services, the costs of this insurance began to rise sharply (Maarse and Okma 2004). The new law of 2015 reduced the number of entitlements and was only dealing with care services for people who need 24-hour care and surveillance, mostly in residential settings. Some of the entitlements of the AWBZ had already been moved to the *Wet Maatschappelijke Onder-steuning Wmo* (Social Support Law) which came in force in 2007. With the new Wlz (Long-Term Care Law) of 2015, a range of other services were moved to the revised Wmo (Social Support Law) of 2015 and to the Zvw (Health Care Insurance Law) of 2006. The AWBZ was based on risk solidarity (as everybody had access on the basis of an assessment of needs), but had only limited income solidarity as premium payments were restricted to a maximum level. The same situation applies to the Wlz (Long-term Care Law): the premiums for this new law are collected via the tax system and are restricted to a maximum. As the insurance by the Long-Term Care Law, which represent a significant part of the total health insurance system, is based on tax contributions (national premiums), the Dutch system is a hybrid of the Bismarck (insurance) and Beveridge (tax based) system.

The overview of the role of solidarity in the Dutch systems presents a rather mixed picture: in spite of ideological claims, the actual role of solidarity in the old health insurance system was limited. The new health insurance law has extended income and risk solidarity to the whole population, but there is no solidarity in the access to complimentary insurance and there is limited solidarity in the long-term care insurance because of the maximum premium levels. Moreover, solidarity within the public insurance programmes is affected by cost sharing like co-insurance and co-payments. In the sickness fund insurance these co-payments were restricted to a maximum. They are still part of the new health insurance by way of a compulsory deductible (€385 per annum in 2016). The AWBZ insurance contained several income-dependent user charges for long-term care and home care. In several cases the patient charges were quite substantial. They could rise to 90 per cent of the costs with a maximum per month (ter Meulen and van der Made 2000). In the new Long-Term Care Law, co-payments are maintained and can range between €160 and €2300 per month. Co-payments are restricting income solidarity as these payments (even when they are income related) are more difficult for lower-income groups than higher-income groups. In fact, these payments further complicate the picture of solidarity in the Dutch system.

4.3   Challenges to Solidarity: Trends in Costs and Income Transfer

In the past decennia, health care expenditure in the Netherlands has risen significantly. In 1970 health care expenditure accounted for 8 per cent of the gross domestic product (GDP), rising to 13 per cent of GDP in 2010 (van der Horst, van Erp and de Jong 2011). More than 50 per cent of these costs were for curative care services, like general practitioners and hospital care. The expenditure for long-term care for older people and people with disabilities were smaller, but were growing faster in this period (idem). The majority of these costs (83 per cent) were paid by collective payments, meaning health insurance premiums and tax payments, while the remaining costs were paid by private payments, including deductibles, co-payments and complimentary insurances.

Though predictions for the future depend on various factors and uncertainties, the *Centraal Plan Bureau CPB* (Central Planning Office) expects that health care expenditure will grow from 13 per cent of GDP in 2010 to 15.5 per cent in 2020 and 22 per cent in 2040, meaning a real growth of 3.2 per cent each year (Van der Horst, van Erp and de Jong 2011). In 2010 an average family paid 23 per cent of their income to collectively financed care (national health insurance and long-term care tax). This figure will rise to 36 per cent in 2040, but this figure might be higher depending on the health of individuals or the costs of better care services (medical technology).

The growth of the GDP per person with 2 per cent a year has led to an increase of health care expenditure per person of 2 per cent a year (van der Horst, van Erp and de Jong 2011). If this expenditure (together with population growth) was the only driving force behind the increase of health care expenditure in general, the total of health care expenditure as part of the GDP would have remained the same. The increasing share of health care in the GDP then must be explained by other factors, namely the demographic process and the increase in the price of care, partly due to the costs of medical technology. Medical technology can contribute to a better quality of care and to more efficiency. Theoretically, it can lead to lower costs in both long-term care and acute care settings, like robot technology in institutional care and routinisation of specialist treatments in hospitals (van der Horst, van Erp and de Jong 2011). However, medical technology is generally driving up the costs of care as the decreasing costs of certain technologies may lead to a more general and widespread use of these technologies (ter Meulen 2008; Maarse and Groot 2008).

The most important reason for rises in cost of care, however, is the demographic process, meaning the rise in the number and proportion of older people in the general population. Life expectancy has risen significantly in the past decades: from 73 years in 1970 to 81 years in 2010 (van der Horst, van Erp and de Jong 2011). As the number of child births decreased, the proportion of people over 75 years of age increased from 3.7 per cent in 1970 to 7.0 per cent in 2010. In the same period the proportion of people under the age of 20 years decreased from 35.8 to 23.6 per cent (idem). The demographic process has been responsible of a change in morbidity and the burden of disease: at a higher age there is an increased risk to be confronted with chronic and debilitating conditions, like neurological conditions (dementia, stroke), heart failure and chronic coronary conditions, muscular-skeletal problems (falls, rheumatoid arthritis), genital-urinary tract problems, and psychiatric problems (depression) (ter Meulen 1995). The elderly are often confronted with loneliness, which may reinforce depression and subjective health status.

According to the CBS, the increasing costs of care for older generations will lead to a substantial pressure on the financial contributions by individuals with an increase of the collective premiums of 7 per cent each year. This development has serious consequences for the *risk* solidarity, meaning the contribution by the 'better' risks (the younger age groups) to the care of the 'bad risks' (persons with high health needs, generally the older generations). In a report on the sustainability of solidarity in health care (Jeurissen 2005) the *Raad voor de Volksgezondheid en Zorg RVZ* (Council for Public Health and Health Care) points at the increase of 'solidarity transfers' from the younger to the older generation in the coming decades. Before the Zvw (Health Care Insurance Law) of

2006 came into force, premiums for health care insurance were increasing rapidly due to the costs of care for older people. The premium for private health insurance rose by 200% per cent between 1989 and 2004. However, the obligatory contribution to the care of the elderly that was included in the private health insurance increased by more than 500 per cent in this period. As opposed to the rising costs of the insurance premium, the costs of cure and care are concentrated in a decreasing part of the population. In 2002 the 10 per cent most expensive patients in the curative health care were consuming 70 per cent of the total health costs, compared to 43 per cent in 1953. This situation was even more extreme in the long-term care sector covered by the AWBZ insurance for long-term care. In 2005, residential patients, who were staying in long-term care services (nursing homes, for example), took 74 per cent of the AWBZ budget while they represent 1.6 % of the population (Jeurissen 2005). This means that the rapidly increasing premiums are meant to pay for the care of a decreasing part of the population. This means not only an increase in risk solidarity, but in intergenerational solidarity (solidarity between the generations) as well.

But there has been, and there will be, an increase in *income solidarity* as well, that is, the contribution by the higher income groups to the health care of the lower income groups. Individuals with a lower level of education have a lower health status and are using more health care than individuals with higher education (Van der Horst and ter Rele 2013). As people with lower education also have lower life expectancy than people with higher education, they need more care than higher educated people (idem). People in the higher educated groups are healthier, but they also make use of privately financed care at home in the later stages of life (instead of going to a residential care setting) (idem). People with a lower education make more use of collectively financed care services. For example, higher educated people were making modest use of AWBZ financed long-term care, around €400 per year measured over the life course. Lower educated people were using €1000–1100 of AWBZ care per year over the life course (idem). These figures are somewhat different for acute care: €1700 for higher incomes and €2200 for lower income groups (idem).

However, looking at the *payments* for health care, we see the opposite picture: individuals in the higher education groups pay twice as much for care as people in the lower education groups. The higher education groups pay not only for their own care, but also, and significantly, for the care of the low education group. On average the difference between the use and the payment of care for people with higher education is €1900 for their entire life course, which is about 10 per cent of their income, also called the 'price of solidarity' (idem). It is expected that in the future the use of care, particularly long-term care, will continue to grow, resulting in higher premiums for health care insurance and for long-term care insurance. Because of the way these premiums are levied, the higher educated groups are expected to make an increasing financial contribution to the costs of care. This is particularly true if the higher costs of care are paid by an increase in the income-dependent part of the premiums (van der Horst, van Erp and de Jong 2011). The other option could be to increase the nominal part of the premium, but that would be much more difficult for the lower education group.

In an interview study by the *Sociaal-Cultureel Planbureau SCP* (Netherlands Institute for Social Research) it appeared that higher education groups are still prepared to contribute to the costs of care of the lower education groups: they understand that it is more difficult for people with lower education to lead a healthy lifestyle (Kooiker and de Klerk 2012). It remains a question whether this will still be the case if the income-dependent premiums will further rise in the future. The premium for health care insurance has risen significantly in the past decades. As noted earlier, the average premium for health insurance has risen by 200 per cent between 1989 and 2004, while the introduction of the national health insurance scheme in 2006 meant a substantial rise in premiums for many individuals and families, too. Though in the first year (2006) of the national health insurance the premium of this insurance was still at a modest level, this premium has risen in the past years, in some cases (2007) with 10 per cent rise of the health insurance premium a year. If these increases continue, they may lead to further pressure on income solidarity and to the willingness of individuals to keep spending an ever increasing part of their income on the costs of care of others.

4.4   Cost Control, Priority-Setting and Needs Assessment

Since the 1970s, successive governments have put great efforts into controlling the costs of health care. An important reason for these policies is that increasing costs are leading to increased pressure on solidarity, particularly income solidarity, as explained in the previous section. Though individuals, particularly in the higher income groups, are prepared to pay an increasing part of their income to the health care of people with lower education, this willingness may decrease in case these contributions become too burdensome. Cost control is essential for preserving solidarity as the basis for the organisation of health care and for the principle of equal and universal access to care.

In the past, governments have applied various instruments to control costs. One can make a general distinction between instruments meant to curb the *supply* of health services, instruments to *control prices* (tariffs) for health care, and instruments to *restrict the demand* for health care (ter Meulen and Maarse 2008). Instruments to *control the supply* of services were, for example, planning of the number of hospital beds (mainly used to reduce the number of beds), the number of specialist units in hospitals, the supply of high-tech medical treatments units, the influx of medical students, etc. Since 1974, many services were limited by fixed budgets. These proved an important source of the 'waiting lists crisis' of the late nineties and early noughties as the fixed annual growth of health care budgets did not keep pace with the growth of health care demand. This policy has never disappeared in Dutch health care: for example, the so-called *zorgaccoorden* (care agreements) of 2013 are meant to limit the growth of the care sector (primary care, mental health care, hospital care and long-term care) with 2 per cent each year and a compensation for the costs of inflation. These agreements also included measures to limit the costs of salaries of health care workers.

The second instrument, *price controls*, has also a long tradition in Dutch health care. Hard negotiations on physician tariffs and the prices of prescription drugs evolved as a recurrent issue in health care policy-making. Perhaps the most dramatic and revolutionary reform was the introduction of fixed budgets for health care provide organisations in 1983 which put a radical end to the open-ended system of hospital financing. The third instrument, *demand controls*, seek directly to influence consumer/patient behaviour. They call explicitly for greater individual responsibility in health care by obligating patients to share in the costs of the use of health services, by co-payments, co-insurance, deductibles and other types of private payments. Medical services like GP care and specialist care were for a long time free of charge for patients covered by statutory health insurance, while co-payments for outpatient prescription have been minimal. However, in the new statutory health insurance (since 2006), the government introduced the 'bonus' (no-claim arrangement), though after two years this measure has been replaced by a compulsory deductible. At the moment this deductible applies to the use of all health care services covered by the national health insurance act. However, there are still co-payments for services and devices like hearing aids. The government determines every year the height of the deductible: in 2016 the deductible is €385, which can be increased by the individual to a maximum of €885 in exchange for a lower nominal insurance premium.

The government decides upon the package of health services which are reimbursed under social health insurance legislation. The government has used this power in the past to reduce the package by removing services from the basic package covered by national health insurance (or the previous sickness fund). Between 1995 and 2000, physical therapy, remedial therapy, dental care and some pharmaceuticals were removed or partly removed from the sickness fund package. These benefits became available in private supplementary health insurances and therefore only accessible to subscribers. In 2011–2012, after a fierce political debate, the popular *rollator* (walker or zimmer frame) and other walking aids were removed from the AWBZ package. In 2012 the government decided to remove gastro-acid reducing medication as well as long-lasting physiotherapy from the basic package. This process of delisting is matched by a *critical assessment* of new treatments before they are (possibly) added to the basic package. The government is advised by the *College Zorgverzekeringen CVZ* (Health Insurance Board) which brings together expertise from various fields in health care and advises the government on all 'package decisions'. CVZ formulates advices to the minister concerning the question which new health care technologies should be included in the package of benefits of the legal health insurance system. The CVZ advice is based on the results of Health Technology Assessments (HTAs), making use of existing HTA projects or commissioned HTA projects.

Since the early nineties, successive governments have aimed to streamline package decisions through a priority-setting process leading to a more modest package of health benefits. The Government Committee *Keuzen in de Zorg* (Choices in Health Care) (1992) was charged with examining how to put limits on new medical technologies and how to deal with problems caused by the scarcity of resources. The committee led by the physician Dunning (often called the 'Dunning committee') proposed four criteria which had to be met to justify the incorporation of a specific health care service in the health benefits package. It had to be necessary, effective, efficient and not classifiable as being an individual's responsibility. The criterion of necessity is viewed from the community-oriented perspective: necessary care enables individuals to join society and to maintain, and if possible, improve their existence. The criteria of necessity and individuals' responsibility are to be determined by politics, in contrast to the principles of effectiveness and efficiency that have a medical-technical character. The government, however, rejected the proposal, holding that the criteria recommended by the committee, particularly the criterion 'necessary care', were too vague.

The RVZ (Council for Public Health and Health Care) published new proposals to prioritise health care services and treatments on the basis of transparent procedures (RVZ 2006; RVZ 2007). The Council report proposed two steps: an *assessment* phase and an *appraisal* phase. In the assessment phase, the cost-effectiveness of a treatment is determined by a calculation of the costs per QALY. The Council proposed to limit the cost per QALY at €80,000 per year. However this limit is also determined by the *necessity* of the treatment, meaning the severity of the disease or disability measured by the burden of disease. The maximum limit may vary according to the burden of disease. Treatments for conditions with a minor burden of disease should not be funded out of collective means (RVZ 2007). By taking the burden of disease into account, the RVZ report added an egalitarian approach to the utilitarian (cost-effectiveness) approach to priority-setting which is typical for the first two medical-technical criteria of the procedure in the Dunning report. The assessment phase is followed by the appraisal phase which determines whether the decision made on the basis of both cost-effectiveness and necessity complies with the principles of justice and solidarity. This phase tries to find out the social impact of a decision and, for example, could decide to leave the treatment to 'private responsibility' (RVZ 2007: 21).

Though priority-setting has been intensively discussed, particularly after the publication of the report of the Dunning committee, it has never been a serious option for the government. At best, the procedures and criteria proposed in the report have played a role in the assessment of new procedures to be included in the basic package. Instead, the government has chosen for *rationing* by limiting the supply of certain services (budget control) and by *needs assessment*, particularly in the field of social and long-term care, formerly covered by the AWBZ but presently by the Wmo (Social Support Law) of 2007/2015, and the Wlz (Long-Term Care Law) of 2015. By assessment of needs and strict criteria for entitlement, the government aims to curb the utilisation of long-term care services. For example, domestic care services, which in the past were covered under the AWBZ, are far more difficult to be entitled to than it was in the past. Under the Social Support Law, domestic care for people who cannot run a household on their own is now the responsibility of the municipalities. One of the criteria in the assessment procedure is the family's capability to provide domestic care to the applicant. However, municipalities are free in how to organise non-residential care and need assessment in their locality (Maarse and Jeurissen 2016). Need assessment may be organised by means of an interview at home: the so-called 'keukentafel gesprekken' (*kitchen table discussions*) between the client, his or her social network and a counsellor of the city council. These discussions include an assessment of the capability of the applicant's social network to provide informal care. Needs assessment is also an essential element in the Wlz, which covers the care for individuals who need permanent supervision to avoid serious damage, and clients who need 24-hour care because of physical problems or problems with self-control (Maarse and Jeurissen 2016).

Delisting, needs assessment and rationing are measures designed to cope with the scarcity of resources. Though they are meant to be fair and just procedures for the allocation of scarce resources, they have resulted in inadequate funding of many services and, by consequence, in waiting lists and poor quality of services. The aggregate effect of the various cost control measures has made it more difficult for individuals to access specific services. This has put a heavy strain on individuals and it may force them to seek private solutions for their health and domestic care problems, particularly for care services which have been denied in the assessment process. It is also important to note that these measures mean a transfer of the burden of the collective financing of health services to the shoulder of the individual citizen, or, in other words, a shift of social solidarity to individual responsibility (ter Meulen and Maarse 2008).

4.5   Personal Responsibility in Social Care

The change in the provision of home care and other long-term care services is an expression of a more fundamental change in the expectations regarding the contributions of individuals to the care of family members. The government has taken the position that the pressure on solidarity has become too big and that solidarity can only be maintained if people take on more individual and social responsibility (Maarse and Jeurissen 2016). The expansion of long-term care on the basis of a generous public funding scheme has created a system in which the citizens have become passive and dependent care receivers. The assumption of the government is that there is a wide and unused potential of social and volunteer networks which can be tapped into when it comes to the delivery of social care. While professional care givers will still be around to deliver care for people in need, a substantial part of the social care can also be delivered by family members, neighbours and friends. The 'kitchen table discussions' (mentioned in the previous section) are meant to explore these possibilities and to make agreements with family members and volunteers to deliver this care.

These policies are implemented as examples of the so-called *participatiesamenleving* (participation society), a concept introduced by the government in the Throne Address by the Dutch King (opening of the parliamentary year) in 2013. The 'participation society' means a society in which everybody who is able to do so takes responsibility for his own life and environment without support or facilitation by the government. The government introduced the paper called *doe demokratie* (do-democracy) which calls for society to organise activities and support by its own means instead of looking at the government for support or being hindered by bureaucratic 'counterforces': citizens must become active and support each other in a 'do-society' (Ministerie van Binnenlandse Zaken en Koninkrijksrelaties 2013). Though the concept includes some emancipatory elements, it is often regarded as an ideology to justify cuts in the care for people at home. The participation society and its emphasis on individual responsibility (instead of relying too much on the state, particularly in social care) is echoed by a recent report by the RVZ (2013). According to the RVZ, solidarity includes *reciprocity*, meaning that the burdens and benefits for social care are distributed fairly. In informal care, reciprocity means that the care receiver and the care giver work together in the caring process. This reciprocity is in fact the basis for solidarity and for the motivation and the personal obligation to display solidarity with the other:

> The person who helps and the person who is being helped, work together and both are finding satisfaction in doing so. This stimulates the preparedness to mutual support and limits the demand for support so that it will be relatively easier to deliver this; it will create then more room to support people who are not able physically or mentally to reciprocity.
>
> (RVZ 2013: 16)

According to the RVZ report, solidarity and reciprocity will create more unity and cohesiveness in society, while lack of reciprocity and overreliance on state support will lead to division and exclusion. In spite of the emancipatory potential of participation and reciprocity, the call for increased involvement of family members and volunteers has much to do with the need to reorganise the care system which has become unsustainable because of its ever growing supply of care services. The RVZ report states that there is a risk that solidarity could disappear because of the inability to limit it: the continuous increase of costs would make it impossible to keep financing the care system (RVZ 2013).

The need to make savings on long-term care is an important reason to shift the decisions about access to care to the municipalities and the involvement of large networks of family care givers and other volunteers (the so-called 'mantel') in the supply of care. Critics argue that the government is too optimistic in its assessment of the potential for family care. Family members do not necessarily have harmonious relations, and neither do they live closely to their dependent parents or other family members or have the time to do so. Though many families are living in harmony with each other, sometimes they can fall apart due to divorce. There is no clear idea about the responsibilities of stepchildren for the parents of their divorced partners (Volkskrant 2016). Children may move away to different parts of the country or to another country. It will be difficult in such situations to deliver family care on a daily basis. Moreover, *within* families the willingness to provide care can be limited, partly because relations between brothers and sisters, parents and children, are often not harmonious. A recent sociological study found out that four of the ten relationships between parents and adult children are not harmonious and that 50 per cent of brothers and sisters have only limited contact or no contact with each other (Hogerbrugge 2016). According to the researcher, the worrying thing is that these relationships do not change over time, and that an increase in caring for parents or other family members may even deepen the conflict between family members (Hogerbrugge 2016). The researcher concludes that this situation does not bode well for the policy of the government to stimulate family care or *mantelzorg* (Hogerbrugge 2016). He also points at the fact that such relations can lead to a decrease in well-being when family members are increasingly engaged in family care giving. An increased involvement in family care may then result in a decrease in well-being in the entire Dutch population.

But the kinds of care people are supposed to give to their family members are not clear either. In a research study with almost 21,000 respondents, 50 per cent of them are willing to supply care for somebody close to them (Mezzo 2013). However, they mention that they are mainly prepared to do domestic support and that they have more difficulty with intimate care. A large majority of the respondents (80 per cent) say that they do not agree with making this kind of care compulsory for family members or other persons close to them (idem).

A recent study found out that the so-called *cold modern* care ideal has increased between the period 2002–2004 and the period 2010–2011. People who adhere to the cold modern ideal think that care giving by family members is undesirable and that men and women should focus on paid jobs. They expect that the government makes this possible by taking over caring tasks (which is opposite to the government's ideas about the 'do-society') (Van den Broek 2016). The cold modern ideal is adhered to mainly by highly educated men and women: at the moment 30 per cent of highly educated men and 35 per cent of highly educated women support this ideal. The *cold modern* ideal differs from the *cold traditional* ideal which says that it is the task of the government to organise the care for dependent family members and there is only a limited role for the family (and then mainly for women according to this traditional ideal). The other ideals are the *warm traditional* and the *warm family ideal*: the former sees a big role for families (and a limited role for the government) on the basis of a traditional view of the role of women as the main care givers, while the warm modern ideal sees family care as a joint responsibility of government and families (Van den Broek 2016). It is the latter which is of course the ideal of recent government policies. The outcomes of this study more or less confirm the findings of a study by the SCP (Netherlands Institute for Social Research) which reports that 33 per cent of the respondents agree with the idea that the government is right to expect that people should take care of individuals with chronic diseases or disabilities, while 35 per cent of the respondents did not agree with this idea (Putters 2014).

Nonetheless, whatever preferences people may have regarding family responsibility, people who care for dependent family members are increasingly confronted with high tariffs by municipalities for the delivery of professional services. Since the new Wmo (Social Support Law) came into force in 2015, as one of the replacements for the AWBZ, the municipalities are responsible for delivering the care for highly vulnerable people. The care services delivered by the municipalities are charged with a tariff that in many cases exceeds the tariff previously charged for the AWBZ services (which were partly funded by the government via the tax system). The background for this development is that the municipalities were confronted with severe 'efficiency cuts' as the government wants to reduce the spending on long-term care. The government justified these cuts (about 25 per cent) with the argument that the municipalities are able to deliver professional care services in a much more cost-efficient way than the previous so-called *zorgkantoor* (regional care-office) within the previous AWBZ (Maarse and Jeurissen 2016). While there is a protection for the lower income groups, the middle and higher incomes have to pay a substantial amount per hour as a contribution for day care and accompaniment. This amount may vary per municipality and can sometimes be €70 per hour in areas where the municipality wants to recoup the total cost price (compare: the previous AWBZ care was charged for only €14.20 per hour; Volkskrant 2015). As other municipalities charge only €20 per hour (or less) this is a typical example of so-called *postcode rationing* (Maarse and Jeurissen 2016). This is a familiar phenomenon in the United Kingdom, where the Clinical Commissioning Group which is linked to postcodes determines access of individuals to medical care and local City Councils determine access to home care. In the egalitarian culture of the Netherlands such procedures are seen as unfair and unacceptable (idem).

Some families have to pay a few hundred euros more per month in the new system (Volkskrant 2015). As a result many of them decline the support by the municipalities due to the high costs. Moreover, 40 per cent of the family care givers experience an increase in the burden of care after the 'kitchen table discussion' (Mezzo 2015). In this way the shift to more personal responsibility comes to fall within the same category as many of the other cost-cutting measures mentioned above. The devolvement of care to a local level becomes another example of *rationing by the purse* in order to limit the costs for the government.

4.6   Private Solutions

The various measures to control costs have resulted in inadequate funding of many services and, by consequence, in waiting lists, rationing and poor quality of services. As the pressures on the health system will continue, the gap between the contributions of the individuals on the one hand and the experienced quality and efficiency of the services on the other hand will increase. Out-of-pocket payments for health in the Netherlands in 2013 (1.5 per cent of final household consumption) are moderate compared to other European countries (for example, in Switzerland it is 4.5 per cent, and in Italy, 3.2 per cent, in 2015; OECD 2015). However, the premium for health care insurance has risen significantly in the past decades: the average premium for health insurance has risen by 200 per cent between 1989 and 2004, while the introduction of the national health insurance scheme in 2006 meant a substantial rise in premiums for many individuals and families as well. In the first year of the national health insurance (2006) the premium of the basic insurance (without the complimentary insurance) was kept at a level of €1027 (including a so-called no-claim bonus). However, the premium has risen significantly in the following years, from €1094 in 2008 to €1288 in 2016. Compared to 2008 (when the no-claim bonus was replaced by a compulsory deductible) the premium has risen with 18 per cent in the past nine years (Vektis 2015). The compulsory deductible increased from €150 in 2008 to €385 in 2016, an increase of more than 150 per cent in six years' time.

The rising costs of the insurance premium causes discontent among the population and can have negative effects on the *trust* of the public in the health care system and on its support for a broad, all comprehensive solidarity. The individual expects a satisfactory return on his 'investments' in the health care system and is not accepting rising premiums if at the same time he is faced with poor performances, like long waiting times or poor quality. The modern patient is a well-informed, critical consumer who wants to get value for money (RVZ 1999). If the health system is not able to deliver, the modern patient-consumer will try to find his own solutions to deal with scarcely available services. In long-term care, private care solutions are already practised on a large scale (Maarse 2004a).

In the Netherlands in 2004, about 2 million persons with handicaps, disabilities or other debilitating problems receive support, 30 per cent of them receiving informal support and 30 per cent of them paying for this support, possibly in combination with informal help. The remaining 40 per cent received publicly funded nursing and care (SCP 2004). The SCP (Netherlands Institute for Social Research) expected in 2004 that the share of private, paid help in the care of the elderly and the chronically ill would increase in the period till 2020. In the period between 2000 and 2020, the demand for long-term care and nursing was expected to grow by 39 per cent. However only a part of this increased demand will be supplied by the public system: privately funded care will rise by 77 per cent (550,000 to 1 million persons), while the public funded care is expected to increase by only 28 per cent (500,000 to 650.000 persons). The office concluded that a vast majority of the coming older generation, particularly the wealthy baby boomer generation, will take refuge to private solutions for future old age dependency, directly or by saving money for the future. These solutions are sought outside the existing public and private health insurances, like the national basic health insurance as well. In fact, the introduction of market forces paved the way for such private arrangements: insurance companies have the freedom to contract home care from any organisation without a compulsory tendering process.

The private solutions discussed here are different than the so-called *Persoongebonden Budgetten* (Personal Budgets) which started in 1995 and which, after many reforms and political conflicts, are currently an integral part of the health care system (Houtepen and ter Meulen 2001). Personal Budgets are cash allowances for people with long-term care needs, most of them elderly and people with learning disabilities and physical disabilities. The Personal Budget is meant for home care and the financial value of it should be equivalent to the *zorg in natura* (care-in-kind) previously delivered to that person. The spending by the individual is limited by this amount, but otherwise individuals have a large discretion of what kind of services they want to buy. The personal budgets are 'private solutions', but they are not based on out-of-pocket payments by the individuals but on the funds in the public insurance for long-term care (AWBZ later followed by the Wlz).

4.7   Market Competition and Individual Responsibility

While increased financial responsibility of individuals can be considered an indirect effect of cost control measures, increased individual responsibility for health is an explicit goal of the market reform introduced with the Zvw (Health Care Insurance Law) of 2006 (ter Meulen and Maarse 2008). A key element of the Zvw is the extension of market competition in health insurance. Market competition was already existent in the private insurance market which covered 35 per cent of the population (see earlier). The new health insurance legislation of 1 January 2006 ended the traditional divide between a private and a public health insurance by introducing one publicly funded basic national health insurance for the whole population giving access to a basic package of services (determined by the government), with a possibility for privately funded complimentary insurances for specific services not included in the basic insurance (Bartholomee and Maarse 2006). The new law extended the competition to the entire health care insurance system. Health insurers – which may operate on a for-profit basis – must compete on premiums, quality of care and type of policy. Consumers have the right to choose their own insurer and type of policy (Maarse and ter Meulen 2006). In addition, they have the right to switch to an alternative policy or another health insurer by the end of each calendar year. In order to guarantee consumer choice, insurers must accept each applicant. Health insurance legislation forbids any form of risk selection by denying access, charging a higher premium or introducing exclusion waivers for pre-existing medical disorders. This part of the legislation is one of the 'public constraints' which are introduced to improve the efficiency and quality in health care and to ensure market competition will not erode access to health care. Other examples of public constraints are the obligation for every citizen to purchase a basic policy and the centralised decision-making structure concerning the package of health services covered by the new health insurance scheme.[3]

Market competition is expected to encourage health insurers to negotiate favourable contracts with health care providers to reinforce their position on the health insurance market. In order to reinforce their negotiating power, insurers are no longer obliged to contract with each provider (selective contracting). However, market competition is expected not only to alter the role of health insurers on the health insurance market, but also to strengthen the role of health consumers as well. The government's basic assumption is that consumers by their choice of health insurer and health plan will gain more influence upon the accessibility and quality of health care and, hence, can realise a greater freedom of choice and individual responsibility.

Though market reform was meant to control costs and to preserve solidarity, it was also driven by the neoliberal ideology of free choice and personal responsibility for health. The state should put aside its paternalistic role of determining what is good for the patient or the way health care should be delivered. Patients are seen as consumers who are able and permitted to make rational choices on health insurance and health services and who can be held responsible for those choices. Health care providers and insurers should also have the freedom to organise and finance the care as they see fit. However, this freedom of choice or freedom of delivery is not unlimited: the public constraints mentioned earlier should guarantee that the health care system stays accessible for all and that the quality of care will be kept at an adequate level. In fact, some of these constraints lead to paternalistic measures which are limiting free choice and personal responsibility (Maarse & ter Meulen 2006).

---

[3] See Section 4.4 in this Chapter.

First, the government has forced individuals to take health care insurance: without insurance, the costs of treatment will not be reimbursed. This obligation is meant to counter the phenomenon of 'free riders', people who do not pay for insurance but who want to benefit from the system of health services. There is no choice not to take a health insurance. Second, as already mentioned, the government determines the package of the services covered by the national health care insurance. This decision is meant to preserve solidarity: a large differentiation of products would result in more individualised packages and reduced solidarity with patients who have a less common disease. There is no choice, then, regarding the basic package, though an individual can choose a lower premium if they choose a larger deductible. However, they do have choice in the complimentary insurance. Third, the government wants to protect individuals against 'wrong decisions' like not including services which the individual thinks he or she will not need.

But there are other limitations to free choice which have to do with the insurance system itself. First, there is a lack of information: health care policies are extremely complicated and people often do not know what to choose. Will they include dental care or physiotherapy in the complimentary insurance or not? Each insurance company is offering a large variety of insurance policies which sometimes look like a labyrinth where one can easily get lost. Individuals find it difficult to switch from one insurance company to another: the so-called transaction costs of comparing different policies and weighing them against each other takes a lot of time and energy. Another difficulty is to assess the quality of the services and treatments of hospitals and other providers contracted by the different insurance companies. This is particularly true for people who can hardly speak Dutch or who have a low level of education.

Individual choice is further restrained by regional concentration and the power of insurance companies. Insurance companies can contract services with local hospitals and other services and professionals. If you do not want to be limited by their choice of providers you have to pay a larger premium. The government and the insurance companies have tried to limit the choice of general practitioner, though this proposal was withdrawn after strong political debate and protests of association of general practitioners and patient groups. Another limitation of individual choice has to do with the choice of the complimentary insurance. Insurance companies are not allowed to refuse patients for basic health insurance, but this is not the case for complimentary insurance. Insurance companies can refuse individuals for these insurances or charge a higher premium. If you are considering changing to another insurer, and you already have a complimentary insurance with your current insurance company, you will think twice before changing if you think you might be refused for a complimentary insurance. You could end up with insurance with the new insurance company and a complimentary insurance with the old insurance company. This is not a desirable situation for many individuals neither for insurance companies who are not happy with clients with only a complimentary insurance. With the introduction of the Zvw (Health Care Insurance Law) in 2006, 18 per cent of the population changed to a different insurance company (Independer 2016). However, in the following years this number went down to between 4 and 6 per cent each calendar year. While choice and change of insurance company was one of the big aims of the Zvw, the majority of the population is staying put.

Health insurance companies have become increasingly powerful by concentration and take-overs: at the moment the market is completely dominated by four large insurance companies (there were 15 insurance companies in 2007). This may lead to *selective contracting* with hospitals and other providers on the basis of quality and costs (Maarse, Jeurissen and Ruwaard 2016). Because of their powerful position, insurance companies could have a countervailing power (with possible cost-saving results) to health care providers (who are merging into larger units too): they can refuse to pay the bill of consultants who fail their patients or who submit exaggerated expense claims. They have also had a strong impact on the costs of pharmaceuticals which have gone down in recent years due to the policies of insurance companies to only reimburse generic or the cheapest versions of medical drugs. However, there is a tendency of insurers to interfere with treatment decisions by individual doctors as they try to determine whether a treatment is indeed needed or could have been better. Many doctors, particularly general practitioners, have complained in recent years about this interference, and also about the huge load of administrative procedures that is coming with a market-based system.

In the early 1990s, when the debate whether to introduce market reform in health care started, the state secretary of health, Hans Simons, argued that market reform was necessary to maintain solidarity in the system. The idea was that market reform would lead to better control of costs and thus would keep insurance premiums and individual payments at a reasonable level. This would be important for the lower income groups for whom higher insurance premiums are more difficult to bear.

However, the costs of care have risen steadily in the past years. This might be the result of the fact that the market reform had no impact on the various developments that are already driving the increase in costs or that market reform has by itself contributed to the rise in costs, for example, because of the increase in administrative procedures. But one things is sure: market reform has not resulted in the greater individual freedom and individual responsibility which was hoped for when the Zvw was introduced.

4.8   Individual Responsibility for Health

An important part of the government policy to alleviate the pressure on the health system is prevention and health promotion. The RVZ published a report *Gezondheid en Gedrag* (Health and Behaviour) in which the relation between health, behaviour and the costs of health care was critically analysed (RVZ 2002). According to the Council the costs of unhealthy behaviour are larger than the costs of healthy behaviour, particularly when not only direct health care costs are taken into account, but also the indirect costs (social costs). As a complement to the right to care, the Council argues that there is a duty to prevent health problems wherever that is possible. Why should people who try to live a healthy life pay for the costs caused by other individuals' unhealthy lifestyles? If a person becomes HIV positive because of unsafe sex, should he or she pay for the costs of treatment? Though the Council has the view that the individuals are responsible for their own health, it recognises the fact that behaviour has many determinants, including genetic factors, environmental influences (social, physical) and psychological determinants. The government should not simply exclude persons from collectively funded treatments, but should promote healthy behaviour and encourage people to take their responsibility.

In the report *Houdbare solidariteit in de zorg* (Sustainable Solidarity in Health Care) the Council further emphasised the need to prevent unhealthy lifestyles (Jeurissen 2005). The effectiveness of the health care system is strongly linked to the behaviour of the population. The Council paid much attention to the behaviour of chronically ill patients. Much could be saved if these patients behaved more appropriately by taking their medications properly (compliance), showed up at scheduled visits and adjusted their lifestyles.

The government has declared prevention and health promotion as cornerstones of its health care policy, but not only that. It is also seen to be each individual's responsibility to stay healthy by adopting a healthy lifestyle. In 2005, the Minister of Health Care foresaw large savings for the National Health Budget when people display more responsible health behaviour. According to the Minister there is need for more individual responsibility for the health care consumer 'since over a quarter of the health problems are related to patterns of lifestyles'. The Minister pointed at disastrous results of obesity, lack of movement, smoking and excessive drinking: 'If the patient can pay for all these bad habits, certainly he can take some more responsibility for his own health care' (Hoogervorst 2004). He gave as his opinion that 'nobody has the right to an unhealthy lifestyle'. Though the Minister said that the increase in individual responsibility is politically 'most difficult to achieve', he saw more scope for it than in earlier periods of time, as the population has a much higher standard of living. However, six years later (2011) another (also liberal) Minister of Care wrote to Parliament that individuals should be allowed to make their own decisions about their lifestyle (De Boer and Kooiker 2012: 140). Decisions about health and healthy living should be given back to the individual citizen (idem).

These ideas are not completely new, of course, as is exemplified by the high taxes on tobacco products and alcohol. However, there are voices advocating the introduction of elements of the equivalence principle into the health insurance legislation. This would be a completely new idea indeed. For instance, the RVZ proposed a 10 per cent variation in the premium rates for the new health insurance scheme to make the premium rate somewhat dependent upon a subscriber's health status. Variations in the premium rates are considered an incentive for adopting a healthy lifestyle.

It is not only the government or its advisory bodies that are putting emphasis on individual responsibility for one's own health. There is a tendency within the population to be stricter on risky and unhealthy lifestyles as a reason to exclude persons from the access to health services, or to let them pay a higher premium. This trend is documented in a survey study by the University of Tilburg (Hansen, Arts and Muffels 2005a,b) in which a large panel of respondents in the Dutch population were asked about the acceptability of various personal criteria like lifestyle, age and genetic factors, to restrict the access to health services (cure, care and prevention). It appeared that solidarity, in the sense of collective funding of various treatments, is still widely shared among the population. However, solidarity is less considered a one-way process: the transfer of funds is regarded as conditional on private contributions and also on certain behaviours. While health professionals wish to treat every person alike, the public wants to make distinctions regarding the funding of treatments on the basis of lifestyle and cultural preferences.

Recent survey studies show that a large part of the population has the opinion that people with an unhealthy lifestyle should be forced to pay a higher premium for their insurance (Kooiker and de Klerk 2012). In a survey study by the Centrale Bureau voor de Statistiek the CBS (Central Statistical Office) about 55 per cent of the interrogated individuals agreed with this idea (Kloosterman 2011). A recent study by the SCP (Netherlands Institute for Social Research) reported that 48 per cent of the respondents thinks it is acceptable to make individuals financially responsible for the consequences of unhealthy behaviour (De Boer and Kooiker 2012). However, at the same time 50 per cent of the respondents in the SCP research find that people with an unhealthy lifestyle have equal right to medical care as people with a healthy lifestyle. There was also a large group who found it difficult to have an opinion about this issue. In an interview study by the SCP many respondents found it difficult to draw a sharp line between healthy and unhealthy behaviour (Kooiker and de Klerk 2012). The researchers concluded that there was no clear consensus about solidarity (or not) with individuals with unhealthy behaviour (idem). They argued that the public probably holds the view that because of the substantial financial contributions, scarce and expensive health care services should be used as efficiently and prudently as possible and that there should be no waste by 'inefficient' behaviour that can be prevented.

4.9   The Future of Solidarity in Dutch Health Care

While solidarity is still seen as the leading principle for the organisation of health care in the Netherlands, one can observe a shift in Dutch health care policy to increased privatisation and more emphasis on individual financial responsibility. This process of privatisation in the financing of access to health and social care is partly the *indirect* result of cost-cutting measures like delisting and rationing whereby individuals are forced to pay out of their own pockets for or to contribute to the payment of certain health and care services. However, the privatisation is also *directly* intended in some areas, for example, in the new insurance system where individuals are encouraged to choose their own insurance company or to take a complimentary insurance. Privatisation in Dutch health care is then both an *implicit* or indirect process as well as an explicit, *policy-driven* process

(Maarse 2004a). The latter may be driven by the (neoliberal) idea that patients, providers and insurance companies should bear a greater responsibility and not rely too much on the state (Maarse 2004a). In the past decade, Dutch health care has also seen a *demand-driven* process where individuals are buying private insurance or buying private care for various private reasons.

An important reason for the privatisation policies is the increase in the costs of care due to the demographic process and the development of new medical technologies. As have been shown, the increase in costs leads to an increase in both income solidarity and risk solidarity. Higher incomes have to pay an increasing part of their income to enable the access to care of the lower income groups (income solidarity), while the 'good risks' (younger generations) are paying an increasing amount for the care of the 'bad risks' (older generations) particularly for care in the final stages of life. As the collective financial responsibility is steadily increasing, there are serious concerns in various Dutch policy documents whether the solidarity-based system is still sustainable: though the higher income groups are still prepared to pay for the costs of the lower income groups, this might change if the costs of premiums for the health insurance and the tax-based premiums for long-term care keep rising (Van der Horst, van Erp and de Jong 2011). Higher income groups could be trying to fund their own health and social care, as they are already doing in the field of long-term care.

There are two options to preserve solidarity: a decrease in the basic package of services (and the increase of the complimentary insurance) or an increase in private financial contributions like co-payments. Another option is to increase the personal involvement in home care for family members or friends and neighbours as envisaged in the Social Support Law and legitimised by the idea of the 'participation society' or the principle of *reciprocity* as advocated by the RVZ (2013). Though there are new initiatives in volunteer care, social research has found that the willingness to provide care for family members is limited and may be often problematic due, for example, to dysfunctional family relations (Hogerbrugge 2016).

The greater emphasis on individual responsibility in health care policy and public opinion might be considered to be in tension with the principles of solidarity and equal access to care that are considered fundamental ethical principles of the Dutch health care system. However, there are voices that argue that increasing individual financial responsibility is the only way to preserve solidarity as the normative basis of the health care system (Van der Horst, van Erp and de Jong 2011). Though this policy may decrease the extent of solidarity, it is meant to preserve a collective system which otherwise could collapse due to the increased burden of collective financial contributions. This process will inevitably result in greater inequalities in access to health care and a *two-tier system of health care* (ter Meulen 1995). Egalitarianism is highly valued in Dutch culture, though respondents in the study of the SCP (Netherlands Institute for Social Research) accepted that some individuals spend their resources on so-called 'luxury care' (that is, care with a higher quality than the care that is supplied in the basic package). However, such 'luxury care' should not have a negative impact on the quality of care for people who cannot afford such 'luxury care' or lead to differences in access to care (Kooiker and de Klerk 2012).

However, differences in access to care have always existed in Dutch health care. As noted earlier, in the previous health care insurance system there were differences in health insurance between the lower income groups with access to the sickness fund insurance (65 per cent) and the better-off who were privately insured (35 per cent). Income solidarity was only existent in the sickness fund, but not in the private insurance, while there was no solidarity between the two insurance systems. Both insurance systems were offering roughly the same package of services, though there were differences in quality of care and in waiting times. In the past years, however, gradual difference have been introduced in access to care by way of individual additional financial contributions. These differences have increasingly been accepted and have been taken over in the new health insurance system by the introduction of a private additional insurance system on top of the basic health insurance.

The emphasis on individual responsibility will make more room for private payments and private health insurance arrangements complimentary to the basic health insurance. In this way, the better-off are offered possibilities to pay their way to services outside the basic package or to higher quality of care. The system has opened up new ways to private funding of health care, and is moving further on the road towards a two-tier system of health care. An important moral argument in defence of a two-tier system is that, provided society is supplying an adequate package of health care services to which all persons have equal access, persons who buy their own services exceeding this package do not offend any ethical principle in doing so (President's Commission 1983). However, there is a risk that in such a mixed system services are moved from the basic tier into the private tier (financed by additional health insurance packages or other private means). This is an attractive option for the government in case of shortage of collective funding (Maarse 2004). However, it could stretch out the individual responsibility too much and could result in a basic package that is not adequate at all. Adequate health care should be based on the principle of solidarity, which includes the collective responsibility for the well-being of the weakest and most vulnerable groups in our society. It should include the protection of human persons whose existence is threatened by circumstances out of their own control, like people with learning difficulties, physical disabilities, people with dementia and psychiatric patients (ter Meulen 1995; ter Meulen 2012). Unfortunately, the care for these groups will more easily be the victim of cost cutting and delisting measures.

Though there is a strong emphasis on private financial contributions and personal responsibility in health behaviour, the policy does not subject the health care system entirely to the mechanisms of free choice and voluntary financial contributions. For example, the public constraints in the Zvw of 2006 make it clear that the vulnerable groups in society should be protected by the prohibition of risk selection and that individuals should not be made fully responsible for their own choices regarding the health care package of their insurance. These public constraints will prevent that disadvantaged groups in Dutch society, like the chronically ill, the handicapped and the low income groups, are abandoned or dumped in low quality care services, and so will lose the opportunity to an autonomous existence. Moreover, the long-term care insurance has been renewed (though substantially limited) in the Wlz of 2015. This law will guarantee care for persons with conditions which require 24-hour care, including residential stay in various care facilities and institutions. Access to these services is based on a needs assessment (by a central office) and the assignment of a *zorg zwaarte pakket* (care burden package) which specifies which services the person is entitled to on the basis of their support needs. At the same time services that were previously provided by the AWBZ but which do not meet the criteria for the Wlz are now provided by the health insurance companies within the Zvw (Health Care Insurance Law) or by the municipalities within the Wmo (Social Support Law).

Still, one needs to be cautious whether the public constraints will be able to protect the position of individuals with low incomes or long-term conditions. For example, there might be a risk of dumping policies of health care providers and of selection by insurance companies. Hospitals are financed directly by way of the *Diagnose Behandeling Combinatie* or

DBC (Diagnosis Treatment Combinations) (Maarse, Jeurissen and Ruwaard 2016) and might be tempted to reduce the length of stay of patients or to offer low-quality care (ter Meulen and Maarse 2003). Health insurers must accept all applicants and premiums cannot vary according to individual characteristics. However, this applies only to the basic insurance and not to the private additional insurance, which is a private insurance and which may be used for risk selection. Insurers can discourage applicants for a basic insurance by refusing access to the additional insurance which is complimentary to the basic insurance. More importantly, if important services are removed from the basic insurance and can only be accessed via the additional insurance, some individuals with poor conditions could face significant problems to access these services. It is still to be seen whether the quality control policy announced by the government will prevent the abuse of individuals' responsibility by care providers. Besides, the system of needs assessment in long-term care may very well hinder the access to long-term services and may put a high burden on patients and family members to take care of their health needs and to supply informal care. This is particularly true in the care provided by the municipalities which is struggling with limited resources and so-called 'efficiency cuts'. Individuals and their families are confronted with increased pressures to provide care via the so-called 'kitchen table discussions'. Services which are difficult or impossible to provide by families or volunteers can be charged by some municipalities for a very high price which can make them unaffordable for some individuals (Volkskrant 2015).

4.10   Conclusion

Though solidarity and equality are often referred to as the most important values in Dutch heath care, their role is being limited due to an increased emphasis on individual responsibility and free choice. Interestingly, the increased emphasis on individual choice and responsibility are justified as a way to preserve the role of solidarity and a system of collectively financed health services which is due to collapse due to the rising costs of demographic change and technology push.

Individual financial responsibility (as opposed to collective responsibility on the basis of solidarity) has been an important part of Dutch health care policy in the past six decades. However, only recently individual responsibility has been translated into an explicit moral goal of Dutch health care policy. In particular, the reform of the health insurance system and the introduction of market forces will give more room for individual health insurance and health care arrangements. Besides, the government and its advisory bodies are emphasising more individual responsibility for one's own health as a way to cope with the scarcity of resources and the increase in risk solidarity. This policy is backed by a decreasing support of solidarity in Dutch society as can be noted in public survey studies. An increasing part of the population has the opinion that one should be stricter on risky and unhealthy lifestyles as a reason to exclude persons from the access to health services, or to let them pay a higher premium. As a result, the health care system in the Netherlands will entrench different patterns of access to care services between the well-off and the less privileged parts of the population in terms of wealth and health situation.

The emphasis on individual responsibility contains important emancipating elements: it can empower individuals to take care of their own needs and to arrange the necessary care services according to individual preferences. Personal autonomy and individual responsibility are very much linked to each other. However, there are groups in our society for whom these ideals are difficult to realise, because of circumstances beyond their own control. One can point at persons unable to care for themselves because of learning disabilities, physical disabilities, dementia or psychiatric disorders. A policy based on individual responsibility can easily result in a basic package of care with poor quality of services and restricted access. While acknowledging the importance of freedom and autonomy, society has a responsibility for disadvantaged groups. Applied to health care, this means that differences in access and quality of care, as may happen in a two-tier system of health care, must benefit the disadvantaged groups.

In this context it might be interesting to refer to the Difference Principle in the Theory of Justice of Rawls[4]. According to Rawls (1989), concepts of justice should uphold a double criterion to judge the outcomes of the distributive process. The first criterion, called the Liberty Principle, is whether the absolute position of the least well-off threatens their capacity to function as autonomous individuals. This means social arrangements, including the distribution of health care should be concerned with the position of the weak and disadvantaged in a society who because of their disadvantage might be significantly limited in their liberty. The second criterion, called the Difference Principle, is whether the relative share of

---

[4] See Section 3.2.

the less privileged is defensible in terms of overall distribution of goods. It is Rawls's belief that it is just to permit differences in the distribution of social goods, provided that these differences promote the interests and enhances the well-being of the most disadvantaged in our society.

One could argue that the increase of private financial responsibility could help to improve the position of the weaker groups as it could give them better access to services and a better quality of these services. However, it is questionable whether this will indeed be the case, as many vulnerable individuals are struggling to have access to adequate services particularly in long-term care and home care. Because of the increased pressures on the collectively financed system, this situation will likely not improve in the near future. Individual responsibility finds its limits in the basic concern with the weaker and vulnerable groups, for whom it is very difficult to realise their personal responsibility for health including financial responsibility. Care services for persons unable to care for themselves because of mental handicaps, dementia or psychiatric disorders, should be an essential part of the publicly funded health care package, with strict control on accessibility and quality of care. The introduction of individual responsibility can only be justified by setting public constraints to safeguard the access and quality of care for weaker groups. In fact, the Dutch government has already implemented public constraints, and will inevitably continue to do so in a future, though commercial interests of insurers and providers are playing a bigger role. While the importance of individual responsibility in health care must be acknowledged, this moral principle has to be balanced against the principle of solidarity with the weaker groups.

Family Solidarity and Informal Care

5.1   Introduction

We have discussed a sociological understanding of solidarity in Chapter 2 and a philosophical understanding of the concept of solidarity in Chapter 3. The philosophical concept of solidarity tries to capture the commitment to the well-being of the other by emphasising the import-ance of recognition of identities and the promotion of dignity in the context of personal relationships. I argued that solidarity focused on the recognition of the identities of others must be regarded as an important corrective to arrangements of health care practices that are based on a just distribution of goods only. Health care policies and arrangements should go beyond merely meeting needs and rights by exploring how people's personal dignity and sense of belonging can be sustained within relations of recognition, reciprocity and support.

In sociology, solidarity is defined as the willingness of individuals to serve and promote the collective interests of a group or of society. This willingness can be based on various motives, for example, because individuals have an interest to do or because they feel a certain responsibility for the fate of others.[1] In sociology, solidarity is an empirical category meant to describe the *social cohesion* in a certain society or group: solidarity describes the extent to which individuals, because of various motivations, are willing to serve and promote the collective interest of the group or of society. Solidarity can be based on an experience of a group identity and a common fate, like, for example, in Durkheim's concept of mechanical solidarity. Solidarity can also be based on the interests of individuals to reach certain goals or to work together to mitigate the costs of illness, disability or redundancy. In such situations the 'strong' perceive an obligation to help the 'weak' by social arrangements like social health care insurance, disability insurance or other forms of social protection. Such arrangements in which the strong support

---

[1]   See Section 2.10.

the weak, may look asymmetrical at a given time, but may serve the long-term interests of the strong, too, in case they might fall ill or lose their job because of disability or redundancy.

Sociologists are generally not much interested in the moral interpretation of solidarity. However, this has not always been the case. The concept of solidarity was developed by French social theorists in response to the excessive individualisation of French society in the nineteenth century. Many theorists, including Comte and Durkheim were driven by moral concerns about the selfishness of individuals. Durkheim, for example, argues that solidarity must be imposed on society to curb the hedonism of individuals which without limitations would lead to a state of anomie. However, since the 1920s, and mainly by the efforts of Max Weber, the moral connotations of sociological concepts and the moralistic motivations of sociologists have disappeared: sociology is supposed to be a 'value-free' discipline, trying to describe and explain social processes without any moral commitment.

While sociologists want to separate themselves from moral views or theories, ethicists are increasingly interested in empirical findings. Particularly in so-called 'empirical bioethics' (Davies et al, 2015) one can find a positive attitude regarding empirical research and the integration of empirical findings in bioethical enquiries. In bioethical debates, sociological research is increasingly used to 'ground' bioethical views or to connect them with professional practices and social values. This is also true for the ethical debate on solidarity in which social theories on solidarity, like Durkheim's theory are referred to understand a particular type of solidarity. This is not a very new development: European traditions of social and ethical thought, in particular, have for a long time tried to combine descriptive and normative claims. The descriptive claim holds that the individual is a product of society and remains tied to other members of society by countless interdependencies. The normative claim defends the importance of values that express and sustain the perception of mutual obligations required for a decent society. Such traditions object to a liberal individualistic interpretation of society on the basis that it does not sufficiently appreciate the need for social integration and mutual obligation. The 'solidarity' approach invites us to consider individual actions in the context of socially structured processes in which individuals are not considered in isolation, but rather as members of a group or collective. This is seen as particularly relevant for care practices and care arrangements in which individuals can be highly dependent on others and where the perception of mutual obligation becomes clearly visible.

Much of the current debate on solidarity has to do with what solidarity means in the context of the increasing individualisation of society (Komter, Burgers and Engbersen 2000), and what kind of obligations individuals have towards each other in terms of providing access to health care and other welfare arrangements (ter Meulen, Arts and Muffels 2001). A special position in this discussion has to do with the interpretation of solidarity in the context of families, meaning solidarity as manifesting the willingness to support the other in the context of family relations, meaning solidarity manifested as mutual obligation in daily practices of engagement and support of other family members who are in need of care. This kind of help and support is called *informal care*, because it offers care in a non-professional way without restrictions and rules set by a central agency. It is a kind of solidarity that can be rather strong even when the pressures to supply informal care are very high (Komter 2005).

It is important to note that both 'family solidarity' and the solidarity that guides health and social care polices share the essential characteristic of solidarity described in Chapter 3, meaning a willingness to support vulnerable individuals, as members of society or as members of a family. However, there are significant differences in the underpinning rationale for this willingness: while 'social' solidarity is seen as a justification for compulsory financial contributions to a national insurance system, family solidarity has a voluntary character, even though there may be a strong sense of duty to supply this care. Furthermore, family solidarity is directed towards a *concrete other*, while the other kind of solidarity has an impersonal character as it is supporting access to health care in society in general.

This chapter will present a combined sociological and philosophical approach to the phenomenon of family care giving. It will consider care giving in family relations from the viewpoint of moral philosophy, highlighting, in particular, the issue of the proper *recognition* of informal carers. For many such carers, recognition is crucial in enabling them to come to terms with their caring role and in supporting their identity both as a care giver and as an individual with their own needs. The chapter will illustrate how an understanding of informal care as an expression of family obligations has important practical implications. At the same time, I will try to underpin this interpretation of solidarity by way of a sociological analysis of family care practices as a specific example of solidarity as well as by modern philosophical theories about reflective solidarity which emphasise the importance of reciprocal recognition of identities and responsibilities.

5.2   Informal Care

Informal care or family care has been documented extensively in a range of documents, particularly by various research institutes in the Netherlands (De Boer 2007; De Boer and Timmermans 2007; De Boer and de Klerk 2013; Dykstra et al. 2006; Fokkema, ter Bekke and Dykstra 2008; Oudijk 2010; Pommer, Woittiez and Stevens 2007; Sadiraj 2009; Timmermans 2003). In these reports and other documents, informal care is being described as mutual, self-evident, unpaid, non-organised help within a social network (Hattinga Verschure 1972). It is care given to somebody who is in need of care by somebody close to that person (Oudijk 2010). It can be care by members from the family or non-family members, like neighbours or close friends. It is a special kind of care because there is a special relationship between those giving care and those receiving it (van den Akker and Luijkx 2004). There exists a certain intimacy and bond between the care giver and care receiver which creates an added value to the care process, but which creates a range of moral dilemmas for both the care givers and care receivers. The latter are gradually losing their autonomy and are becoming dependent on their partner. The former are facing new moral dilemmas because of the change in the relationship with their partner (or parent). Instead of a relationship of equals, it changes into a relationship of a care giver with a dependent person who needs to be taken care of (van den Akker and Luijkx 2004).

Informal care can have special qualities that are difficult to offer by professional care givers: a special attention, personal knowledge of the patient including her or his habits, preferences and wishes, and a personal affective relationship (CEG 2004). A professional care giver is working according to professional norms and standards, and must always keep her or his distance from the patient. The differences between both types of caring relationships can be the source of many frictions and communication problems and, in some cases, a power struggle between the family care giver and the professional (van den Akker and Luijkx 2004).

Informal care is supposed to be based on a personal decision to supply this care. However, in practice such a decision is often not as voluntary as it looks like, as individuals may be led by a strong moral duty to supply this care (CEG 2004). Family members can be very emotionally involved in the care of their ill or disabled partners or parents, and will often find it very difficult *not* to support and help them. Spouses who are caring for their partner suffering from dementia may try to keep caring for them as long as possible, as they see it as their moral duty to do so as an act of personal solidarity. Many of them feel guilty and depressed when their partner needs to be admitted to a care home if family care becomes too difficult and burdensome (van den Akker & Luikx 2004).

Informal care is a widespread phenomenon. According to the OECD, more than 10 per cent of adults in European countries provide unpaid, informal care, defined as providing help with personal care or activities of daily living for people with functional limitations (Colombo et al. 2011). The contribution of informal care givers varies between the countries, particularly between the North and South of Europe. In some countries in the South like Spain and Italy, 15.3 and 16.2 per cent of the population respectively are providing informal care for people with limitations. In Scandinavian countries, on the other hand, the figures are 9.3 per cent for Denmark and 8 per cent for Sweden. In between are countries like the Netherlands, Belgium, France and Germany where approximately 11–12 per cent of the population are providing informal care (Colombo et al. 2011). These differences can be explained by the different *care regimes* for the supply of long-term care: on the one hand, a state-based model with universal access to public services, which is typical for the Northern countries, and on the other hand, a family-based model with high responsibilities for family members and volunteers to provide care and a residual role for the state (Carrera et al. 2013). The latter is typical of countries in the South of Europe. In some countries between the Northern and Southern areas there is a mix of state-provided services and family responsibilities. In the Netherlands, however, as discussed in Chapter 4, the government has reduced the entitlements to state-funded long-term care services and is shifting a large share of the responsibility to family members via the so-called 'kitchen table discussions'. A similar change in policy may happen in other continental countries where the pressures on institutional long-term care services are growing (Ranzi and Pavolini 2013).

The 2001 Census in the United Kingdom found that there were 5.9 million carers (approximately 11 per cent of the population) involved in family care in England, Wales, Scotland and Northern Ireland. This number has increased to 6.5 million in 2011 with over 1 million people (1.4 million) caring for 50 hours or more per week (Carers UK 2014). Women are more likely to be carers than men: 58 per cent of the carers in the United Kingdom are women, compared with 42 per cent who are men (Carers UK 2015). In the Netherlands in 2000, 32 per cent of the population of 50–69 years was involved in informal care for the older generation with middle aged daughters and daughters-in-law constituting the largest group (NIZW 2004). In 2008, there were 1.1 million people giving long-term, intensive informal care (Oudijk et al. 2010). According to the SCP (Netherlands Institute for Social Research), in 2012, 20 per cent of the adult (18 years and above) Dutch population was involved in long-term and intensive care for family members, household members or acquaintances (De Boer and de Klerk 2013). Like the United Kingdom, women are more likely to be a care provider: in the Netherlands 60 per cent of the carers are women. Half of them are between 45 and 65 years of age (De Boer and de Klerk 2013). Compared with men, women perform more domestic duties and tasks in the area of personal and intimate care, while men tend to do more work around the house, deal with financial tasks and offer moral support. Only in cases where their wives are severely and chronically ill do men perform the same domestic and personal care tasks as women (Duijnstee et al. 1998). Informal carers live nearby or in the same house as the dependent person; they often live in shared households; they generally belong to lower-income groups or have no income of their own at all; and they tend to have a lower level of education (Duijnstee et al. 1998). A substantial number of women care for their dependent elderly parents as well as for their children. They are sometimes called, the 'sandwich generation' (Abel 1991: 116) as they may have caring duties towards, parents, children and partner at the same time. As a result, they are prone to have health problems of their own.

The physical and emotional burden of informal care can be very high. The most physically demanding tasks cited include lifting the dependent person, helping him or her to the toilet or to turn over in bed, extra household tasks and travelling to and from the hospital (Kuyper 1993). These burdens are particularly heavy in the informal care of people with dementia who not only need personal care, but may also need to be continually supported and to be protected throughout the day. Apart from physical burdens, providing this level of care, especially for a partner with dementia, will often lead to significant emotional problems, because of the impact on the carer's own life and sense of identity. Often care givers have to give up a paid job or have to reduce hours with significant loss of income (Timmermans 2003). Research by the SCP (Netherlands Institute for Social Research) found out that between 150,000 and 200,000 family care givers in the Netherlands felt overburdened while 9 per cent of all family care givers had become ill or burnt out by their caring tasks (Timmermans 2003; De Boer and de Klerk 2013). A recent study by Peetom et al. (2016) revealed several problem areas related to providing informal care for relatives. The following issues are reported by this group of researchers: informal care appears to be time-consuming, while combining informal care with work and other daily activities is burdensome. The list of care tasks is for some care givers too extensive, and most care givers lack support from siblings. Care givers have a sense of continuous responsibility and need for prepared-ness which increases the burden of care. They are feeling totally 'absorbed' by the care situation (Peetom et al. 2016: 26–27). The behav-iour of the care recipient can also increase the burden, especially when the division of roles between the partners changes or when concerns about safety begin to dominate the caring relationship. Health com-plaints of care givers also pose difficulties in their performance of care tasks. Adaptations in the home environment are expensive, and arran-ging for them is time-consuming. There are also concerns about financial consequences particularly amongst care givers who are spouses of care recipients (Peetom et al. 2016: 26–27). Because of the heavy burdens, family care givers may have to give up care giving and have to let their spouse be admitted to an institution. Another risk may be neglect or abuse in the caring relationship (Bakker 2001).

While the burden of care is growing, the demographic process is reducing the number of people available to give informal care. Changes to the nuclear family have reduced the number of close family members potentially available to provide care, while many families are now also geographically dispersed. Many children of dependent older people have moved away from their parents to other cities or regions, have their own family life, or are divorced and may have a new partner or family (HM Government 2008). If families are living at some distance, it is difficult to assess the needs of parents or other family members who in many cases are reluctant to ask for help as they do not want to be a burden for their children or for their partner (van den Akker and Luijkx 2004).

In the course of time, family care may be experienced as an increas-ingly burdensome situation, in which the carer feels they have few choices and from which it is difficult to escape. This phenomenon has been described as *role captivity* (Aneshensel, Pearlin and Schuler 1993) or the *informal care clamp* (Knipscheer 2010). They have the feeling that they have to fulfil too many tasks, lost their independence and are increasingly confronted with health problems of their own (De Boer and de Klerk 2013). This is particularly the case in family care for people with long-term progressive conditions like dementia. Some carers may have started caring out of affection or other intrinsic motivation, but feel they are increasingly trapped in the process of care giving, and worried about what would happen if they were to refuse further care (Department of Health 1999). In such cases, the 'voluntariness' of the care's actions may derive more from a lack of formal legal obligation than from a genuine sense of ongoing free choice.

5.3   A Different Type of Solidarity

To get a better understanding of 'family solidarity', as demonstrated through the provision of informal care, it is important to compare this manifestation of solidarity with other manifestations of solidarity from a sociological point of view. As we have seen in Chapter 2, a classical contribution to the concept of solidarity was made by Emile Durkheim which we will summarise briefly. In the *Division of Labour* Durkheim described the transition from traditional to modern society as involving a transformation of traditional forms of cooperation and social relationships between individuals (Durkheim 2014). The traditional or preindustrial societies are characterised by what Durkheim called *mechanical* solidarity: the solidarity and the social cooperation based on it, is spontaneous, in the sense of 'not reflected upon': it is a normal or natural thing to help and support each other. Examples of such mechanical solidarity can still be found in modern times, particularly in rural communities or those with a strong common religious belief, where the help of neighbours from within the community is spontaneous in times of hardship or natural disaster.

In a situation of mechanical solidarity, there is a uniformity of beliefs and values within the social group, which may be enforced by strict mechanisms of authority and social control. With the development of the division of labour, social relationships begin to change: the societal structure becomes differentiated and social functions become specialised. In this modern society, individuals become highly dependent on each other because of this specialisation. Durkheim called this kind of cooperation *organic* solidarity to express the modern situation of functional and complementary interdependence between individuals. Organic solidarity is accompanied by a process of individualisation, including a diversification of individual values which replaces the collective conscience of traditional society. Thus, solidarity in a modern context means not only that individuals have become highly interdependent on each other, but also need to cooperate for their own and society's interests. This organic solidarity enables the collective interest to take priority over the interests of individuals. European health care systems can be seen as an example of organic solidarity in so far as the individuals are under the obligation to contribute to the interest of the community as a whole, that interest being understood as equal access to health care for all who are in need.

Family solidarity in the form of family care does not fit neatly in either of the two categories of solidarity distinguished by Durkheim, although it shares the essential characteristic of a willingness to help those who are vulnerable in the context of a relationship. The solidarity which is expressed in family care has a personal, concrete meaning that is different from the organic solidarity which tries to organise collective interests in an abstract way. Though it is tempting to understand family solidarity as an expression of mechanical solidarity, as the care for a spouse or family member seems a 'natural' or self-evident thing to do, this type of solidarity seems not applicable either. The personal expression of solidarity in contemporary family care is different from the mechanical solidarity that is typical of pre-modern societies. The individualisation process has resulted in a change in family structure as well as in the social structure of neighbourhoods. The need or duty to care for another dependent person, a family member or a neighbour, is no longer self-evident as it would be in a situation of 'mechanical solidarity'. In the case of families, this is not only true for the relationship between parent and child, but also, and increasingly, between partners. In the remote past the family was an institution that was primarily meant to promote reproduction and to provide economic support, with a hierarchical structure and fixed obligations. In the recent past however, families have evolved away from these traditional patterns and have turned into affective relationships (Knipscheer 1992). However, this change of interdependency does not result in a total disappearance of relations of support and assistance, nor of the preparedness to offer this support. In fact, the decline of the compulsory nature of this support has made room for individual initiatives to provide this support on the basis of negotiation and personal autonomy. One may speak here of a different manifestation of solidarity that is not based on compulsion, but rather on voluntary choice: it tries to help people who are in need by way of concrete, personal service. This does not mean that there is not a sense of obligation to supply this support. However, individuals take on this obligation because they have voluntarily agreed to do so and not because of an entirely spontaneous response which is typical of mechanical solidarity.

For similar reasons, family solidarity in the supply of care cannot be interpreted as a kind of *communal solidarity* as it was defined by Weber in his book *Wirtschaft und Gesellschaft* (2012). Weber made a distinction between two types of 'solidary' social relationships: the communal and the associative relationships.[2] Relationships are *communal* if they are based on subjective feelings (traditional or affectual) that one belongs together. Relationships will be called *associative* if they are motivated by self-interests or other rational motivations. The associative relationships are typical for the market, in which individuals are encouraged to acts of exchange and competition. The associative relationship rests on a rational agreement by mutual consent in which there is an obligation for each party to adhere to the agreement or a rational expectation that the other party will live up to it (Weber 2012).

Communal relationships may rest on various types of affectual, emotional or traditional bases. While Weber mentions various examples of such relationships (religious brotherhood, an erotic relationship, a relation of personal loyalty, etc.), the most typical case of a communal relationship is in his view the family. However, modern families have moved away from the loyalty and communal relations and obligations as perceived by Weber. Solidarity within families and between generations is not 'self-evidently experienced as positive' (Komter 2005: 160). According to Komter (2005), the receiving and accepting of care are not without problems, as care may even be experienced as a burden or a kind of control. There are still obligations, but much of the care giving is subject to negotiating between care givers and receivers, with each having their own interests and perspectives based on personal autonomy.

The (widespread) manifestation of personal solidarity in family care provides a strong argument against the thesis of authors who argue that the individualisation of society and the lack of consensus on shared values has led to a decline in other-directness and concern for persons who are in need of support. This concern about individualisation is typical amongst communitarian authors who refer to the moral concept of solidarity as a feeling of commonality and belonging together which is positioned against the individualism of our contemporary society. It is also directed towards the excessive individualism of the market in which individuals are alleged to be interested only in their own claims and interests and not feeling responsible for the needs of others. In the view

---

[2] See Section 2.9.

of many communitarian thinkers, this excessive individualisation is a morally doubtful process that tends to undermine the organic ties in society and therewith the reciprocal social responsibilities to which the concept of solidarity refers (Bellah et al. 1985). On this view, a society built on individualism is going in the direction of *anomie* as defined by Emile Durkheim in his major volume on suicide (Durkheim 1897). This term describes a condition in which, due to a lack of shared social and moral norms, society is becoming fragmentised and social and community ties are breaking down. When individuals cannot connect themselves to shared values, they try to find meaning in their own private lives, particularly by self-cultivation and consumption-oriented choices, often as a defence against a dangerous and heartless world (Bellah et al. 1985).

However, the fear of communitarians of excessive individualisation is only justified when individualisation is taken in its negative moral connotation. In this negative meaning, individualism refers to hedonism, privatism, consumerism and the 'I' culture (Lasch 1979), and stands in opposition to solidarity as a normative concept (in the meaning of companionship, altruism and defence of the weakest). However, such an interpretation of individualism fails to appreciate that individualism also has a positive connotation in which it refers to self-realisation, individual responsibility and emancipation from the traditional social ties of family, class or religion. Individualisation in this positive meaning can go together with solidarity, and can even contribute to an 'ethics of commitment', that is a feeling of responsibility towards the weakest in society or in one's own family or neighbourhood. It is exactly this positive connotation of individualism that is characteristic of informal care and the family solidarity it represents.

5.4   Professional Support and Recognition in Informal Care

The extent to which a person is able to provide (and to continue providing) informal care is dependent on various social and emotional factors (Knipscheer 1992). One important factor is that there is enough *support* for the informal carer: not only emotional support from relatives and friends, but also professional support offered by the public health care system, particularly home-based care. Practical support can alleviate the physical burden of care, and, importantly, may help safeguard the emotional relationship between partners which is in many cases the moral basis of the provision of informal care. Professional help for physical care will also enable the informal carer to have more time for him or herself, for the lack of personal free time is an important part of the burden of informal carers.

However, some family care givers are reluctant to ask for support by professional care givers, for example, because they do not want strangers in their homes (van der Lyke & Morée 2004). Sometimes, the relationship between the family care giver and the care receiver may be very close, not allowing any 'intrusion' by a stranger. In other cases, care givers are too proud to ask for help or feel ashamed to do so, or they fear to lose control as professionals have their own professional opinions and standards of how to provide care (idem).

As already mentioned, family care can lead to many sacrifices and great costs for care givers, like social isolation and increased psycho-logical and physical burdens. This is particularly true in cases where the family care giver does not want professional care givers to intervene in the care-giving process. In many cases, family care can become too stressful and burdensome, leading to the breakdown of the care-giving process because the carer can no longer cope. It may potentially also lead to the physical and emotional abuse of the older person who is supposed to be cared for (Bakker 2001; Soares, Barros, Torres-Gonzales et al. 2010). Temporary breaks from caring may diminish the emotional and physical strain and the personal ties between the patient and the carer can be strengthened or at least kept at an adequate level. Such relief can be realised by respite care and outpatient care offered by nursing homes and community centres.

The report by the Nuffield Council, *Dementia: ethical issues* (2009) points at the problems of changing and maintaining identity of family care givers when caring for people with dementia. Many care givers need time to grow in their role as care giver and to assume a new identity as such. Some care givers may even reject their 'carer' identity altogether, and continue to see themselves as a daughter and not as a care giver (Nuffield Council on Bioethics 2009; Goldsteen et al. 2007). At the same time many care givers face difficulties in maintaining their *own* identity when caring for their relative: in taking on the identity of a care giver they risk losing aspects of what it means to be themselves. It is therefore crucial that mechanisms are in place in order to allow care givers to hold on to their own identity, for example, through access to regular respite services in order to give them free space to be themselves and pursue their interests outside their caring role. Carers need to be recognised as individuals with their own needs. In taking on the identity of a carer people often risk losing aspects of what it meant to be themselves. As a partner in care, the carer should be able to feel that they are not solely responsible, and that it is legitimate for them to have some time to themselves while others provide the necessary care for their loved one (ter Meulen and Wright 2012). They also should be made aware that their own interests are important when difficult decisions need to be made. This is particularly true for the care for people with dementia, where there is a strong tendency to give priority to the interests of the person with dementia, due to their decreasing capacity and the need to take decisions for them (idem).

The most important support of informal carers is the *recognition that they are partners in the care of the dependent person* (RMO/RVZ 1999). The work of informal carers is indispensable to the care system: without the contribution of informal carers, the formal public care system would be completely overwhelmed. Yet, many informal carers feel that there is little respect and appreciation for their work: their contribution is taken for granted, and their own needs ignored. Institutional care services should recognise the contribution of the family care givers and to prevent tensions and conflicts between the professional and the family care givers. Instead of a paternalistic approach which tells informal carers how to care for their spouse or family member, professional care givers should acknowledge the valuable contribution of the family care giver (idem). On the other hand, the family carer should be open to professional advice and not reject the professional advice out of hand: both kinds of care are mutually dependent on each other (van der Made, ter Meulen and van der Burg 2001).

According to the report by the Nuffield Council on Bioethics, it is crucial that professionals and care givers work together in genuine partnership to ensure that people with dementia benefit from their joint expertise and joint knowledge. Such a partnership would reflect the solidarity shown within the family:

> We believe that an attitude of working *with* families and other carers, supporting them in their own care of the person with dementia, is more conducive to the interests of the person with dementia and better recognizes the centrality of relationships with family and friends for many people with dementia.
>
> (Nuffield Council on Bioethics 2009: 41)

Such a partnership would involve a relationship of trust between professionals and care givers, based on mutual respect for each other's role and expertise, as well as on the premise that all concerned are seeking to help the person to live as well with their dementia as possible. As a 'partner' in care, family care givers should be able to feel that they are not solely responsible, and that it is legitimate for them to have some time to themselves while others provide the necessary care for their loved one (ter Meulen and Wright 2012).

5.5   Communitarianism Revisited

We have identified family solidarity as a different manifestation of solidarity as compared to the mechanical solidarity of traditional communities and the organic solidarity guiding health care and welfare arrangements in modern society. Family solidarity is directed at the concrete other and is perceived as based on free choice, albeit often accompanied by a strong sense of personal duty (Oudijk et al. 2011). An important moral element of family solidarity is the need for recognition of family care givers, not only of their concrete practical efforts, but also of their own identity as care givers and as individuals. According to the Nuffield Council Report on the ethical issues in dementia, the recognition of carers and the essential role they play, both in the life of those they care for and in the wider community, is an important way in which they can be supported in their solidarity with those for whom they care. By taking on the identity of a carer, care givers risk losing aspects of what it means to be themselves. Care givers make an *appeal* to our solidarity to be recognised as people with a specific identity as care givers and with concrete and particular needs to fulfil their role and to express their identity.

However, the need for recognition of specific identities constitutes a challenge to conventional notions of solidarity. These notions have a tendency to emphasise the unity and coherence of the group as a way to protect the group from threats from outside (ter Meulen, Arts and Muffels 2001). Conventional notions of solidarity suggest an exclusion of 'others' by the construction of 'us' against 'them'. The range of individual differences and of their expression in different identities is restricted by the effort to maintain the unity of the group. Communitarian thinkers advocate this conventional manifestation of solidarity as an important context for the development of identities. They are generally led by the belief that individuals can only reach fulfilment or a valuable life by commitments and relationships in a community (Kymlicka 2002). Individuals are 'embedded' or 'situated' in social roles and practices: they do not decide to enter such practices, but they are inevitably deeply immersed in them. Instead of taking an outsider position, communitarian authors encourage individuals to further immerse themselves in practices and communal relationships as a way to realise their own personal good. For this reason, communitarian authors argue for a 'politics of the common good', which is conceived as 'a substantive conception of the good life which defines the community's way of life' (Kymlicka 2002: 220). Rather than adjusting itself to the pattern of preferences of individuals, the common good provides a standard by which those preferences should be evaluated (idem).

As highlighted in Chapter 3, certain communitarian authors have a tendency to emphasise the cohesiveness of the group and to reduce the importance of individual autonomy. An example is Michael Sandel who argues that liberal authors have a false view of individual autonomy, particularly when they argue that the self is prior to social and individual values. An example is Rawls who argues that the 'self is prior to the good',[3] meaning that the self is prior to social roles and relationships and can freely judge these roles and social expectations from a distance (Kymlicka 2002: 221). Sandel, on the other hand, argues that the self is not prior to the good, but that it is constituted by the ends and values that we discover by virtue of being embedded in a shared social context (Kymlicka 2002: 224). Instead of the 'unencumbered self' which is underlying liberal philosophy, Sandel argues that the self is to a great extent constituted by social values and ends: we can only discover who we are, not by the choices we make or have made, but by reflecting on the goals and ends of the communities which we are part of.

The ideas of Sandel about the constitutive role of communities in regard to personal ends and values are criticised as leading to inclusiveness and disregard of individual differences.[4] They are accused of a romantic return to the cosiness of the small community (Tönnies' idea of 'Gemeinschaft') and even to totalitarian thinking in which the goals of individuals are subservient to the goals of the community or the state. They seem to remind us of the romantic conservatism of political writers in the first part of the nineteenth century like De Bonald in France and Herder in Germany. As discussed in Chapter 2, De Bonald argued against the 'Protestantism' of French society by its emphasis on individual autonomy and the lack of respect for communal values. Instead of the

---

[3] See Section 3.2.   [4] See Section 3.9.

social fragmentation post-Revolution, French society should return to the social structures of the *ancien régime* in which the evil tendencies of individuals were suppressed by the state. According to De Bonald, society was prior to the individual, a thought echoed in the communitarian position of Sandel.

According to Kymlicka (2002), communitarian thinkers are claiming that, once the assumption that autonomy as a general value has been dropped, religious and cultural groups should be allowed to protect their members' constitutive ends by restricting individual rights. Sandel (1990), for example, has defended the right of the Amish to have their own teaching practices and to be exempted from mandatory education laws. According to Sandel, the freedom of conscience should be understood as the freedom to pursue once constitutive ends, not to rationally revise one's religion (Kymlicka 2002: 240). Sandel regards religious affiliation as so constitutive of people's identity that protecting and advancing that identity is more important than protecting individual's rights and autonomy.

The communitarian approach is often criticised because it offers only limited and rigid categories of identity. Conventional (including communitarian) notions of solidarity risk to ignore the need for autonomous choice by individuals and for expression and recognition of their individualities. Such an expression of solidarity, for example, would not help those who are caring for the needs of another family member, as it would limit their possibilities for individuality and would not offer them the recognition they seek.

However, the strong emphasis on the role of community in shaping and protecting people's identity is not shared by all communitarian authors. Benhabib (1992) makes a distinction between two different strands of communitarian response to the liberal ideal of justice and individual rights. On the one hand, there is what she calls 'integrationist' communitarianism. This is the type of communitarianism that argues that the problem of individualism, anomie and alienation in our modern societies can only be solved by a recovery or revitalisation of some kind of value scheme (Benhabib 1992). It is a brand of communitarianism that reflects the claims of political Romanticism in early nineteenth century as well the conservative reaction (De Bonald, Le Maistre) in post-Revolutionary France. It is typical for modern communitarian authors like Sandel who emphasise the role of values and common ends to shape the moral character of individuals. According to Benhabib, 'it is characteristic of the integrationist view that it emphasises value revival, value reform, or value regeneration and neglects institutional solutions' (Benhabib 1992: 77).

On the other end of the communitarian spectre, Benhabib discerns the 'participationist' communitarianism: this type of communitarianism sees the problems of modernity in the sense of a loss of belonging, lack of solidarity and feelings of oneness, 'but more in the sense of a loss of *political agency and efficacy*' (Benhabib 1992: 77). The loss of political efficacy is not a consequence of the separation of the personal from the political or of the differentiation of modern societies into various spheres (political, economic, civic and familial-intimate). Instead the loss may be the result of contradictions between the various spheres, limiting the agency of individuals in one sphere because of the position in another sphere (idem). As an example, Benhabib mentions the duties of motherhood in the familial sphere which limit the public aspirations in the sphere of the economy, politics or academia. She refers to the work of communitarian authors like Michael Walzer and Charles Taylor who take the view that modern societies are not communities integrated around one single conception of the good or 'even a shared understanding of the value of belonging to community itself' (Benhabib 1992: 79). Instead of the dominance of one conception of the good, which should be shared and adhered to by everybody, participatory communitarianism encourages the participation of individuals in the political debate to reduce the contradictions between spheres. According to Benhabib, participatory communitarians like Taylor and Walzer acknowledge that 'societies are marked by a "plurality" of visions of the good and of the good itself' (Benhabib 1992:79). They do not regard social differentiation and the existence of different identities as a problem that need to be overcome by value education or other policies to implement common values. Instead of the homogeneity and harmonisation of the integrationist communitarians, participatory communitarians argue for political participation in which people have a say in the economic, political and civic arrangements which define our lives. A vibrant participatory life can become central to the formation and flourishing of one's self-identity and the revitalisation of certain values (Benhabib 1992).

There are modern accounts of communitarianism which distance themselves from the integrationist tendencies of communitarianism. Etzioni (1998), for example, argues that the 'new communitarians' have been concerned with the balance between community and autonomy, between individual rights and social responsibilities. They want to explore the conditions under which the common good and individual rights need to be adjusted to each other rather than assuming that the community 'is and should be supreme' (Etzioni 1998: xi). Etzioni criticised communitarians like Sandel and Nisbet who stressed the importance of communities for the development of individuals, but did not explore the 'opposite danger: that a community may be oppressive, authoritarian, and may unduly penetrate the individual' (idem).

In his later work Bellah (1998) also rejects the idea that society should become a *Gemeinschaft* in which there is complete consensus about values and goals:

> While community-shared values and goals do imply something more than procedural agreement – they do imply some agreements about substance – they do not require anything like total or unarguable agreement. A good community is one in which there is argument, even conflict, about the meaning of the shared values and goals, and certainly about how they will be actualized in everyday life. Community is not about silent consensus; it is a form of intelligent, *reflective* life, in which there is indeed consensus, but where the consensus can be challenged and changed – often gradually, sometimes radically – over time.
>
> (Bellah 1998:16; italics added)

According to Bellah, a good group or community is not a contractual association (which is typical for liberal thought), but is a group that continually asks the question '[what] will make this group a *good* group' (Bellah 1998: 16). When it reaches agreement about the good it is supposed to realise, it becomes a community with some common values and goals. However, these goals and values will always be contested and are open to further debate (idem).

5.6   Reflective Solidarity

When we try to understand the solidarity at the level of caring practices, and particularly the relation between solidarity and recognition of identities in these practices, it will not be helpful to resort to traditional accounts of solidarity which emphasise the role of homogeneity and uniformity as, for example, in integrationist types of communitarianism. However, this does not mean we should leave the notion of solidarity all together. As we have seen there are strands in communitarian thought which argue for a participatory approach to solidarity in which heterogeneity of values and differences in identities are not considered as something that needs to be erased or homogenised, but as important values in itself which should be promoted by an inclusive, participatory approach.

However, these participatory approaches are not clear about *how* such a participatory approach could lead to a recognition of identities and at the same time to a shared understanding of the good. The way forward to such a reconciliatory approach is proposed by Jody Dean in her theory of *reflective solidarity* as we discussed in Chapter 3.[5] Dean develops her theory of reflective solidarity on the basis of the theory of the social self as developed by the social (behaviourist) psychologist George Herbert Mead in the first decades of the twentieth century (Mead 1970). Particularly relevant to Dean's theory is Mead's concept of the 'generalised other' which Mead introduces to describe how the organised community or social group gives unity to the self. It is the attitude of the whole community as it enters into the experience of the individual members of the group (Mead 1970: 154). Mead regarded the self essentially as a social structure which arises and is formed in social experience. The self can be solitary, but it can never arise outside of social experience (Mead 1970). The individual experiences himself from the particular standpoints of other individual members of the same social group, or from the generalised standpoint of the social groups as a whole to which he belongs (idem). The individual enters his own experience of the self not directly, but by taking the attitudes of others to himself within a social environment or context of experience in which both he and the other individuals are involved:

> The individual possesses a self only in relation to the selves of the other members of his social group; and the structure of his self expresses or reflects the general behaviour pattern of this social group to which he belongs, just as does the structure of the self of every other individual belonging to this social group.
>
> (Mead 1970: 164)

According to Mead, an individual can only develop a complete self by taking the attitudes of the organised social group to which he belongs towards the organised, co-operative social activity or set of activities in which that group is involved. The individual takes on the attitude of the generalised other towards himself and the attitudes of other members of his group towards behaviour. By taking this perspective, the individual governs his own conduct accordingly.

---

[5] See Section 3.10.

The essentially social formation of the self does not mean that individuals are completely conditioned by their social surroundings. The individual does not only have a 'self' but also a 'me' or 'I' that reflects on the self and on the social expectations of the generalised other. Each individual has to take the attitude of the community, but has also the capacity to reply to the community and to try to change the attitudes of the community:

> We can reform the order of things; we can insist on making the community standards better standards. We are not simply bound by the community. We are engaged in a conversation in which what we say is listened to by the community and its response is one which is affected by what we have to say.
>
> (Mead: 1970: 168)

Mead's theory of the social self, and of the way social expectations are becoming part of the self, provides an interesting perspective on the social psychological basis of solidarity: being able to recognise and sympathise with the expectations of others as well as to assess and appraise one's own contributions to a social group in terms of the expectation of others are essential conditions for solidarity (Komter 2005).

Mead's behaviourist theory allows for a critical reflection on the social expectations which create social solidarity. This point is further developed in Dean's theory of reflective solidarity and particularly her theory of the 'Third'. According to Dean, the standpoint of the 'generalised other' means taking the standpoint of relationships between the members of a group and of the expectations they have towards one another (Dean 1996). It includes a common understanding of what it means to identify as a member of a group and of the way one is expected to fulfil the various social roles as part of the mutual collaboration. The generalised other can be institutionalised as a specific societal role like the judge or the police officer. But according to Mead's theory, there is always the possibility of reflection and revision of the expectations we have in society of such professions and roles (and as a member of a specific profession as well). There are different ways to interpret the expectations that are tied to these social roles and functions. For example, the police officer is expected by middle class individuals to protect their property and securing peace. For lower classes a police offer may present repression and brutal force to keep them in their place.

According to Dean, once we have recognised the openness and variety of interpretations of the generalised other, once we realise there are different generalised others, we can understand that our identities will never completely fulfil the expectations of the generalised other: 'Instead, we adopt an interpretation of it, an interpretation which arises out of our understanding of identity in the context of the relationships in which we are situated' (Dean 1996: 37). Dean argues that reflective solidarity must be understood 'dialogically': 'the expectations organized within the generalized other can always be brought up for questioning' (Dean 1996: 37). Dialogue is not a threat to solidarity, but can strengthen it by our shared engagement in dialogue (idem). Reflective solidarity then strengthens social ties as well as it opens the possibility for reflection on social expectations and personal identity.

According to Dean, solidarity can never be viewed as fixed or as given: achieving solidarity means that we open the membership of a group or community to dialogue and communicative reflection. Solidarity requires self-understanding of and reflection on who 'we' are. Dean introduces the concept of the 'Third' as part of this continuous reflection. The perspective of the 'Third' helps to break open the homogeneity and isolation of the social group and to redefine solidarity as something else than a group mentality with insiders and outsiders. The third means that we are not just dealing with a situation of 'you' and 'me', but that we need to bring in the perspective of the 'they' or 'she' or 'he'. The attitude of reflective solidarity 'will never enable us to fully include the voices and experiences we exclude' (Dean 1996: 34). Nonetheless, if we adopt this perspective, we take account of our exclusions, attempt to include excluded others in our 'we' (idem). When we take this perspective, 'we are able to expose the omissions and blind spots within the narratives of our shared identity' (idem). We will 'acquire the capacity to criticize and question the expectations of our group' (idem). The perspective of the hypothetical 'Third' and of reflective solidarity that is based on it, are central to our ability to conceive of a 'we' that moves beyond the narrow and closed context of conventional solidarity (idem).

Dean opens the interpretation of solidarity as a communicative process, creating a 'we' in the process of reflection on expectations regarding the generalised other. In this process identities are affirmed and recognised as different ways of interpretation and meeting of these expectations:

> In conventional solidarity our appeal is based on our common interests, concerns, and struggles. With reflective solidarity we appeal to others to include and support us because our communicative engagement allows us to expect another to take responsibility for our relationship. Here we recognize the other in a way that is neither immediate nor restrictively

mediated. We recognize her in her difference, yet understand this difference as part of the very basis of what it means to be one of 'us'... we take
the attitude of the group, but we take it reflectively, attuned to the
standpoint of the situated, hypothetical third.

(Dean 1996: 39)

Once we take a reflective attitude towards this shared understanding, we
realise that citizenship in a pluralist society requires support of the other
in her difference.

5.7 Reflective Solidarity and Care

As we have discussed in Chapter 3, contemporary accounts of solidarity
focus on reciprocal recognition of identities and responsibilities. For
example, in Honneth's work, solidarity means an interactive relationship
in which individuals mutually sympathise with each other's different ways
of life because they esteem each other in reference to a shared value horizon.
While the group is the first instance for such recognition of individual
differences, and for the self-esteem resulting from it, such solidarity can be
extended to other members of society. In Chapter 3, we have argued that a
modern conceptual framework for solidarity should include issues of reciprocal recognition of identities and mutual responsibilities. The importance
of reciprocal recognition of identities and responsibilities is being emphasised in other contemporary theoretical accounts of solidarity (ter Meulen
and Houtepen 2012). Particularly in feminist theory (Benhabib 1992; Young
1997), there have been various efforts to challenge the gender bias in theories
of justice and universal rights, which should be supplemented with a policy
of recognition and a sensitivity to individual differences.

A practical theory of solidarity should not primarily focus on the
moral rights and obligations of individuals only, but also engage the
question what it takes from institutions to organise health care arrangements along communicative and participatory lines. What is needed is an
approach that combines the need for individual recognition with an
inclusive understanding of solidarity as opposed to the tendency of
exclusion in traditional accounts of solidarity. Solidarity is not about
fixed values or identities: it is a communicative and participatory process
in which values and identities are subject to continuous reflection.

Reflective solidarity as advocated by Jody Dean represents an important approach to an inclusive kind of solidarity in the context of health
and social care practices, and particularly in the context of family care.

The way in which care services are provided may have unforeseen or even adverse consequences for the identities of the individuals involved. Care needs, caring and care services reflect and affect the identities of care recipients in diverse and unpredictable ways. Reflective solidarity implies continuous reappraisal of the way that institutions and services affect the people involved in caring practices. In conjunction with the recognition of the centrality of the needs of the care recipient, this calls for a degree of flexibility of caring arrangements.

For example, in the care of people with dementia, reflective solidarity may be realised through involving both family care givers and recipients in decisions about the distribution and delivery of professional care services. Care recipients should not just be seen as passive bearers of rights or mere carriers of disease or disability, but as citizens with specific views on their own care. The needs of both care recipients and their family carers should be addressed by their active involvement and critical reflection on the services provided for them. What is needed, then, is a continuous reflection on what is 'good care' and what it means to be a 'good care giver'. While solidarity in the past resulted in homogenised care services without any involvement of those they aimed to benefit, modern reflective solidarity sees care recipients and family carers as active citizens who need our support and solidarity, but who also want to be included as critical citizens with their own views as to how solidarity with the concrete other should be practised, and how 'good care' should be delivered. This means, for example, that there should be more openness and trust between family care givers on the one hand and professional health and social care givers on the other hand, and that family care givers should have access to confidential medical and psychological information about the person they care for where this is necessary for them to carry out their caring role. Reflective solidarity might also lead to more innovative ways of providing or facilitating care, such as giving people in need of care and support the opportunity of managing their own personal budgets in order to purchase the services that would best meet their own needs (Houtepen and ter Meulen 2001).

This critical and reflective approach to family solidarity finds support in the UK Government Report *Caring about Carers* (1999), which states that

> recognition of their contribution to the care of someone else and to society more widely is important to many carers. They value involvement in discussions about the help provided to them and the person they are caring for, as well as practical help with the tasks of caring.
>
> (Department of Health 1999: 22)

Institutional providers of care thus need to recognise the contribution of informal carers and ensure tension is not created between paid care givers on the one hand and informal carers on the other hand. Instead of a paternalistic approach, professionals providing care in the home carers (such as district nurses) should acknowledge the contribution of the family carer. In turn, the family carers should be open to professional advice and not reject professional care out of hand.

5.8   Conclusion

Solidarity is essentially a relational concept: it is about the mutual obligations that individuals may perceive towards each other in the context of a specific community. This is particularly true of solidarity as expressed in the context of family care giving. While solidarity in welfare arrangements has to do with societal and political arrangements to support individuals in times of need and dependency, solidarity as expressed in family has to do with personal relations and mutual responsibilities.

Family solidarity is to a large extent based on personal and autonomous choices, even though individuals might feel pressured to deliver care because the other is in need and there is nobody else around to help (or they do not want any help). This will increasingly be the case as municipalities or other institutions are cutting back support. However, family solidarity is a type of solidarity that needs to be maintained and supported by professional help by nurses, paramedics, home helps and day care centres. This professional help is a necessary condition for informal care givers to keep caring for their partners, parents, neighbours and friends. Waiting lists, high financial contributions and diminishing professional support will weaken this preparedness (van der Made, ter Meulen and van der Burg 2001). However, government policies at the moment are built on the belief that family care or informal care will be able to complement or substitute the withdrawal of professional care. As we have seen in Chapter 4 by the example of the Netherlands, governments are increasingly limiting the entitlements to long-term care which are seen as too generous, particularly in the field of home care. Families are believed to step in as a substitution for professional help which has become too expensive. However, instead of this 'substitution model', family care or non-professional care should be considered from the idea of 'communicating vessels' (Muffels and Verburg 2001: 269). This idea sees the care system as an open system that is in frequent contact with the surrounding environment and that is heavily influenced by the structural and context changes (idem). The idea of the communicating vessels implies that the supply of care may diminish or 'leak away' due to context changes as mentioned earlier (changing family networks, individualisation and increased participation of women in the labour force). It also implies that a low level of care in the 'professional vessel' might correspond with a low level of care in the 'family care vessel' (Muffels and Verburg, 2001: 269; see also Oudijk et al. 2011).

Komter (2005) does not talk about 'communicating vessels' but about the 'complimentary thesis', which 'holds that higher levels of formal care go together with higher levels of informal care' (Komter 2005: 164). Komter refers to her own research in the Netherlands (Komter, Burgers and Engbersen 2000) which corroborated the complimentary thesis for the Netherlands. Künemund and Rein (1999) compared five developed countries to examine whether the amount of support for older people is shaped by a 'crowding out' process, meaning that generous welfare systems displace family solidarity. They found out that there was no support for the 'crowding out' thesis. Instead, they found more evidence that supports the reverse hypothesis, namely that the relationship between the state and the family may be described as a process of 'crowding in': generous welfare systems which give resources to elderly people help to increase rather than undermine family solidarity (Künemund and Rein 1999). On the basis of research in France, Arber and Attias-Donfut (2000) come to similar conclusions: 'family support given to elderly disabled parents does not diminish when these parents receive professional support, but on the contrary, in such cases it has a tendency to increase' (Arber and Attias-Donfut 2000: 13). They argue that 'the hypothesis whereby one form of support crowds out the other can be rejected' (idem). Support by the public care system does not substitute or replace the care supplied by family members, but in fact reinforces and increases the likelihood of this type of solidarity. Family care has a higher chance to develop when it is not seen as a residual kind of support but as an essential component that needs to be supported by the public care system and recognised as a serious partner in the supply of care for older and dependent persons.

Solidarity in family care should be recognised and adequately supported by the provision of material, practical, emotional and professional support. This is not only important from a moral, but also from a pragmatic, point of view, as the health and social care systems would collapse without the support offered by family care givers to dependent others. The severe cuts to council funding for social care by the

Government in the United Kingdom are 'writing on the wall': the shortage of funds for social care at home are leading to dramatic problems in the NHS which is at 'breaking point' as it is not able to cope with the care for older people who are not able to be discharged from hospital as there is no adequate social care available. As family care givers 'pick up the bill' for what are to a large extent societal obligations, they have a justified claim to be adequately supported by professional care givers. However, this professional support should take into account the needs and identities of the people supplying informal care and not 'colonise' this care by paternalistic approaches. Carers and persons cared for should be included in the delivery of care and empowered as citizens to deliver their care according to their own perspectives and identities.

6

Why We Need Solidarity

According to many, solidarity is something that seems to be missing in contemporary society: individuals think only about their own interests and seem to have no interest in the needs and concerns of others. While one could regard this as a somewhat exaggerated picture of modern social life, there are sociologists like Zygmunt Bauman who confirm the idea that the modern individual is leading the life of a consumer, preoccupied with the satisfaction of his own selfish needs and wishes. Instead of cooperating, individuals are antagonistic towards each other and not very much interested in social cooperation which is a key component of the idea of solidarity (Bauman 2001). In view of these hyper individualistic and consumerist drives, one could question the point of arguing for solidarity as a principle for social and moral policies (Taylor-Gooby 2011). Is solidarity, with its emphasis on the interest of the group, the common good, and social justice not an outmoded concept which is 'out of touch' with our individualised society? Instead of clinging to his 'old idea' with its socialist and Christian denotations (Chapter 1), should we not abandon it altogether and replace it with moral concepts that are more 'realistic', meaning more accommodating to the emphasis on individual choice, freedom and autonomy which are typical for the 'modern world'?

In the preceding chapters, I have tried to argue that individualisation and solidarity are not necessarily antagonistic towards each other, and that, for example, *reflexive* approaches may help to accommodate the interests and perspective of the group with the emphasis on individuality and recognition of differences. Moreover, I have tried to argue that, even if our society is getting more and more individualised, emphasising rational self-interest and consumerist choice, we still need a moral perspective that promotes the interests of vulnerable individuals who are *not* able to make such choices because of their medical or social predicament. I have also tried to argue that the idea of justice alone is not enough to safeguard the interests of vulnerable groups. But before drawing conclusions, let us summarise the various insights and views from the perspective of the five claims presented at the end of Chapter 1.

6.1   From the Social to the Moral (Claim One)

Concerns about the individualisation of society and the lack of solidarity are not new: social theorists and critics in nineteenth century France were advocating the need for solidarity and social responsibility to turn around the unfettered individualism and huge social inequalities of post-Revolution France. The concept of solidarity was imported from the legal domain to define the moral obligations of the individual towards others and to create more unity in society. The word solidarity expressed the idea that individuals are mutually connected with each other, not just as an empirical fact, but also from a moral point of view: Because individuals are connected with each other, they have also a *moral responsibility* towards the well-being of other human beings. This is what I called the first claim of solidarity.

The combination of mutual connectedness and moral responsibility was a central feature in the writings of social theorists like Auguste Comte and Charles Gide. Comte emphasised that the accomplishments of individuals are, to a large extent, the result of their dependence on the division of labour within society (Gide 2010). This mutual dependence and the cooperation resulting from it, creates a *moral debt* of individuals, not only towards contemporary society, but also to societies of the past. Comte and Gide argued for a cognitive process in which individuals come to insight in their social connectedness ('solidarité-fait' or factual solidarity) which would lead to recognition of their mutual obligations ('solidarité-devoir' or moral solidarity) (Reisz 2007). This process would result in social engagement with and acceptance of a political process in which the injustices of the social cooperation were mitigated and resolved. This idea was further elaborated by Léon Bourgeois in his theory of 'solidarism'. Bourgeois made a distinction between 'natural solidarity' and 'moral solidarity': natural solidarity is the web of social relations and interdependencies which is in principle blind, 'amoral' and unjust (Bourgeois 1896). This natural situation must be superseded by moral solidarity based on a 'quasi-contract' in which the injustice of the natural solidarity is redressed by way of reciprocal duties.

The efforts by French theorists to connect social dependencies and moral obligations, were criticised by the Jesuit writer Heinrich Pesch who argued that they tried to make a short cut from the factual interdependencies of individuals to their moral obligations towards each other (Große Kracht 2007). As they did not explain how the gap between the factual and the moral should be bridged, Pesch accused the French theorists of a *naturalistic fallacy* in which moral duties are based on empirical observations. The fact that Pesch was developing a rather dated and particularistic scholastic perspective on solidarity (his own theory of 'solidarism'), does not mean that these comments are out of date. In fact, they point at an important philosophical problem: if solidarity is a normative duty, what is the philosophical basis for this duty? The fact that we are connected by many social dependencies does not mean that we do have a moral duty towards each other. One could also argue the other way: because of the social connectedness, one could try to liberate oneself from them by a selfish attitude. As pointed out by Pesch, the solutions by the French theorists for this problem were philosophically unsatisfactory and based on arbitrary arguments. Bourgeois, for example, introduced the idea of individual consent or self-interest as the basis for the social contract, but, as Pesch rightly argued, this was a pure voluntary act which could always be recalled if individuals had an interest to do so.

What Pesch tried to argue was that solidarity should not just be based on some arbitrary or contractual decision (based on self-interest) but on a *philosophical anthropology* which gives a philosophical account of our place in the world and our relations with other human beings. On the basis of such a philosophical anthropology, we will be able to define human rights and obligations. These definitions might be informed by empirical findings, but the philosophy leading to these definitions has an autonomous status and cannot be reduced to knowledge of the facts. In Chapter 3 I argued for an anthropology based on the essential relatedness and social embeddedness of the human person. I referred to the work of Jaeggi (2001) who situated solidarity in the 'ethical life' of individuals referring to Hegel's idea of *Sittlichkeit*. The ethical life are the relations where the individual finds his or her own self (Theunissen 1981). Individuals see themselves in relation with the other, who is not the limitation but the precondition of one's own freedom. This relational anthropology, which is typical for many representatives of continental philosophy, argues that we have a duty to solidarity and support of the other *because such a support and commitment is an important value in itself*, not just because we have an interest to do so as, for example, many contemporary liberal theorists are arguing. Solidarity based on interest and calculation is arbitrary and 'shallow' (Jaeggi 2001): individuals can withdraw their support as soon as they have an interest to do so in the same way as they can change sides in a coalition. This was essentially the critique of Pesch on Bourgeois' solidarism.

The concept of solidarity expresses this commitment for the other, particularly for others who are in need of it due to circumstances out of their control. Solidarity at a concrete, personal level might look different than solidarity which is underlying arrangements of the welfare state. This type of solidarity is generally seen as based on common interest and a shared goal (Van Oorschot 1998). Self-interest will play an important role in this type of solidarity: individuals contribute to the support of others as they expect to be supported when they are in need themselves. This is the type of solidarity underlying the gift relationship as identified by Marcel Mauss (2011). On the basis of his anthropological studies in non-Western cultures of the role and meaning of the gift, Mauss concluded that the gift is never pure: It is driven by personal interests and utilitarian calculations which benefits both parties and creates a bond between them (Chapter 2). However, though self-interest and strategic calculations play an important role in the support of welfare state arrangements, at a fundamental level these arrangements also express a deeper commitment and an identification with the needs of the vulnerable other (Jaeggi 2001).

6.2   Solidarity and Justice (Claim Two)

The view of the human person as related to and dependent on the other, which we have identified as an important philosophical foundation of the idea of solidarity, can also help to better explain the importance of solidarity as a value distinct from the principle of justice. The second claim discussed in Chapter 1 was that when we are dealing with the moral problems of justice in health care we do not need the concept of solidarity. According to Bayertz, for example, we should better refer to the concept of justice as this is much better understood than the concept of solidarity which is another word for 'institutionalized support by the state' (Bayertz 1999: 22). The view of Bayertz and other philosophers is that instead of solidarity we should embrace the perspective of distributive justice based on rational deliberations, particularly 'behind the veil of ignorance' as proposed by John Rawls in his *Theory of Justice* (1989).

However, the liberal theory of justice expresses a different view of man than the anthropology that is underlying the concept of solidarity. While solidarity expresses the view of man as essentially in relation with others, liberal justice sees man as an isolated being focused on his own interests.

The relations between individuals are not based on mutual support or commitment to help the other, but on rational calculations and deliberations who should get which 'share of the cake'. Liberal philosophers tend to present the idea of justice as based on a neutral theory or a 'thin' theory of the good without much reference to personal values and concerns of individuals. However, as Nagel argues, such a theory is not as neutral as it looks, as it is based on an individualistic view of man according to which the best that can be wished for is the unimpeded pursuit of his own interests as long as this does not interfere with the rights of others (Nagel 1989).

Liberal theories of justice ignore the relational commitments between individuals which are typical for the concept of solidarity. The concept of solidarity expresses this commitment to the other, who deserves our support as he or she is in need of it due to circumstances out of their control. As commitment to others, solidarity is an important value *in itself*, and is not something we agree with merely because we have an interest to do so. However, this does not mean that solidarity should replace liberal justice: the perspective of justice protects the rights and interests of individuals as autonomous beings. Solidarity concerns the commitments and recognition of the well-being of the other without personal interest. Following Honneth's work (1995) on solidarity and recognition, I argued that solidarity represents the 'Sittlichkeit' or 'ethical life' of Hegel, while justice represent the 'Moralität' of Kant. Both concepts are distinctive, but both concepts are needed for the moral interpretation of institutional arrangements in contemporary society and particularly in health care. Habermas sees justice and solidarity as 'two sides of a coin': justice concerns the rights and liberties of autonomous, self-interested individuals, whereas solidarity concerns the mutual recognition and well-being of individuals who are connected in the life world (Habermas 1989; Houtepen and ter Meulen 2000b).

While liberal theories are based on a one-sided view of man (as motivated by enlightened self-interest only), it does not mean that there is no concern among liberal authors for the disadvantaged in our society. For example, Rawls cannot be accused of a lack of concern of the disadvantaged in society. His *Theory of Justice* presents an egalitarian scheme which is supposed to benefit all members of society, particularly the position of the least well-off. However, the weakness of liberal theories lies in the negative identification with the 'receiver' of goods. While Rawls may have endorsed high standards for collective distribution of basic goods to mitigate natural and social inequalities, I have argued in Chapter 3 that there is a tendency in some types of liberalism, particularly in opportunity-based liberalism, to restrict standards of provisions and obligations for support of less advantaged individuals to a minimum. The support to them is, in many cases, based on a scrutiny of their needs and of the opportunities that have been open to them (Houtepen and ter Meulen 2000b; Pasini and Reichlin 2001; Wolff 1998).

Though a pattern of distribution may be just in terms of benefit to the most disadvantaged individuals, it might at the same time be humiliating in the way this type of justice is delivered. As Margalit argued, in order to evaluate whether a just society is also a *decent* society, it is important to make a distinction between the *pattern* of distribution and the *procedure* to obtain the just distribution (Margalit 1996). The distribution may be just and efficient, but it may still lack compassion and a supportive attitude. In practice, justice may become very calculating about what is just, instead of being humane and gentle. Margalit argues that the just society as defined by Rawls is, in spirit, a decidedly decent society. However, Rawls cannot avoid that, in practice, the just society may be an indecent society, particularly in the *procedures* of how goods are distributed to needy individuals. An example are the recently introduced 'kitchen table discussions' in the Netherlands between the client, his social network and a counsellor of the city council (Chapter 4). These discussions are meant to assess the capability of the applicant's social network to provide care at home. Similarly, access to long-term care facilities in institutions like nursing homes is severely restricted, as admissions are based on a scrutiny of the potential within families to deliver care at home.

In Chapter 3 I presented the work of Honneth who (in line with Hegel's idea of 'Sittlichkeit') defines solidarity as an interactive relationship in which individuals recognise each other's identities and mutually sympathise with each other's ways of life. Health and social care arrangements may ignore or hinder such relationships as they may be based on humiliating procedures which lack the commitment and support that are typical for solidarity. A practical theory of solidarity then does not focus on rights and obligations of individuals only, but also wants to engage with the question how to promote relations of responsibility and recognition at an institutional level.

A practical theory of solidarity should pay special attention to solidarity with vulnerable groups in society. I have called this type of solidarity *humanitarian* solidarity which is solidarity based on identification with the values of humanity and responsibility for the other. Humanitarian solidarity is a strong candidate for the common cause which, according to authors like Taylor, is needed in contemporary societies: it is a value that goes beyond the self-interest and the indifference which are typical for a society which is based on liberal rights only (Taylor 1997). I argued that humanitarian solidarity is a commitment that can define a particular society and should never be abandoned in favour of the rational self-interest of the liberal discourse. Humanitarian solidarity is the basis for building just institutions in health care and accepting these institutions as an expression of a commitment to responsibility and recognition of individual needs and differences. It acts as a *corrective force* for justice, particularly when these institutions are at risk to fall below the standards of decency and humanity. Humanitarian solidarity helps to create an ethical society, in which individuals are not humiliated and are connected with society on the basis of humanitarian solidarity or 'shared humanity' (Margalit). As Schuyt (1998) argued, when welfare states are reduced and governments must make difficult decisions regarding solidarity-based arrangements, their main responsibility shall be that nobody falls below the standards of decency: 'While decency is a notch below prosperous, may not make people happy, and does not provide protection from all of life's accidents and inconveniences, it will safeguard citizens from humiliation and servitude' (Schuyt 1998: 311).

6.3   Solidarity and Subsidiarity (Claim Three)

The ageing of the population and the increasing costs of care which can be associated with this process are leading national governments to rethink the financing of care by restricting entitlements and increasing private financial contributions from individuals. Moreover, families are increasingly under pressure to provide home care and personal care for their dependent family members. The shift from care by professional caregivers paid by the state towards care by family members, is part of process in which societal solidarity is increasingly limited by a reduction of entitlements supplied by the welfare state.

The ideological legitimisation of these reductions refers to the idea that the reduction of involvement of the state may create 'real solidarity' within families and small communities. This is what I called the third claim of solidarity, that governments have no role to play in solidarity and should leave this to the lower levels of society, particularly families and social networks. In Chapter 4, I referred to the idea of 'reciprocity' as put forward by the RVZ, the Dutch Council for Public Health and Care

(RVZ 2013). According to the Council, reciprocity in informal care means that the care receiver and the care giver work together in the caring process whereby the burdens and benefits are distributed fairly between them. This reciprocity will support the motivation to provide care and the personal obligation to display solidarity with the other. Moreover, reciprocity-based solidarity will create more unity and cohesiveness in society, while lack of reciprocity and overreliance on state support will lead to division and exclusion. However, as the Council admits, the background of this moral appeal is the need to cut costs and to limit entitlements to care.

Though the Council for Public Health cannot be associated with neoliberal ideas and policies, the idea of reciprocity and of pushing solidarity back to families and social networks concurs with the neoliberal call for reduction of the involvement of the state and the reinforcement of the self-reliance of individuals instead of their dependency on state supported institutions. According to neoliberal ideology (Hayek 2012), individuals should take more initiative in organising their life and they should turn to their families and to small civic societies when they need help instead of relying on the welfare agencies of the state: the 'minimal state' is the best way to generate social solidarity and the flourishing of personal virtues and good character.

The principle of subsidiarity, as advocated in catholic social teaching (Verstraeten 1998), argues in a comparable way, that state sponsored solidarity should only be offered when individuals and their social network are not able to organise care themselves. Subsidiarity means that the best help that society can offer is the help that results in self-help: individuals should be stimulated to develop their own talents and potential instead of relying on help by the state. The latter would lead to dependency and obstruction of the self-development of the individual. The principle of subsidiarity prescribes that society should only provide social support on a supplementary basis, and only to help a person to overcome his troubles by using his own powers and resources.

The application of principles like subsidiarity and 'reciprocity' may be tempting as it seems to lead to emancipatory outcomes like increased individual autonomy and personal solidarity with the other. However, there is a risk that a rather restricted interpretation of this principle may throw the care for their dependent family members back to individuals who are already overburdened by this type of care. Moreover, as women are usually the main informal care givers, it may very well hinder the emancipation of women who are forced to give up their jobs or are under the extreme pressure of being in a 'sandwich situation' (Abel 1991): on the one hand caring for children who are growing up and on the other hand caring for their parents (or parents-in-law) or their partners who are becoming increasingly dependent on the help by others.

In Chapter 5 I defined family care or informal care as based on a willingness to help a vulnerable and dependent other in the context of a relationship. It is a different type of solidarity than the solidarity that is underlying the arrangements of the welfare state (Knipscheer 1992). Solidarity in welfare arrangements has to do with societal and political arrangements to support individuals in times of need and dependency. Solidarity as expressed in family care has to do with personal relations and mutual responsibilities. Family solidarity is not based on compulsion, but on a voluntary choice to help another human being who is in need of support by way of a concrete and personal service. This does not mean that there is not a sense of obligation to supply this support. However, individuals take on this obligation because they have voluntarily agreed to do so, even though they might feel pressured because of the lack of support by municipalities or family members.

However, it is important for family care givers to be supported by professional caregivers: a withdrawal of professional support will lead to reduced willingness to support dependent family members (Muffels and Verburg 2001; Komter 2005). However, government policies at the moment are built on the belief that family care or informal care will be able to complement or substitute the withdrawal of professional help which has become too expensive. Instead of this 'substitution model' family care or non-professional care should be considered from the idea of 'communicating vessels': a low level of care in the 'professional vessel' might correspond with a low level of care in the 'family care vessel' (Muffels and Verburg 2001). In Chapter 5, I argued that family care can only fulfil its role in the care system when it is not seen as a residual kind of support but as an essential component of the care for dependent people which needs to be supported by the professional system organised and funded by national and local governments. Subsidiarity or 'reciprocity' should not mean total withdrawal of professional support for family caregivers, but should mean adequate support to enable family caregivers to provide the solidary support for their dependent family member.

Apart from pragmatic arguments, there is also an important moral argument to support family care. Family care giving can be characterised as the type of personal solidarity which, according to Honneth (1995), is an important basis for self-esteem and recognition of the other (Chapter 3). However, it is not the solidarity of the strong communal ties which is promoted by some communitarian authors (Kymlicka 2002). Family solidarity is the type of solidarity in which self-esteem and recognition of individual difference are important ethical principles (Honneth 1995). However, as mentioned above, this personal solidarity can only flourish when it is supported by the solidarity-based arrangements for health and social care. Health and social care policies should not be based on rational interests solely, but should also express the general willingness to contribute to the personal solidarity in family care giving directed to the 'concrete other' (Benhabib 1992). This support is another way to promote the common goal of humanitarian solidarity as the type of solidarity which is concerned with the needs and interests of vulnerable individuals in our society.

6.4 Solidarity and Individuality (Claim Four)

The fourth claim regarding solidarity is that it stiffens individuality and overrules the autonomy of the individual in favour of the interests of the group. This claim is particularly directed towards some communitarian authors who argue that the individual needs the social surrounding of the group to develop his or her identity and to become an active member of the social and political community (Kymlicka 2002). This critique, however, is not entirely fair. There are indeed communitarian authors like Michael Sandel (1990) who argue that the self of individuals is to a large extent constituted by social values and ends of their communities. Individuals can only discover who they are, not by the choices they are making, but by reflecting on the goals and ends of the communities they are part of. Such communitarian ideas about the constitutive role of communities in regard to personal identities can indeed be criticised as leading to inclusiveness and a disregard of individual differences. These ideas seem to reflect a romantic nostalgia to the cosiness of the small community ('Gemeinschaft') or even to totalitarian ideologies.

The communitarian call for solidarity as inclusiveness reminds us of the romantic conservatism of political writers in the first part of the nineteenth century like De Bonald and De Maistre in France, Burke in the United Kingdom and Herder in Germany, as (partly) presented in Chapter 2. According to Burke, the individualisation of society would result in a loss of traditional norms and clear guidance for the individual who, as a result, would only be interested in the pursuit of his own interests. De Bonald argued in a similar way against the emphasis on individual autonomy and the lack of respect for communal values. Instead of the social fragmentation post-Revolution, French society should return to the social structures of the old times (meaning pre-Revolution) in which the evil tendencies of individuals were suppressed by the state (de Jager 1980). According to De Bonald, society is prior to the individual, a thought that seems to be echoed by Sandel when he says that the self is not prior to the good, but that the self is constituted by the ends and values that are part of the social context.

However, as already mentioned, these conservative tendencies are not typical for all contemporary communitarian authors. Etzioni (1998), for example, takes a distance from the view that the group is the supreme authority. He argued that 'new communitarians' are trying to find a balance between community and autonomy, between individual rights and social responsibilities and to explore the conditions under which the common good and individual rights could be adjusted to each other. In Chapter 5 I referred to the distinction made by Benhabib (1992) between 'integrationist' and 'participatory' communitarianism. 'Integrationist' communitarianism is the type of communitarianism that argues that the problem of individualism, anomie and alienation in our modern societies can only be solved by a revitalisation of values and homogeneous communities. 'Participatory' communitarians argue for a process of political participation in which people have a say in the economic, political and civic arrangements which define their lives. A vibrant participatory life will help the formation and flourishing of one's self-identity and the revitalisation of certain values.

In Chapter 5, I have argued that participatory communitarianism is an important step towards an understanding of solidarity that recognises individual differences and supports the recognition of individual identities in health and social care practices. I have presented Jody Dean's concept of 'reflective solidarity' as an important way forward to reconcile the recognition of identities and sharing a conception of the good. Dean (like Honneth) argues for a dialogic approach in which individuals discuss their expectations and interpretations of the 'generalised other' a term introduced by Mead (1970). The recognition of different interpretations of the generalised other (which can be a specific societal role or ideal) leads to the understanding that our identities will never completely fulfil the expectations of the generalised other and that we constantly need to question the expectations we have of the generalised other. Such a dialogue is not a threat to solidarity, but can strengthen it by our shared engagement in dialogue. Reflective solidarity is a communicative process which strengthens social ties as well as opens the possibility for reflection on social expectations and personal identity.

The idea of reflective solidarity concurs with the emphasis on reflexivity by Giddens and Beck as the condition of individuals in modern societies which I presented in Chapter 1.[1] According to Giddens, social and individual life in modern times is characterised by reflexivity, meaning that these practices are constantly examined and reformed in the light of incoming information about these practices, thus constantly changing the character of these practices (Giddens 1990). Like Beck (2007) and Bauman (2001), Giddens argues that in modernity nothing is certain and everything is in constant revision and examination. Identities are not fixed or based any more on traditional social roles and patterns: they are formed and redefined in a constant process of revision and reflection in the context of social and intimate practices. People are comparing various lifestyles in search of their true identity or of authenticity. This reflexive approach concurs with the idea behind reflective solidarity: solidarity means reflections on personal identities by way of interpretations of the generalised other and other information. This reflectively applied knowledge will lead to recognition of individual differences as well as a shared understanding of the common goals of practices.

Solidarity in health care practices does not mean resorting to traditional, integrationist accounts of communitarianism which obliterate individual differences and personal autonomy: by taking a participatory and reflective approach it will be possible to develop common understandings and communal practices while at the same time recognising and supporting individual differences and personal autonomy.

6.5   Solidarity: An Exclusive European Value? (Claim Five)

It is often claimed that solidarity represents a typical European approach to the arrangement of health and social care services and other systems of social support. The typical 'European' aspect is the support of the idea of a common good and the willingness of individuals to put their interests in second place in order to help others who are less well-off. In health and social care, this means individuals with higher incomes make a larger financial contribution to the health care insurance system in order to

---

[1] Please note that Dean uses the word 'reflective' while Giddens and Beck use the word 'reflexive'. Both writing styles are being used when comparing their approaches.

enable disadvantaged and vulnerable groups in society to have access to good quality health and social care services. Though in many countries the solidarity-based systems of health and social care are under increased tension, solidarity seems to stay strong and intact in spite of reforms like the introduction of market forces and financial payments (Maarse and Paulus 2003). European citizens are, in general, happy with solidarity as the basis of health and social care as it leads to better protection and access to care as compared to other systems in the world. They are, in general, dismayed about health care in the United States where, until the recent introduction of the Affordable Care Act (Patient Protection and Affordable Care Act 2010), a large group of the population did not have access to health care or only care of poor quality. In contrast to the alleged individualism of the United States, which they hold responsible for this unacceptable situation, Europeans boast that they have 'solidarity', meaning a mentality that supports the common goals including the support of the weak by the strong.

However, one can raise several questions regarding this claim. First, it is not clear whether 'solidarity' is a shared value all over Europe. Many countries which offer universal access to health and social care do not speak about solidarity. This is particularly true for the United Kingdom which developed the universally accessible National Health Service (NHS) in the 1940s on the basis of tax contributions and not on a Bismarck-inspired national health insurance model. The word 'solidarity' is an unfamiliar term in the United Kingdom: instead one speaks of 'community responsibility' or 'communitarianism' to describe the concerns and support for the poor and vulnerable individuals in society (Johnson and Cullen 2001: 108). The architects of the National Health Service, including the reformer William Beveridge, tried to meet the obligation of society for all its members and particularly those most in need without speaking of solidarity (Johnson and Cullen 2001:109). Moreover, one can ask whether these policies were based on real concerns and commitments with the poor and vulnerable or just political pragmatism, meaning preventing the working class from falling apart due to ill health and premature death (idem).

This does not mean that solidarity was or is not existent at the level of personal relations and responsibilities in British society. In his famous book *The Gift Relationship* (1970), Richard Titmuss argued that the Second World War resulted in the development of a community spirit in British society with an increased concern for the welfare of others (Campbell and Jones 2001: 406). Titmuss (1970) argued that an altruistic attitude towards the needs of others was an important factor in the willingness of many British citizens to give blood to strangers and, more generally, to support the development of the National Health Service and the Welfare State. Titmuss recognised that this solidarity was also driven by (long-term) personal interests and he argued that the gift-relationship was in fact based on a mix of altruism and self-interest (Titmuss 1970: 214–15).[2] This combination of social responsibility and individual interest as the basis for social support of the Welfare State shows much resemblance to the solidarity in continental Europe. However, as noted earlier, the word 'solidarity' is not referred to in the British policy discourse.

Scandinavian countries do not justify their universal health and social care systems in terms of solidarity either. Sweden, for example, has for a long time been regarded as the country with the most widely developed welfare state including a system of universally accessible, good quality health and social care services. Most of these services are free of charge and are meant to support the needy and vulnerable. The financial burden is distributed according to ability to pay through a system of income taxes and employer fees. However, the word 'solidarity' is not used in the Swedish context to legitimise these policies and arrangements. Instead, one speaks of equality and democracy (Bergmark, Lindberg and Thorslund 2001: 77). Solidarity has no meaning in the Swedish health and social care model. It is a term usually reserved to characterise certain romantic individuals or radical social movements (Bergmark, Lindberg and Thorslund 2001: 97).

However, while the United Kingdom and the Scandinavian countries do not use the word 'solidarity', they have been able to develop health care systems that are offering universal access to care which, particularly in the case of Scandinavia, are similar or perhaps to some extent superior to the insurance-based systems which do refer to solidarity like Germany, the Netherlands, Belgium, France and Switzerland. The word 'solidarity' does not guarantee the best possible system of health and social care, as even solidarity-based systems might fail some people, particularly people with chronic and long-term needs. Equally, it is not true that countries

---

[2] Titmuss's ideas were strongly influenced by the work of Marcel Mauss on the gift relationship (Sykora 2009). Mauss discovered that the gift is never purely altruistic: it is also driven by personal interests and utilitarian calculations which benefits both parties and creates a bond between them (see Chapter 2). Like Mauss, Titmuss argued that the gift relationship is a driving force for social cohesion.

which are not referring to 'solidarity' have not developed systems of health and social care to support individuals who are in need. I am not referring here about the tax-based systems of the United Kingdom and Scandinavia, but to the United States where, in spite of the dominance of the market model, there are services organised by the federal government to help the vulnerable and poor individuals to get access to health and social care (Callahan 2008). Examples are the Medicare Programme (funding of health care for all individuals over 65), the Medicaid programmes (jointly funded by the federal and state governments), and the Veterans Health Administration (a large programme to accommodate the medical needs of veterans of the military). The Affordable Care Act signed into law by President Obama has improved the access of many Americans to health insurance by a mandatory insurance programme with a minimum coverage of essential medical services without the possibility of risk selection by insurance companies. The Affordable Care Act has resulted in a drop of uninsured people from 18 per cent of the population of 310 million inhabitants in 2010 to 11 per cent of 320 million in 2016 (Marken 2016). Though this means that there are still 30 million people in the United States without health insurance (these are not just poor people, but include also 'free riders'), the Affordable Care Act can be regarded as an act of solidarity with vulnerable people in the United States. However, not many in the United States will refer to 'solidarity', as the term is still widely associated with socialism.[3]

Europeans are, in general, proud of the universal access to health and social care, and they have no high opinion of what they regard as the individualism and lack of solidarity in the United States, which they see as an important reason for the lack of universal access to health care (though the Affordable Care Act is regarded as an important achievement). However, one can question the claim that there is no solidarity in American society and that this society is composed of egoistic individuals

---

[3] This 'anti-socialism' is responsible for a resistance among parts of the American population against state interventions in health care and for the resistance and resistance against the Affordable Care Act leading to the rescinding of this Act by the Trump administration. It remains to be seen what the impact will be of this decision, but the expectation is that it will lead to a sharp increase in the number of uninsured individuals as well as to risk selection and financial obstacles for people with pre-existing conditions and older people applying for a health insurance. Though of course this effort to remove the Affordable Care Act can not be seen as an example of solidarity, this change in policy does not mean that solidarity is disappearing from American society (as can be shown by the strong resistance to this decision by the Trump administration).

who have no commitments to common goals including the well-being of vulnerable others. This is a superficial stereotype that does not fit with the character and reality of American culture. I have referred in Chapter 2 to the observations by Alexis de Tocqueville during his travel through the United States in the mid-nineteenth century. According to De Tocqueville, individuals in American communities had to look to their own affairs and to concern themselves with public matters. They were doing so because of 'enlightened self-interest', meaning a view of one's own interests which takes basic rights of others into account (Siedentop 1994). De Tocqueville argued that enlightened self-interest is not a bad thing as long as chasing one's own interests includes some sacrifice to help others. Such a modest sacrifice would be in the interest of both the giver as the receiver. Enlightened self-interest is not the same as egotism which leads to excesses and chaos. Instead, a reasonable amount of self-interest combined with some self-sacrifice could be the solid basis of a morally acceptable society (de Tocqueville 2010).

The observations by De Tocqueville are quite remarkable as they put the alleged difference between Europe and the United States in another light. In fact, the motive of American citizens to engage with their communities (as observed by De Tocqueville) is not much different than the motive underlying solidarity of individuals in modern European societies, which is to a large extent based on enlightened self-interest. Nonetheless, there are concerns that the bonds in American communities are withering and that Americans have lost their engagement with the life of their communities. According to Putnam, Americans have gradually been 'pulled out from one another' and their communities (Putnam 2000). He argues for a revival of the 'social capital' in American society, meaning the strengthening of communal bonds and mutual commitments.

However, as Dickenson has argued, there is a risk that such social capital can lead to 'in group solidarity' with the 'us' against the 'them' (Dickenson 2013: 17). One can also question whether the decline of community life has indeed resulted in a lack of commitment for common causes. For example, the Civil Rights Movement in the 1950s and 1960 is a clear sign of collective commitment with the cause of the Black community (Dickenson 2013: 16). Another example are grassroots groups trying to promote better access to health care for people without insurance or limited access within Medicaid (Jennings 1990). Oregon Health Decisions was one of the grassroots movements which, in the 1980s and 1990s, was the driving force behind the Oregon Health Care Plan, which attracted worldwide attention because of its prioritisation of health care services on the basis of cost-effectiveness and values of the population. This prioritisation, in combination with affordable health insurance, was meant to expand access to health care for vulnerable groups in Oregon in the Medicaid Programme (ter Meulen 1993). Though the process is often accused as 'the haves' deciding about the 'have-nots', it can be regarded as expressing the feelings of responsibility and social concerns of many American citizens with the lack of access and the poor quality of care for the most disadvantaged individuals in their society (Garland 1993).

Though individualism can go hand in hand with a commitment to a common cause, there is a risk that individualism leads to a centring on the self with less commitment with others. According to Charles Taylor, there is a 'dark side' of individualism 'which both flattens and narrows our lives, makes them poorer in meaning, and less concerned with others or society' (Taylor 1991: 4). Taylor refers to De Tocqueville, who also warned against the threat that individuals would close themselves off in the solitude of their own lives (idem). This retreat into the self, which according to Taylor is a mistaken interpretation of the ideal of authenticity, leads to a 'facile relativism' and moral subjectivism according to which one ought not to challenge other people's values (Taylor 1991: 14).

Bellah et al. argue that many Americans are concerned to find meaning in life not primarily through self-cultivation 'but through intense relations with others' (Bellah et al. 1985: 291). They conclude from their research that in American life, there is a desire for 'intense relationships with others' and an attempt 'to move beyond the isolated self'. However, they also found that the language of individualism, which they called 'the primary language of American self-understanding' makes the communal interests difficult to articulate (Bellah et al. 1985: 290–291). Moreover, they notice a split between the public world in which individualistic competition is rife, and the private world or 'lifestyle enclaves' where personal relationships and the search for meaning are meant to make the competitive striving bearable (Bellah et al. 1985: 292).

The 'flat and narrow' individualism criticised by Taylor can, to some extent, be linked with the arrival of narcissism as a predominant personality type in modern societies. According to Christopher Lasch, modern culture is witnessing the arrival of the narcissistic personality which can be characterised by illusions of omnipotence and a 'grandiose self'. The modern narcissist is constantly seeking the audience of others to admire his or her individual accomplishments or to attach himself to those who radiate celebrity, charisma and power (Lasch 1979: 38). The modern individual has fallen in love with himself: the prevailing passion is 'to live for the moment ... to live for yourself' (Lasch 1979: 30). Similar observations are made by Jean Twenge and Keith Campbell in *The Narcissistic Epidemic* (2009). Twenge and others criticise the 'narcissistic inflation of the self' and 'the road of narcissism' marked by 'greed, self-centredness, shallow relationships, vanity, social isolation, phony economics, bailouts, and blame' (Twenge and Foster 2008; Twenge and Campbell 2009, xii; Dickenson 2013). They argue that we can walk a 'different path', which leads us to responsibility for ourselves and others, which brings us joy without harming others, such as close relationships, strong communities, hard work, and passions or hobbies' (Twenge and Campbell 2009: xii).

However, narcissism is not the same as individualism. The narcissist personality sees the other as a mirror for him or her own grandiose personality without feeling any responsibility for the other. This is not the case in individualism, even when it is based on 'enlightened self-interest'. As De Tocqueville argued, individualism based on self-interest is not the same as 'egoism': it can go together with sacrifices to help the other and thus to solidarity. This type of solidarity, which has a long tradition in American culture, is not much different than solidarity based on self-interest which is dominant in many European countries. It may be corrupted by consumerism and narcissism, but that threat is not typical for American society only.

6.6   Conclusion

The principle of solidarity has been guiding the building of welfare states in many European countries, including the arrangements of health and social care. However, this principle does not provide specific answers how to deal with the pressure on these arrangements, for example, the scarcity of resources and the problem of limiting and rationing health care. Usually, limits in health care are set on the basis of utilitarian outcome measures like cost-effectiveness studies or (often arbitrary and political) calculations about what individuals should pay out of their own pockets. For example, in the United Kingdom, the National Institute for Health and Care Excellence (NICE) gives recommendations to the NHS about new treatments on the basis of an assessment of evidence regarding the clinical effectiveness and cost-effectiveness of health technologies including new pharmaceutical treatments, clinical procedures, medical devices and diagnostic agents.

We need to accept that, in view of limited resources, choices have to be made regarding the kind of health care services society should provide to its citizens. However, such choices should not just be led by economic and clinical evidence only. Access to health and social care, and guidance about the quality of this care, should also be led by the principle of *humanitarian solidarity*. This principle can be defined as a responsibility to protect those persons whose existence is threatened by circumstances beyond their control, particularly natural fate or unfair social structures. The claim for humanitarian solidarity is based on a philosophical understanding of human beings as fundamentally related with each other: existing as a human being means essentially being related to the other and to have commitments to the other. The concept of humanitarian solidarity expresses this relational commitment, particularly for those individuals who are in distress and need our support because they are not able to help themselves. One can think of people with dementia, psychiatric illness and intellectual disabilities. As commitment to others, solidarity is an important value *in itself*, and is not something we agree with merely because we have an interest to do so.

Paternalism, lack of respect and ignoring the needs and wishes of the vulnerable and indigent are common, even within health care systems that are based on principles of just distribution. An important way to prevent humiliating and indecent care is to involve individuals in the decision-making and delivery of their care. Care recipients should not merely be addressed as abstract bearers of rights or mere carriers of disease or disability. Their care should be geared to their specific needs and directed to their capacities as responsible persons (even when they have diminished capacity). Caring practices should focus on how to communicate with individuals and how to respect their identities and responsibilities in the process of care. A relevant concept in this context is 'reflective solidarity' (Dean) which means that decisions should be taken with a continuous reflection on the way institutions and services affect the identities of people involved in caring practices. In conjunction with recognition of the centrality of the needs of the care receiver, this calls for a degree of flexibility of caring arrangements based on feedback and involvement of the persons involved in the caring process on the conditions of one's action.

Reflective approaches see solidarity as a communicative process which strengthens social ties as well as opens the possibility for reflection on social expectations and recognition of personal identities. It is not the solidarity of the strong communal bonds as promoted by some communitarian authors: such a type of solidarity is not acceptable any more in a society which emphasises the importance of individuality and the recognition of individual differences. Reflective solidarity can help to promote concrete practices in which self-respect (rights) and self-esteem (solidarity) are the main ethical principles (Honneth).

The solidarity of concrete practices can only flourish when it is supported by specific arrangements in the policy and delivery of health and social care. This means that policies in the (public) health system should not distance themselves from concrete practices of solidarity because of a strong belief in subsidiarity or adherence to a neoliberal ideology. Instead, these policies should express the general willingness to contribute to the goals of solidarity by specific support of certain care policies and health and social care arrangements. This means, for example, the support of family care givers for people with dementia. Support for family care givers is an important condition for recognition of their identities as partners in the care for their dependent family members. This recognition is an important condition for their willingness to keep providing care for their family members. In view of the growing numbers of patients suffering from Alzheimer's disease in the near future,[4] the support by family givers, but also the support *for* family givers, should be essential elements of care policies and practices.

Solidarity does not replace justice, but acts as a *corrective force* for justice, particularly when these institutions are failing in respect with common standards of decency and humanity. It is not aiming at formulating general levels of care services as a measure of justice, but it seeks to prevent that care for dependent individuals, which becomes humiliating and indecent. It expresses a commitment to sustain the life of fellow human beings, particularly when their conditions are becoming difficult to bear. Solidarity, particularly humanitarian solidarity, helps to create an ethical society in which individuals are not humiliated and are connected with society on the basis of 'shared humanity' (Margalit). This is why we need solidarity.

---

[4] Research shows that, in 2013, there were 815,827 people with dementia in the United Kingdom (www.alzheimers.org.uk). 773,502 of these people with dementia were aged 65 years or over. This represents 1 in every 79 (1.3 per cent) of the entire UK population and 1 in every 14 of the population aged 65 years and over. In 2015, there will be 856,700 people with dementia in the United Kingdom in 2015 at the current rate of prevalence. If current trends continue and no action is taken, the number of people with dementia in the United Kingdom is forecast to increase to 1,142,677 by 2025 and 2,092,945 by 2051, an increase of 40 per cent over the next 12 years and of 156 per cent over the next 38 years.

REFERENCES

Abel, E. (1991). *Who Cares for the Elderly? Public Policy and the Experiences of Adult Daughters.* Philadelphia: Temple University Press.

Akker, P. van den, Luijkx, K. (2004). De mantelzorgontvanger. Wederkerigheid als complicerende factor. In: K. Knipscheer, ed., *Dilemma's in de Mantelzorg.* Utrecht: NIZW Nederlands Instituut voor Zorg en Welzijn, pp. 19–31.

Alzheimer's Society. (2014). *Dementia Report 2014.* London: Alzheimer's society. Available at: www.alzheimers.org.uk. [Accessed 7 Oct. 2016].

Anderson, J. (1995). Translator's Introduction. In: A. Honneth, ed., *The Struggle for Recognition: The Moral Grammar of Social Conflict.* Cambridge: Polity Press, pp. x–xxi.

Aneshensel, C.S., Pearlin, L.I., Schuler, R.H. (1993). Stress, role captivity and the cessation of caregiving. *Journal of Health and Social Behavior*, 34(1), pp. 54–70.

Arber, S., Attias-Donfut, C., eds. (2000). *The Myth of Generational Conflict: The Family and State in Ageing Societies.* London and New York: Routledge.

Bakker, H. (2001). *Ontspoorde Zorg: Overbelasting en Ontsporing in Mantelzorg aan Ouderen.* Utrecht: Nederlands Instituut voor Zorg en Welzijn.

Baldwin, P. (1990). *The Politics of Social Solidarity: Class Bases of the European Welfare State 1875-1975.* Cambridge: Cambridge University Press.

Bartholomée, Y., Maarse, J. (2006). Health insurance reform in the Netherlands. *EuroHealth*, 12(2), pp. 7–9.

Bauman, Z. (1998). *Leven met Veranderlijkheid, Verscheidenheid en Onzekerheid.* Amsterdam: Boom.

(2001). *The Individualized Society.* Cambridge: Polity Press.

Bauman, Z., Galecki, L. (2005). The unwinnable war: an interview with Zygmunt Bauman. *Open Democracy*, 2 December 2005. Available at: www.opendemocracy.net/globalization-vision_reflections/modernity_3082 .jsp [Accessed 10 Oct. 2016].

Bauman, Z., May, T. (1990). *Thinking Sociologically.* Oxford: Blackwell.

Bayertz, K. (1999). Four uses of 'solidarity'. In: K. Bayertz, ed., *Solidarity: Philosophical Studies in Contemporary Culture.* Amsterdam: Kluwer Academic Publishers, pp. 3–28.

Beauchamp, T., Childress, J. (2012). *Principles of Biomedical Ethics*, 7th Ed. New York: Oxford University Press.

Beck, U. (2007). *Risk Society: Towards a New Modernity*. Reprint of the 1992 Edition. London: Sage.

Beecher, J. (1986). *Charles Fourier: The Visionary and His World*. Berkeley: University of California Press.

Bellah, R.N., Madsen, R., Sullivan, W.M., Swidler, A., Tipton, S.M. (1985). *Habits of the Heart: Individualism and Commitment in American life*. New York: Harper and Row.

Bellah, R.N. (1998). Community properly understood: a defence of 'democratic communitarianism'. In: A. Etzioni, ed., *The Essential Communitarian Reader*. Lanham: Rowham & Littlefield Publishers, pp. 15–19.

Benhabib, S. (1992). *Situating the Self: Gender, Community and Postmodernism in Contemporary Ethics*. New York: Routledge.

Bergmark, A., Lindberg, E., Thorslund, M. (2001). Solidarity and Care in Sweden. In: R. ter Meulen, W. Arts, R. Muffels, eds., *Solidarity in Health and Social Care in Europe*. Series Philosophy & Medicine Vol. 69. Dordrecht: Kluwer, pp. 77–105.

Bernstein, E. (1899). *Die Voraussetzungen des Sozialismus und die Aufgaben der Sozialdemokratie*. Stuttgart: J.H.W. Dietz.

Bioethics (2012). Special issue: the role of solidarity in bioethics. *Bioethics*, 26(7), pp. ii–iv, 343–394.

Boer, A. De, Timmermans, J. (2007). *Blijvend in Balans Een Toekomstverkenning van Informele Zorg*. Den Haag: Sociaal en Cultureel Planbureau.

Boer, A. de, ed. (2007). *Toekomstverkenning Informele Zorg*. Den Haag: Sociaal en Cultureel Planbureau.

Boer, A. de, Kooiker, S. (2012). Zorg. In: V. Veldheer, J-J. Jonker, L. van Noije & C. Vroman, eds., *Een Beroep op de Burger: Minder Verzorgingsstaat, Meer Eigen Verantwoordelijkheid?* Sociaal en Cultureel Rapport 2012. Den Haag: Sociaal en Cultureel Planbureau, pp. 140–160.

Boer, A. de, Klerk, M. de (2013). *Informele Zorg in Nederland Een Literatuurstudie Naar Mantelzorg en Vrijwilligerswerk in de Zorg*. Den Haag: Sociaal Cultureel Planbureau.

Boorse, Ch. (1977). Health as a theoretical concept. *Philosophy of Science*, 44(4), pp. 542–573.

Bourgeois, L. (1896). *Solidarité*. Paris: Armand Colin. Available at: http://classiques.uqac.ca/classiques/bourgeois_leon/solidarite/bourgeois_solidarite.pdf [Accessed 9 July 2015].

Broek, Th. van den (2016). Langdurige zorg in Nederland: beleid en publieke opinie. *Demos*, 32(1), pp. 6–7.

Burke, E. (1988 [1792]). *Reflections on the Revolution in France*. London: Penguin.

Bussemaker, J. (1993). *Betwiste Zelfstandigheid: Individualisering, Sekse en Verzorgingsstaat.* Amsterdam: SUA.

Callahan, D. (1988). *What Kind of Life: The Limits of Medical Progress.* New York: Simon and Schuster.

—— (2003). Individual good and common good: a communitarian approach to bioethics. *Perspectives in Biology and Medicine,* 46(4), pp. 496–507.

—— (2008). Europe and the United States: contrast and convergence. *Journal of Medicine and Philosophy,* 33, pp. 280–293.

Campbell, A., Jones, S. (2001). The historical and philosophical background of 'solidarity' in UK social welfare. In: R. ter Meulen, W. Arts, R. Muffels, eds., *Solidarity in Health and Social Care in Europe.* Series Philosophy & Medicine Vol 69. Dordrecht: Kluwer Academic Publishers, pp. 397–415.

Care Quality Commission (2016). *The State of Health Care and Adult Social Care in England 2015/16.* London: Care Quality Commission. Available at: www.cqc.org.uk/sites/default/files/20161013b_stateofcare1516_web.pdf [Accessed 14 October 2016].

Carrera, F., Pavolini, E., Ranci, C., Sabbatini, A. (2014). Long-term care systems in comparative perspective: care needs, informal and formal coverage, and social impacts in European countries. In: C. Ranzi, E. Pavolini, eds., *Reforms in Long-Term Care Policies in Europe. Investigating Institutional Change and Social Impacts.* Dordrecht: Springer Press, pp. 23–52.

Carers UK (2014). State of caring 2014. *Policy briefing May 2014.* London: Carers UK. Available at: www.carersuk.org/for-professionals/policy/policy-library/state-of-caring-2014. [Accessed 13 October 2016].

—— (2015). *Facts about Carers: Policy Briefing October 2015.* London: Carers UK. Available at: www.carersuk.org/for-professionals/policy/policy-library/facts-about-carers-2015. [Accessed 25 October 2016].

CEG (2004). *Mantelzorg, Kostenbeheersing en Eigen Verantwoordelijkheid: Signalering Ethiek en Gezondheid.* Den Haag/Zoetermeer: Centrum voor Ethiek en Gezondheid, pp.127–151.

Centesimus Annus (1991). *Encyclical Letter from Pope John Paul II to his Venerable Brother Bishops in the Episcopate the Priests and Deacons, Families of Men and Women Religious, all the Christian Faithful, and to all Men and Women of Good Will on the Hundredth Anniversary of Rerum Novarum.* Rome: Vatican. Available at: http://w2.vatican.va/content/john-paul-ii/en/encyclicals/documents/hf_jp-ii_enc_01051991_centesimus-annus.html. [Accessed 23 Sept 2016].

Chadwick, R. (1999). Genetics, choice and responsibility. *Health, Risk & Society,* 1, pp. 293–300.

Chadwick, R., Berg, K. (2001). Solidarity and equity: new ethical frameworks for genetic databases. *Nature Review Genetics,* 2/4, pp. 318–321.

Colombo, F., Llena-Nozal, A., Mercier, J., Tjadens, F. (2011). *Help Wanted? Providing and Paying for Long-Term Care*. OECD Health Policy Studies. Paris: OECD.

Companje, K.-P., Hendriks, R., Verachtert, K., Widdershoven, B. (2009). *Two Centuries of Solidarity: German, Belgian and Dutch Social Health Insurance 1770–2008*. Amsterdam: Aksant.

Comte, A. (1864). *Cours de Philosophie Positive*, Vol IV. Paris: Bachelier.

  (1976 [1832–1842]). Cours de Philosophie Positive. In: K. Thompson, *Auguste Comte: The Foundation of Sociology*. London: Nelson.

  (1998 [1825/1826]). Considerations on the Spiritual Power. In: H.S. Jones, *Auguste Comte: Early Political Writings*. Cambridge: Cambridge University Press, pp. 187–227.

Daniels, N. (1985). *Just Health Care*. Cambridge: Cambridge University Press.

  (2007). *Just Health. Meeting Health Needs Fairly*. Cambridge: Cambridge University Press.

Davies, R., Ives, J., Dunn, M. (2015). A Systematic Review of Empirical Bioethics Methodology. *BMC Medical Ethics*, 16:15.

Dean, J. (1996). *Solidarity of Strangers: Feminism after Identity Politics*. Berkeley: University of California Press.

Department of Health (1999). *Caring about Carers: A National Strategy for Carers*. London: HM Government Crown Office.

Dickenson, D. (2013). *Me Medicine vs We Medicine: Reclaiming Biotechnology for the Common Good*. New York: Columbia University Press.

Donzelot, J. (1994). *L'Invention du social: Essai sur le déclin des passions politiques*. Paris: Éditions du Seuil.

Doran, K. (1996). *Solidarity: A Synthesis of Personalism and Communalism in the Thought of Karol Wojtyla/John Paul II*. New York: P. Lang.

Dorr, D. (1983). *Option for the Poor: A Hundred Years of Vatican Social Teaching*. Dublin: Gill & Macmillan.

Duijnstee, M. A., Van den Dungen, A., Cuijpers P., Maliepaard, R. (1998). The Role, the Burden and the Support of Informal Care. In: A.J.P. Schrijvers, ed., *Health and Health Care in the Netherlands. A Critical Self-Assessment by Dutch Experts in the Medical and Health Sciences*. Maarssen: Elsevier/De Tijdstroom, pp. 20–32.

Durkheim, E. (1889). Ferdinand Tonnies. Gemeinschaft und Gesellschaft. Abhandlung des Communismus und des Socialismus als empirischer Culturformen. Leipzig, 1887: xxx–294. *Revue Philosophique de la France et de l'Étranger*, 27, pp. 416–422. Available at: www.jstor.org/stable/41075054. [Accessed 26 February 2015].

  (1897). *Le suicide: Étude de sociologie*. Paris: Félix Alcan.

  (1972). *Selected Writings. Edited with an Introduction by Anthony Giddens*. London: Cambridge University Press.

(1972 [1925]). *L'Éducation morale: Cours de sociologie dispensé à la Sorbonne en 1902-1903. Avertissement de Paul Fauconnet*. Paris: Presses Universitaires de France.

(2014 [1893]). *The Division of Labor in Society*. Translation by W.D. Hall. New York: Free Press.

Dworkin, R. (1981). What is equality? Part I: equality of welfare; part II: equality of resources. *Philosophy and Public Affairs*, 10(3/4), pp. 185–246; 283–345.

Dykstra, P.A., Kalmijn, M., Knijn, T.C.M., Komter, A.E., Liefbroer, A.C., Mulder, C.H. (2006). *Family Solidarity in the Netherlands*. Amsterdam: Dutch University Press.

Ederer, R.J. (1991). Heinrich Pesch, solidarity and social encyclicals. *Review of Social Economy*, 49(4), pp. 596–610. Available at: www.jstor.org/stable/29769586. [Accessed 21 April 2015].

Elias, N. (1971). *Sociologie en geschiedenis en andere essays*. Amsterdam: Van Gennep.

Engelhardt, H.T. (1974). The disease of masturbation: values and the concept of disease. *Bulletin of the History of Medicine*, 48(2), pp. 234–248.

(1986). *The Foundations of Bioethics*. Oxford, New York: Oxford University Press.

Etzioni, A. (1998). Introduction. In: A. Etzioni, ed, *The Essential Communitarian Reader*. Lanham: Rowham & Littlefield Publishers, pp. ix–xxiv.

Eurostat (2015). *Statistics explained. Mortality and life expectancy statistics*. Available at: http://ec.europa.eu/eurostat/statistics-explained/index.php/Mortality_and_life_expectancy_statistics. [Accessed 4 April 2016].

Fokkema, T., Bekke, S. ter, Dykstra, P.A. (2008). *Solidarity between Parents and Their Adult Children in Europe: Report Netherlands Interdisciplinary Demography Institute*. Amsterdam: Koninklijke Academie van Wetenschappen.

Fries, J. (1980). Ageing, natural death and the compression of morbidity. *New England Journal of Medicine*, 303(3), pp. 130–135.

(2005). The compression of morbidity. *Milbank Quarterly*, 83(4), pp. 801–823.

Garland, M. (1993). Grenzen stellen aan de gezondheidszorg. Ervaringen uit Oregon. In: R. ter Meulen, H. ten Have, eds., *Samen kiezen in de zorg. Het voorbeeld Oregon*. Baarn: Ambo, pp. 34–64.

Giddens, A. (1971). *Capitalism and Modern Social Theory: An Analysis of the Writings of Marx, Durkheim and Max Weber*. Cambridge: Cambridge University Press.

(1972). Introduction: Durkheim's writings in sociology and social philosophy. In: *Emile Durkheim*, Selected writings: Edited with an Introduction by Anthony Giddens. Cambridge: Cambridge University Press, pp. 1–50.

(1990). *The Consequences of Modernity*. Cambridge: Polity Press.

(1991). *Modernity and Self-Identity: Self and Society in the Late Modern Age*. Cambridge: Polity Press.

(1998). *The Third Way: The Renewal of Social Democracy*. Cambridge: Polity Press.

Gide, Ch. (2010). *Solidarité. Les œuvres de Charles Gide Volume XI.* Textes présentés et annotés par Patrice Devillers. Serie Phiolosophie Sciences Politiques. Paris: L'Harmattan.

Goldsteen, M., Abma, T., Oeseburg, B., Verkerk, M., Verhey, F., Widdershoven, G. (2007). What is it to be a daughter? Identities under pressure in dementia care. *Bioethics*, 21(1), pp. 1–12.

Gouldner, A. (1970). *De naderende crisis van de Westerse sociologie.* Bilthoven: Ambo.

Government Committee on Choices in Health Care (1992). *Choices in Health Care.* Rijswijk: Ministry of Welfare, Health and Cultural Affairs.

Große Kracht, H.-J., Karcher, T., Spieß, Ch., eds. (2007). *Das System des Solidarismus. Zur Auseinandersetzung mit dem Werk von Heinrich Pesch SJ.* Berlin: LIT Verlag.

Große Kracht, H.-J.(2007). Zwischen Soziologie und Metaphysik. Zur Solidarismus-Konzeption von Heinrich Pesch SJ. In: H.-J. Große Kracht, T. Karcher, Ch. Spieß, eds., *Das System des Solidarismus. Zur Auseinandersetzung mit dem Werk von Heinrich Pesch SJ.* Berlin: LIT Verlag, pp. 59–89.

Gruenberg, E.M. (1977). The failures of success. *Milbank Memorial Quarterly/ Health and Society*, 55(1), pp. 3–24.

Habermas, J. (1989). *De nieuwe onoverzichtelijkheid en andere opstellen.* Meppel: Boom.

Hansen, J., Arts, W., Muffels, R. (2005a). Wie komt eerst? Een vignetonderzoek naar de solidariteitsbeleving van Nederlanders met patiënten en cliënten in de gezondheidszorg. *Sociale Wetenschappen*, 48 (1/2), pp. 31–60.

(2005b). Solidair tegen (w)elke prijs? Een quasi-experimenteel onderzoek naar de voorkeuren van Nederlanders voor ruimere of beperkter pakketten in de zorgverzekering. *Sociale Wetenschappen*, 48 (1/2), pp. 61–84.

Harris, A.L. (1946). The Scholastic Revival: the Economics of Heinrich Pesch. *Journal of Political Economy*, 54, pp. 38–59.

Hattinga Verschure, J.C.M. (1972). Ontwikkeling van zorgcriteria voor herstructurering van de gezondheidszorg. *Het Ziekenhuis*, 2, pp. 500–504.

Hayek, F. (2012 [1944]). *The Road to Serfdom: Condensed Version with Contributions by John Blundell, Edwin J. Feulner and Walter E. Williams.* London: The Institute of Economic Affairs.

Hayward, J.E.S. (1959). Solidarity: the social history of an idea in nineteenth century France. *International Review of Social History*, 4(2), pp. 261–284.

(1961). The official social philosophy of the French Third Republic: Léon Bourgeois and solidarism. *International Review of Social History*, 6(1), pp. 19–48.

Hechter, M. (1987). *Principles of Group Solidarity.* Berkeley: University of California Press.

Held, V. (2006). *The Ethics of Care: Personal, Political and Global.* New York: Oxford University Press.

HM Government (2008). *Carers at the heart of 21st-Century Families and Communities*. London: HM Government, Crown Office.

Hofstadter, R. (1944). *Social Darwinism in American Thought*. Boston: Beacon Press.

Hogerbrugge, M. (2016). Continuïteit in familiebanden. *Demos*, 32(1), pp. 1–3.

Honneth, A. (1995). *The Struggle for Recognition: The Moral Grammar of Social Conflicts*. Cambridge: Polity Press.

Hoogervorst, H. (2004). *Speech on the OECD Conference Paris, May 13, 2004*. Available at: www.minvws.nl. [Accessed 23 February 2016].

Horst, A. van der, Erp, F. van, Jong, J. de (2011). *Zorg blijft groeien. Financiering onder druk*. CPB Policy Brief /Trends in Gezondheid en Zorg. 2011/11. Den Haag: Centraal Planbureau.

Horst, A. van der, Rele, H. ter (2013). *Solidariteit onder druk. Zorg op maat heeft de toekomst*. CPB Policy Brief 2013/01. Den Haag: Centraal Planbureau.

Houtepen, R., Meulen, R. ter (2000a). New types of solidarity in the European welfare state. *Health Care Analysis*, 8, pp. 329–340.

(2000b). The expectations of solidarity: matters of justice, responsibility and identity in the reconstruction of the health care system. *Health Care Analysis*, 8, pp. 355–379.

Houtepen, R., Meulen, R. ter, Widdershoven, G. (2001). Beyond justice and moralism; modernity and solidarity in the health care system. In: R. ter Meulen, W. Arts, R. Muffels, eds., *Solidarity and Health Care in Europe*. Series Philosophy & Medicine Vol. 69. Dordrecht: Kluwer Academic Publishers, pp. 339–363.

Houtepen, R., Meulen, R. ter (2001). Personal budgets for the elderly: a case study in Dutch solidarity. In: R. ter Meulen, W. Arts, R. Muffels, eds., *Solidarity and Health Care in Europe*. Series Philosophy & Medicine Vol. 69. Dordrecht: Kluwer Academic Publishers, pp. 339–363.

Hume, D. (1978). *Treatise on Human Nature (1739–1740)*. Oxford: Clarendon Press.

Humphries, R., Thorlby, R., Holder, H., Hall, P., Charles, A. (2016). *Social Care for Older People: Home Truths*. London: Kings Fund and Nuffield Trust.

Illingworth, P., Parmet, W. (2012). Solidarity for Global Health. *Bioethics*, 26(7), pp. ii–iv.

Independer (2016). *Overstapmonitor* Available at: www.independer.nl/zorgverzekering/info/overstapmonitor.aspx. [Accessed 18 February 2016].

Ionescu, G. ed. (1976). *The Political Thought of Saint-Simon*. Oxford: Oxford University Press.

Jaeggi, R. (2001). Solidarity and Indifference. In: R. ter Meulen, W. Arts, R. Muffels, eds., *Solidarity in Health and Social Care in Europe*. Series Philosophy & Medicine Vol. 69. Dordrecht: Kluwer Academic Publishers, pp. 287–308.

Jager, H. de (1980). *Mensbeelden en maatschappijmodellen*. Leiden: Stenfert Kroese.

Jennings, B. (1990). Grassroots bioethics revisited: health care priorities and community values. Special supplement. *Hastings Center Report*, 20(5), p. 16.

Jeurissen, P. (2005). *Houdbare solidariteit in de gezondheidszorg*. Zoetermeer: Raad voor de Volksgezondheid en Zorg.

Johnson, M., Cullen, L. (2001). Solidarity and care in the United Kingdom. In: R. ter Meulen, W. Arts, R. Muffels, eds., *Solidarity in Health and Social Care in Europe*. Series Philosophy & Medicine Vol. 69. Dordrecht: Kluwer, pp. 107–131.

Jones, H.S. (1998). *Auguste Comte. Early political writings*. Cambridge: Cambridge University Press.

Kautsky, K. (1910). *Ethik und materialistische Geschichtsauffassung*. Stuttgart: J.H.W. Dietz.

Kloosterman, R. (2011). *Solidariteit in de zorg. Bevolkingstrends, derde kwartaal 2011*. Den Haag: CBS Centraal Bureau voor de Statistiek.

Knipscheer, K. (1992). Demografische veranderingen en het zorgvermogen van de samenleving. In: N. van Nimwegen, J. de Jong Gierveld, eds., *De demografische uitdaging: Nederland in Europa op weg naar de 21ste eeuw*. Houten/ Zaventem: Bohn Stafleu Van Loghum, pp. 89–107.

ed. (2004). *Dilemma's in de Mantelzorg*. Utrecht: NIZW Nederlands Instituut voor Zorg en Welzijn.

(2010). Weerkaatst plezier. *TSG*, 88 (6), pp. 306–308.

Komter, A., Burgers, J., Engbersen, G. eds. (2000). *Het cement van de samenleving. Een verkennende studie naar solidariteit en cohesie*. Amsterdam: Amsterdam University Press.

Komter, A. (2005). *Social Solidarity and the Gift*. Cambridge: Cambridge University Press.

Kooiker, S., Klerk M. de. (2012). *Meebetalen aan de zorg. Nederlanders over solidariteit en betaalbare zorg*. Den Haag: Sociaal en Cultureeel Planbureau.

Künneman, H., Rein, M. (1999). There is more to receiving than needing: theoretical arguments and empirical explorations of crowding in and crowding out. *Ageing and Society*, 19(1), pp. 93–12.

Kuyper, M.B. (1993). *Op de achtergrond. Een onderzoek naar de problemen van partners met een chronische ziekte*. Nijmegen: Katholieke Universiteit Nijmegen.

Kymlicka, W. (2002). *Contemporary Political Philosophy. An Introduction*. 2nd Ed. Oxford: Oxford University Press.

Laborem excercens (1981). *Encyclical of Pope John Paul II to His Venerable Brothers in the Episcopate to the Priests to the Religious Families, to the sons and daughters of the Church, and to all Men and Women of good will, on Human Work on the ninetieth anniversary of Rerum Novarum.* Rome: Vatican. Available at: w2.vatican.va/content/john-paul-ii/en/encyclicals/documents/hf_jp-ii_enc_14091981_laborem-exercens.html. [Accessed 23 Sept. 2016].

Lafortune, G., Balestat, G. (2007). *Trends in Severe Disability among Elderly People: Assessing the Evidence in 12 OECD Countries and the Future Implications. OECD Working Paper 26.* Paris: OECD.

Lasch, Ch. (1979). *The Culture of Narcissism. American Life in an Age of Diminishing Expectations.* New York: Warner Books.

Leroux, P. (1840). *De l'Humanité, de son principe et de son avenir, où se trouve exposeé la vraie définition de la religion et où l'on explique le sens, la suite et l'enchaînement du mosaïsme et du christianisme.* Published by le CDI Alsacienne. Available at: http://gallica.bnf.fr. [Accessed 9 July 2015].

Lijphart, A. (1975). *The Politics of Accommodation: Pluralism and Democracy in the Netherlands.* Berkeley: University of California Press.

Lorrain, J. (1979). *The Concept of Ideology.* London: Hutchinson.

Lukes, S. (2014). Introduction to this edition. In: E. Durkheim, *The Division of Labor in Society,* New York: Free Press, pp. xxv–xlvi.

Lycke, S. van der, Morée, M. (2004). De mantelzorger. Over gevangen zitten en grenzen stellen. In: K. Knipscheer, ed., *Dilemma's in de mantelzorg.* Utrecht: NIZW Nederlands Instituut voor Zorg en Welzijn, pp. 33–49.

Maarse, H., Paulus, A. (2003). Has solidarity survived? A comparative analysis of the effect of social health insurance reform in four European countries. *Journal of Health Politics, Policy and Law,* 28(4), pp. 585–614.

Maarse, H. (2004a). The changing balance between public and private in health care: an introduction. In: H. Maarse, ed., *Privatisation in European Health Care: A Comparative Analysis in Eight Countries.* Maarssen: Elsevier, pp. 16–31.

    (2004b). Towards a comparative analysis of privatisation in European health care. In: H. Maarse, ed., *Privatisation in European Health Care: A Comparative Analysis in Eight Countries.* Maarssen: Elsevier, pp. 169–198.

Maarse, H., Meulen, R. ter (2006). Consumer choice in Dutch health insurance after reform. *Health Care Analysis,* 14, pp. 37–49.

Maarse, H., Groot, W. (2008). Productinnovatie en arbeidsproductiviteit in de zorg. *Economisch-statistische Berichten,* Jaargang 90, nr 4452.

Maarse, H., Jeurissen, P. (2015). The policy and politics of the 2015 long-term care reform in the Netherlands. *Health Policy,* 120(3), pp. 241–245.

Maarse, H., Meulen, R. ter (2006). Consumer choice in Dutch health insurance after reform. *Health Care Analysis,* 14, pp. 37–49.

Maarse, H., Okma, K. (2004). The privatisation paradox in Dutch health care. In: H. Maarse, ed., *Privatisation in European Health Care: A Comparative Analysis in Eight Countries.* Maarssen: Elsevier, pp. 97–116.

Maarse, H., Jeurissen, P., Ruwaard, D. (2016). Results of the market-oriented reform in the Netherlands. *Health Economics, Policy and Law*, 11(2), pp. 161–178.

Made, J., van der, Meulen, R. ter, Burg, M. van den (2001). Solidarity and care in the Netherlands. In: R. ter Meulen, W. Arts, R. Muffels, eds. *Solidarity in Health and Social Care in Europe*. Series Philosophy & Medicine Vol. 69. Dordrecht: Kluwer Academic Publishers, pp. 229–253.

Margalit, A. (1996). *The Decent Society*. Cambridge, MA: Harvard University Press.

(2002). *The Ethics of Memory*. Cambridge, MA: Harvard University Press.

(2010). *On Compromise and Rotten Compromises*. Princeton, NJ: Princeton University Press.

Marken, S. (2016). U.S. Uninsured Rate at 11.0%, Lowest in Eight-Year Trend. *Gallup Poll*. Available at: www.gallup.com [Accessed 7 October 2016].

Mater et Magistra (1961). *Encyclical of Pope John XXIII on Christianity and Social Progress*. Rome: Vatican. Available at: w2.vatican.va/content/john-xxiii/en/encyclicals/documents/hf_j-xxiii_enc_15051961_mater.html. [Accessed 23 September 2016].

Mauss, M. (2011 [1925]). *The Gift: Forms and Functions of Exchanges in Archaic Societies*. Mansfield Centre, CT: Martino Press.

Mead, G.H. (1970 [1934]). *Mind, Self and Society: From the Standpoint of a Social Behaviourist: Edited and with an Introduction by Charles W. Morris*. 17th Edition. Chicago: The University of Chicago Press.

Meulen, R. ter (1988). *Ziel en zaligheid. De receptie van de psychologie en van de psychoanalyse onder de katholieken in Nederland 1900–1965*. Nijmegen/Baarn: Ambo.

(1993). Het Oregon health care plan: feiten en achtergronden. In: R. ter Meulen, H. ten Have, eds., *Samen kiezen in de zorg. Het voorbeeld Oregon*. Reeks Gezondheidsethiek No. 8. Baarn: Ambo, pp. 19–33.

(1995). Limiting solidarity in the Netherlands: a two-tier system on the way. *Journal of Medicine and Philosophy*, 20, pp. 637–646.

(2000). Solidarity in health care. In: W. Derkse, J. van der Lans, S. Waanders, eds., *In Quest of Humanity in an Globalising World: Dutch Contributions to the Jubilee of Universities in Rome*. Leende: Damon, pp. 92–103.

(2008). Is rationing the inevitable consequence of medical advance? *Journal of Medicine and Law*, 27(1), pp. 71–82.

(2011). How 'decent' is a decent minimum of healthcare? *Journal of Medicine and Philosophy*, 36, pp. 612–623.

(2015). Solidarity and justice in health care: a critical analysis of their relationship. *Diametros*, 43, pp. 1–20. Available at: www.diametros.iphils.uj.edu.pl/index.php/diametros/issue/view/45.

(2016). Solidarity, justice and recognition of the other. *Theoretical Medicine and Bioethics*, 37, pp. 517–529.

Meulen, R. ter, Made J. van der (2000). The extent and limits of solidarity in Dutch health care. *International Journal of Social Welfare*, 9, pp. 250–260.

Meulen, R. ter, Arts, W., Muffels, R., eds. (2001). *Solidarity in Health and Social Care in Europe*. Series Philosophy & Medicine Vol. 69. Dordrecht: Kluwer Academic Publishers.

(2001). Solidarity, health and social care in Europe. Introduction to the volume. In: R. ter Meulen, W. Arts, R. Muffels, eds., *Solidarity in Health and Social Care in Europe*. Series Philosophy & Medicine Vol. 69. Dordrecht: Kluwer Academic Publishers, pp. 1–11.

Meulen, R. ter, Maarse, H. (2003). De diagnose behandelings combinatie. Een gevaar voor de solidariteit? *Tijdschrift voor Geneeskunde en Ethiek*, 13(1), pp. 25–27.

(2008). Increasing individual responsibility in Dutch health care: Is solidarity losing ground? *Journal of Medicine and Philosophy*, 33, pp. 262–279.

Meulen, R. ter, Houtepen, R. (2012). Solidarity. In: R. Chadwick, ed., *Encyclopaedia of Applied Ethics*. Amsterdam: Elsevier, pp. 198–205.

Meulen, R. ter, Wright, K. (2012). Family solidarity and informal care: the case of people with dementia. *Bioethics*, 26 (7), pp. 361–368.

Mezzo (2013). Panel Een vandaag: Helft is bereid tot mantelzorg. Available at: www.mezzo.nl/pagina/voor-professionals/thema-s/cijfers-informele-zorg/resultaten-nationaal-mantelzorgpanel/panel-eenvandaag-helft-is-bereid-tot-mantelzorg. [Accessed 24 October 2016].

(2015). Mantelzorger wel vaker gezien, maar niet gehoord. Available at: www.mezzo.nl/artikel/mantelzorger-wel-vaker-gezien-maar-niet-gehoord. [Accessed 24 October 2016].

Moore G.E. (1903). *Principia Ethica*. Cambridge: University Press.

Ministerie van Binnenlandse Zaken en Koninkrijksrelaties (2013). *De doe-demokratie. Kabinetsnota ter stimulering van een vitale samenleving*. Den Haag: Ministerie van Binnenlandse Zaken en Koninkrijksrelaties.

Monbiot, G. (2016). Neoliberalism. The ideology at the root of all our problems. *The Guardian*, April 15, 2016. Available at: www.theguardian.com/books/2016/apr/15/neoliberalism-ideology-problem-george-monbiot. [Accessed 23 September 2016].

Muffels, R., Verburg, R. (2001). Reforms in health and social care in Europe: the challenge to policy. In: R. ter Meulen, W. Arts, R. Muffels, eds., *Solidarity in Health and Social Care in Europe*. Series Philosophy & Medicine Vol. 69, Dordrecht: Kluwer Academic Publishers, pp. 255–276.

Nagel, Th. (1989). Rawls on justice. In: N. Daniels, ed., *Reading Rawls*, 2nd ed. Stanford: Stanford University Press, pp. 1–16.

Nell-Breuning, O. von (1978). *Soziallehre der Kirche. Erlaüterungen der lehramtlichen Dokumente*. Wien: Katholische Sozialakademie Österreichs.

NIZW (2004). *Vergrijzing en informele zorg*. The Hague: Nederlands Instituut voor Zorg en Welzijn.

Nozick, R. (1974). *Anarchy, State, and Utopia*. New York: Basic Books.

Nuffield Council on Bioethics (2009). *Dementia: ethical issues*. London: Nuffield Council on Bioethics.

Nussbaum, M. (1992). Human functioning and social justice: In defense of Aristotelian essentialism. *Political Theory*, 20, pp. 202–246.

———— (2011). *Creating Capabilities: The Human Development Approach*. Harvard: Belknap Press.

OECD (2015) *Health at a Glance 2015: OECD Indicators*. Paris: OECD. Available at: http://dx.doi.org/10.1787/health_glance-2015-en. [Accessed 18 February 2016].

Oorschot, W. van (1998). *Shared Identity and Shared Utility: On Solidarity and Its Motives*. Tilburg: Tilburg Institute for Social Sciences.

Oorschot, W. van, Komter, A. (1998). What is it that ties? Theoretical perspectives on social bond. *Sociale Wetenschappen*, 41(3), pp. 5–24.

Oudijk, J., Boer, A. de, Woittiez, I., Timmermans, J., Klerk, M. (2010). *Mantelzorg uit de doeken. Een actueel beeld van het aantal mantelzorgers*. Den Haag: Sociaal Cultureel Planbureau.

Oudijk, D., Woittiez, I., Boer, A. de (2011). More family responsibility, more informal care? The effect of motivation on the giving of informal care by people over 50 in the Netherlands compared to other European countries. *Health Policy*, 101, pp. 228–235.

Pasini, N., Reichlin, M. (2001). Solidarity, citizenship and selective distributive justice in health care. In R. ter Meulen, W. Arts, R. Muffels, eds., *Solidarity in Health and Social Care in Europe*. Series Philosophy & Medicine Vol. 69. Dordrecht: Kluwer Academic Publishers, pp. 309–331.

Peetom, K., Lexis, M., Joore, M., Dirksen, C. Witte, L. de (2016). The perceived burden of informal caregivers of independently living elderly and their ideas about possible solutions. A mixed methods approach. *Technology and Disability*, 28, pp. 19–29.

Pesch, H. (1902). Solidarismus. *Stimmen aus Maria Laach*, 63, pp. 38–60; 307–324.

Pollock, A. (2016). This deadly debt spiral was meant to destroy the NHS. There is a way to stop it. *The Guardian*, 5 July 2016.

Pommer, E., Woittiez, I., Stevens, J. (2007). *Comparing Care: The Care of the Elderly in Ten EU-Countries*. Den Haag: Sociaal Cultureel Planbureau.

Prainsack, B., Buyx, A. (2011). *Solidarity: Reflections on an Emerging Concept in Bioethics*. London: Nuffield Council on Bioethics.

———— (2017). *Solidarity in Biomedicine and Beyond*. Cambridge: Cambridge University Press.

President's Commission for the Study of Ethical Problems in Medicine and Biomedical and Behavioral Research (1983). *Securing Access to Health Care: A Report on the Ethical Implications of Differences in the Availability of Health Services*. Washington, D.C.: U.S. Printing Office.

Putnam, R.D. (2000). *Bowling Alone: The Collapse and Revival of American Community*. New York: Simon and Schuster.

Putters, K. (2014). *Rijk geschakeerd. Op weg naar de participatiesamenleving*. Den Haag: Sociaal Cultureel Planbureau.

Quadragesiomo Anno. (1931). *Encyclical of Pope Pius XI on Reconstruction of the Social Order to our Venerable Brethren. The Patriarchs, Primates, Archbishops, the Bishops, and Other Ordinaries, in Peace and Communion with the Apostolic See, and Likewise to all the Faithful in the Catholic World*. Rome: Vatican. Available at: https://web.archive.org/web/20060902085107/ http://www.vatican.va/holy_father/pius_xi/encyclicals/documents/hf_p-xi_enc_19310515_quadragesimo-anno_en.html. [Accessed 19 October 2016].

Ram Tiktin, E. (2012). The right to health care as a right to basic human functional capabilities. *Ethical Theory and Moral Practice*, 15(3), pp. 337–351.

Ranzi, C., Pavolini, E., eds. (2013). *Reforms in Long-Term Care Policies in Europe. Investigating Institutional Change and Social Impacts*. Dordrecht: Springer Press.

Rawls, J. (1989). *A Theory of Justice*. 11th Ed. Oxford: Oxford University Press.

Reisz, G. (2007). Der solidarische Staat. Solidaritätsdeutungen in Deutschland und Frankreich und ihre politische Bedeutung heute. In: H.-J. Große Kracht, T. Karcher, Ch. Spieß, eds., *Das System des Solidarismus. Zur Auseinandersetzung mit dem Werk von Heinrich Pesch SJ*. Berlin: LIT Verlag, pp. 31–58.

RMO/RVZ. (1999). *Zorgarbeid in de toekomst. Advies over de gevolgen van demografische ontwikkeling van vraag en aanbod zorg(arbeid)*. The Hague/Zoetermeer: Raad voor Maatschappelijke Ontwikkeling/Raad voor de Volksgezondheid en Zorg.

Rousseau, J.-J. (1762). *Du Contrat Social*. Paris: Garnier Flammarion. Available at: http://classiques.uqac.ca/classiques/Rousseau_jj/contrat_social/Contrat_social.pdf. [Accessed at 17 October 2016].

RVZ Raad voor de Volksgezonheid en Zorg (1999). *De trend, de traditie en de turbulentie*. Zoetermeer: Raad voor de Volksgezondheid en Zorg.

(2002). *Gezondheid en gedrag*. Zoetermeer: Raad voor de Volksgezondheid en Zorg.

(2006). *Zinnige en duurzame zorg*. Zoetermeer: Raad voor de Volksgezondheid en Zorg.

(2007). *Rechtvaardige en duurzame zorg*. Zoetermeer: Raad voor de Volksgezondheid en Zorg.

(2013). *Het belang van wederkerigheid...solidarteit gaat niet van zelf*. Den Haag: Raad voor de Volksgezondheid en Zorg.

Sadiraj, K., Timmermans, J., Ras, M., Boer, A. de (2009). *De toekomst van de mantelzorg*. Den Haag: Sociaal en Cultureel Planbureau.

Sandel, M. (1984). Introduction. In: M. Sandel, ed., *Liberalism and Its Critics*. New York: New York University Press, pp. 1–11.

ed. (1984). *Liberalism and Its Critics*. New York: New York University Press.

(1990). Freedom of conscience or freedom of choice? In: J. Hunter, O. Guiness, eds., *Articles of Faith, Articles of Peace*. Washington: Brookings Institute, pp. 74–92.

(1998). *Liberalism and the Limits of Justice*, 2nd Ed. New York: Cambridge University Press.

Schuyt, C. (1998). The sharing of risks and the risks of sharing: solidarity and social justice in the welfare state. *Ethical Theory and Moral Practice*, 1(3), pp. 297–311.

SCP Sociaal en Cultureel Planbureau (2004). *Verpleging en Verzorging Verklaard*. Den Haag: Sociaal en Cultureel Planbureau.

Sen, A. (1990). Justice: means versus freedoms. *Philosophy and Public Affairs*, 19 (2), pp. 111–121.

Siedentop, L. (1994). *Tocqueville*. Oxford: Oxford University Press.

Soares, J., Barros, H., Torres-Gonzales, F., Ioannidi-Kapolou, E., Lamura, G., Lindert J., Dios Luna, J. de, Macassa, G., Melchiorre. M.-G., Stankunas, M. (2010). *Abuse and Health Among Elderly in Europe*. Kaunos: Lithuanian University of Health Sciences.

Stjernø, S. (2004). *Solidarity in Europe: The History of an Idea*. Cambridge: Cambridge University Press.

Swaan, A. de (1989). *Zorg en de Staat. Welzijn, onderwijs en gezondheidszorg in Europa en de Verenigde Staten in de nieuwe tijd*. Amsterdam: Bert Bakker.

Swart, K.W. (1962). 'Individualism' in the mid-nineteenth century (1826–1860). *Journal of the History of Ideas*, 23(1), pp. 77–90.

Sykora, P. (2009). Altruism in medical donations reconsidered: the reciprocity approach. In: M. Steinmann, P. Sykora, U. Wiesing eds., *Altruism Reconsidered: Exploring New Approaches to Property in Human Tissue*. Farnham: Ashgate, pp. 13–49.

Taylor, Ch. (1984). Hegel: history and politics. In: M. Sandel, ed., *Liberalism and Its Critics*. New York: New York University Press, pp. 177–199.

(1991). *The Ethics of Authenticity*. Cambridge MA: Harvard University Press.

(1997). *Philosophical Arguments*. 2nd Ed. Cambridge MA: Harvard University Press.

Taylor-Gooby, P. (2011). Does risk society erode welfare state solidarity? *Policy & Politics*, 39(2), pp. 147–161.

Theoretical Medicine and Bioethics (2016). Special Issue: Solidarity and Autonomy: Two Conflicting Values in English and French Health Care and Bioethics Debates? *Theoretical Medicine and Bioethics*, 37(6), pp. 441–529.

Theunissen, M. (1981). *Selbstverwirklichung und Allgemeinheit*. Berlin: de Gruyter.

Thompson, K. (1976). *Auguste Comte: The Foundation of Sociology*. London: Nelson.

Timmermans, J., ed. (2003). *Mantelzorg. Over de hulp aan mantelzorgers*. Den Haag: Sociaal Cultureel Planbureau.

Titmuss, R. (1970). *The Gift Relationship. From Human Blood to Social Policy*. London: George Allen & Unwin.

Tönnies, F. (1887). *Gemeinschaft und Gesellschaft*. Leipzig: Fues's Verlag.

Toqueville, A. de (1984 [1835/1840]) *Democracy in America: Specially Edited and Abridged for the Modern Reader by Richard D. Heffner*. New York: Mentor (Penguin Putnam).

(1861–1866). *Œvres Complètes*. Paris: Gallimard.

Tronto, J. (1993). *Moral Boundaries: A Political Argument for an Ethic of Care*. New York: Routledge.

Twenge, J.M., Foster, J.D. (2008). Mapping the scale of the narcissism epidemic: Increases in narcissism 2002–2007 within ethnic groups. *Journal of Research in Personality*, 42, pp. 1619–1622.

Twenge, J.M., Campbell, W.K. (2009). *The Narcissism Epidemic: Living in the Age of Entitlement*. New York: Free Press.

Vektis (2015). Verzekerden in beeld. *Zorgthermometer*, 20, April 2015.

Verburg, R., Meulen, R. ter (2005). Solidariteit of rechtvaardigheid in de zorg? Een spanningsveld. *Sociale Wetenschappen*, 48 (1/2), pp. 11–30.

Verstraeten, J. (1998). De betekenis van solidariteit en subsidiariteit in kerkelijke documenten. *Ethische Perspectieven*, 8, pp. 210–220.

(2005). Solidariteit in de katholieke traditie. In: E. de Jong, M. Buijssen, eds., *Solidariteit onder druk? Over de grens tussen individuele en collectieve verantwoordelijkheid*. Annalen van het Thijmgenootschap 93(1). Nijmegen: Valkhof Pers, pp. 26–53.

Volkskrant (2015). Zorg via gemeenten kan tot vijf keer duurder uitvallen. *Volkskrant*, 22nd of December 2015.

(2016). Familierelaties zijn vaak te slecht voor mantelzorg. *Volkskrant*, 6th of February 2016.

Wal, G. van der (1988). Solidair, hoe en waarom? Over de betekenis van solidariteit bij de bekostiging van de gezondheidszorg. In: F. Jacobs, G. Van der Wal, eds, *Medische schaarste en het menselijk tekort*. Reeks Gezondheidsethiek No. 3. Baarn: Ambo, pp. 79–111.

Walzer, M. (1984). Justice and the good. In: M. Sandel, ed., *Liberalism and Its Critics*, New York: New York University Press, pp. 200–218.

Weber, M. (1919). *Wissenschaft als Beruf*. München und Leipzig: Von Duncker & Humblot.

(1920 [1904/1905]). Die protestantische Ethik und der Geist des Kapitalismus. *Archiv für Sozialwissenschaft und Sozialpolitik*, 20 Band, Heft 1, 1–54; 21 Band, Heft 1, pp. 1–110; Edited and re-published in *Gesammelte Aufsätze zur Religionssoziologie, Band 1*, Tübingen: Mohr Siebeck, pp. 17–206.

(2012 [1947]). *The Theory of Social and Economic Organisation. Translated by A.M. Henderson and Talcott Parsons. Edited with an Introduction by Talcott Parsons*. Mansfield Centre, CT: Martino Publishing.

Wolff, J. (1998). Fairness, respect and the egalitarian ethos. *Philosophy and Public Affairs*, 27(2), pp. 97–122.

Young, I.M. (1997). *Intersecting Voices. Dilemmas of Gender, Political Philosophy, and Policy*. Princeton, NJ: Princeton University Press.

INDEX

abuse, physical and emotional, 152
ABWZ. *See* Exceptional Medical
    Expenses Law
Affordable Care Act, 29, 179, 181
alcohol, 133
Algemene Wet Bijzondere Ziektekosten
    AWBZ. *See* Exceptional Medical
    Expenses Law
alienation, 22
American Indians, 62
Amish, 156
anarchism, 42
ancient regime, 31, 33
anomie, 151
anti-essentialism, 79
anti-solidarist bias, 41–42
Arber, S., 165
aristocracy, 37
Aristotelianism, 78–79
Aristotelian-Thomistic philosophy,
    48–49
associative relationships, 65–66, 150
Attias-Donfut, C., 165
autonomy, 176
    contextual approach to, 2
    individual responsibility and, 139
    liberalism on, 1
    local, 38
    neglect of, 79
    neoliberalism and, 17
    principle of respect for, viii
awful individualism (*l'odieux
    individualisme*), 37

baby-boom generation, 127–128
Balestat, G., 13
banking crisis, 14

Bauman, Zygmunt, 19, 167
Bayertz, K., 23–24, 170
Beck, Ulrich, 18–19
Bellah, Robert, 98, 158, 183
Benhabib, S., 104–105, 156–157
Bernstein, Eduard, 6
Beveridge, William, 11
bioethics, viii. *See also* Nuffield Council
    on Bioethics
    dissatisfaction with mainstream of, 1
    empirical, 142
    Four Principles of Bioethics, 1
    liberal and libertarian views in, viii
Bioethics (journal), 1
BIOMED 2, ix
biomedical sciences, 76
bio-statistical model of health, 76
von Bismarck, Graf Otto, 10–11, 109
blaming the victim, 84
Blanc, Louis, 44
De Bonald, Louis Viscount, 32–34,
    155–156, 176–177
Bonaparte, Napoleon, 41–42, 44
Boorse, Christopher, 75–76
Bourgeois, Léon, 4–5, 168
    liberalism of, 50
    on society, 46
    on solidarism, 43–47
brotherhood, 31
Burke, Edmund, 32, 176–177
Buyx, Alena, 1–2

Callahan, Daniel, 29, 98–99
Campbell, Keith, 183–184
capabilities, 77–81
capitalism, 66
care regimes, 145

Caring about Carers (UK Government Report), 163
Catholicism, 7–10, 111
Centesimus Annus (Pope John Paul II), 8
Centraal Plan Bureau CPB (Central Planning Office), 115
Chadwick, Ruth, 1
children, 124
Christianity, 40–41, 49
Civil Rights Movement, 182
Code Civil of 1805 (Bonaparte), 41–42
cold modern ideal, 125
cold traditional ideal, 125
collective consciousness, 54–55
  in mechanical solidarity, 58
  in modern era, 57
  in organic solidarity, 58–59
College Zorgverzekeringen CVZ (Health Insurance Board), 120
communal relationships, 65–66, 150
communal solidarity, 150
communicating vessels, 175
communitarian thinkers, 21, 103, 154–158, 176–177
  criticism of, 27–28
  on individualism, ix
  on individualisation, 150
  on integrationist and participatory communitarianism, 177
  integrationist communitarianism, 156–157, 178
  on liberalism, 96–101
Comte, Auguste, 33–34, 42, 168
  birth of sociology and, 51–54
  Considerations on the spiritual power, 54
  on individualisation, 35
  concerns about solidarity, 11–12
concrete other, 143, 154, 176
conservatism, 16
Considerations on the spiritual power (Comte), 54
consumers, 19, 167
corporatism, tripartite, 111
cost control, 118–122
Council for Public Health and Health Care (RVZ)

Health and Behaviour report by, 132
  report by, 123–124
Counter-Enlightenment, 31

Daniels, N., 75–77, 79–80
  on opportunity, 81
  on Sen and Nussbaum, 80–81
DBC. *See* Diagnosis Treatment Combinations
Dean, Jody, 28, 102, 159
  on generalised other, 160
  reflective solidarity from, 162–163, 177
  on Third, 161–162
debilitating conditions, 13
debt, 68
  generational, 46
  social, 43
The Decent Society (Margalit), 87–89
delisting, 120, 122, 134
demand controls, 119
dementia, 115
  care for, 153
  Nuffield Council on Bioethics on, 1
  support for, 2
Dementia: ethical issues (Nuffield Council on Bioethics), x, 152
Democracy in America (De Tocqueville), 38
demographic change, 27
deontological philosophy, 73
Diagnosis Treatment Combinations (DBC), 137–138
Dickenson, D., 182
Dictionnaire (Diderot), 41
Diderot, Denis, 41
difference principle, 77, 82–83, 139–140
disability. *See also* expansion of disability theory
  care for, 125
  elderly populations trends in, 12–13
  humiliation and intellectual, 106–107
  insurance, 23
disease, burden of, 116, 121
distribution of goods
  of primary goods, 88
  procedures of, 172
  Rawls on, 171–172

distributive justice, 83, 99
division of labour, 56–57
    changing realities of, 60
    dependence on, 168
    increasing individualisation from, 58
    morality and, 60
    in traditional societies, 57–58
Division of Labour (Durkheim), 148
do-democracy, 123
Dunning committee, 120–121
Durkheim, Emile, 5, 30, 148
    on anomie, 151
    mechanical solidarity and, 141
    on organic solidarity, 20
    on solidarity, 54–62
Dutch constitution, 111–112
Dworkin, Ronald, 83–84

economic crisis, 15
education, 36, 117
    higher and lower groups of, 118
    of informal carers, 146
L'Éducation morale (Durkheim), 61
efficiency cuts, 125–126, 138
egalitarianism, 74, 85, 136
egotism, 182
    individualism distinction from, 38
    society suppression of, 34
elderly populations, 116
    care of, 117
    disability trends among, 12–13
    increasing costs of care for, 173
Elias, Norbert, 91
EMU. See European Monetary Union
Engelhardt, H.T., 86
enlightened self-interest, 69–70
    morality of, 38–39
    as motivation, 39–40
    some sacrifice and, 182
    in US, 69
equality, opportunity approach to, 83
equitable access to health care, vii–viii
ethics, 185
    ethic of care theory of, 95
    Hegel on, 104–105, 169–170
    of liberalism, 105
    morality distinct from, 106
    of socialism, 6

The Ethics of Memory (Margalit), 106
Etzioni, A., 157–158
European Commission, ix
European Monetary Union (EMU), 14
European values, 28–29, 178–184
Exceptional Medical Expenses Law
    (ABWZ), 113–115, 120–122
    replacements for, 125
expansion of disability theory, 12–13

fairness as justice, utilitarianism and, 73
family care
    family solidarity and, 149
    givers of, 146–147
    morality and, 175–176
    personal solidarity in, 150
    sacrifices from, 152
    substitution model of, 164
    support for, 186
family solidarity, 26, 143, 148, 154
    basis of, 164, 175
    family care and, 149
    in modern era, 150
feminist theory, viii, 162
financial responsibility, 17
Fourier, Charles, 35–36, 40
free choice
    emphasis on, vii
    limitations on, 130–131
free speech, limitations of, 44
freedom
    freedom-in-relation-to-others, 80–81
    negative, 77, 80–81
    paradox of, 56
    positive, 80–81
    in republican societies, 105
French Revolution
    huge social inequalities after, 168
    individualism after, 3–4
    individualisation after, 31–37
full theory of the good, 75

GDP. See gross domestic product
Gemeinschaft to Gesellschaft, 21–22,
    57, 66, 101
generalised other, 159–160, 177–178
Giddens, A., 18, 55, 178
Gide, Charles, 43, 168

The Gift (Mauss), 62
gift relationship, 62–64, 170
gross domestic product (GDP),
  115–116
group mentality, 27
Gruenberg, E.M., 13
Gundlach, Gustav, 50

Habermas, J., viii–ix, 26, 94, 104
  on justice, 95
  on solidarity, 171
Hayek, Friedrich, 15
Hayward, J.E.S., 41
Health and Behaviour report (RVZ),
  132
Health Care Insurance Law of 2006
  (Zorgverzekeringswet Zvw), 112,
  116–117, 128
Health Insurance Act of 2006
  (Netherlands), 16
Health Insurance Board. *See* College
  Zorgverzekeringen CVZ
Health Technology Assessments
  (HTAs), 120
healthy behaviour, 132, 134
Hechter, M., 21
Hegel, G. W. F., viii, 93
  ethical life notion of, 104–105,
  169–170
high income groups, 118–119
historic materialism, 66
home care, 90–91
  in Netherlands, 27
Honneth, Axel, viii, 93–95, 102–104,
  171
hospital beds, 119
HTAs. *See* Health Technology
  Assessments
human development, three stages of,
  52
humanitarian solidarity, ix, 107,
  172–173, 185
Hume, David, 48
humiliation, 87–89, 91
  avoiding, 185
  humiliating procedures of welfare
  states, 87
  intellectual disabilities and, 106–107

identity, 18, 97–98
  recognition of, 158
Illingworth, P., 3, 28–29
inclusive solidarity, 162
income solidarity, 112–113, 136
  increase in, 117
income transfer, 115–118
individual responsibility, 132–134
  autonomy and, 139
  collective responsibility replaced by,
  109–110
  emphasis on, 136
  financial, 135–136, 138–139
  limits of, 140
  market forces and, 128–132
  in social care, 122–126
individualism, 85, 156–157
  communitarian thinkers on, ix
  egotism distinction from, 38
  emphasis on, vii
  after French Revolution, 3–4
  in modern era, 98
  positive connotation of, ix
  Taylor on, 183
  in US, 179
  weakness of, 99
individualisation
  communitarian thinkers on,
  150
  Comte on, 35
  from division of labour, 58
  fight against, 51
  after French Revolution, 31–37
  increasing rates of, 143
  negative connotation of, 151
  reflexivity and, 18–22
  structures changed by, 149
individuals
  basic rights of, 73
  becoming consumers, 19
  conformity of, 61
  dependence on states by, 37
  Elias on, 91
  fundamental interdependency of, viii
  in high income groups, 118–119
  interdependence of, 25
  motivations of, 69–70
  obligations agreed to by, 84

individuals (cont.)
  recognition of differences in,
    101–104, 162
  relational realisation of, 169–170
  self-reflexive biographies of, 19
  in social roles, 154–155
  society reciprocal with, 7
  vulnerable individuals and morality,
    167–168
industrialisation, 4, 35
  disruption caused by, 36
  problems resulting from, 40
informal care, 143, 148, 151–154
  clamp, 147
  women giving, 174–175
initiatives for mutual support, 10
insurance, disability, 23
insurance based systems, 11
interest groups, 31
interest solidarity, 22–24, 39, 92

Jaeggi, Rahel, viii, 92–93, 95
John Paul II (Pope), 8
  criticism of welfare state by, 9
John XXIII (Pope), 8–9
Just Health (Daniels), 75–76
Just Health Care (Daniels), 75–76

Kant, E., 94
  morality of, 96–97, 104–105, 171
Kautsky, Karl, 6
Keynesian economic policies, 15
kitchen table discussions, 122–123, 138,
    145, 172
Komter, A., 20, 65, 150, 165
kula, 62
Künemund, H., 165
Kymlicka, W., 82–83, 86–87, 156

Laborem Exercens (Pope John Paul II),
    8
Lafortune, G., 13
laissez-faire politics, 4, 34, 53
Lasch, Christopher, 183–184
laws, 37
leftist authors, 35
Leninist theory, 6–7
Leroux, Pierre, 40–41

De l'Humanité (Leroux), 40–41
liberalism, viii, 42, 91, 170–172. *See also*
    neoliberalism
  of Bourgeois, 50
  central ethic of, 105
  choice and circumstance in, 83
  communitarian thinkers on, 96–101
  contractual, vii–viii
  criticism of, 92
  failures of, 79–81
  on interpretation of autonomy, 1
  justice, viii–ix
  on justice, 2–3
  laissez faire policies of, 4, 34, 53
libertarianism, 42
  in bioethics, viii
  challenge from, 86–87
  on justice, 2–3
  New Right and, 86–87
Liberty Principle, 139
life expectancy, 12–13
life world, 94–95
liquid society, 19
local initiatives, 109
long-Term care, 90–91
  expansion of, 122
  limiting of entitlements to, 164
  in Netherlands, 27
  savings on, 124
  services, 117
Long-term Care Law of 2015 (Wlz),
    112, 114, 121, 137
love, 93
  Christian, 7
  of poor populations, 40–41
Lukes, S., 20
luxury care, 136

de Maistre, Joseph-Marie Count, 31–34
Margalit, Avishai, 87–89, 106, 172
market forces, 16
  forced on NHS, 17
  as guiding principles, 10, 15
  increasing influence of, 110
  individual responsibility and,
    128–132
Marx, Karl, 6
  historic materialism of, 66

Mater et Magistra (Pope John XXIII), 8
Mauss, Marcel, 62–64, 170
Mead, Georg Herbert, 28, 102–103, 159–160
mechanical solidarity, 58, 141, 148–149
Medicaid, 181
medical technology, 115–116
    costs of, 13–14
Medicare Program, 181
Middle Ages, 100–101
middle classes, 23
    New Right support from, 87
minimum wage, 36
von Mises, Ludwig, 15
modern era, 18, 63
    collective consciousness in, 57
    family solidarity in, 150
    individualism in, 98
    rationalisation of, 67
    reflexivity in, 178
morality, 69, 168
    authority of, 69–70
    debt towards society and, 68
    dilemmas of, 144
    division of labour and, 60
    of enlightened self-interest, 38–39
    ethics distinct from, 106
    family care and, 175–176
    Kant on, 96–97, 104–105, 171
    obligations of, 49–50, 61, 70
    sociology and, 42, 69
    of two-tier system of health care, 136
    vulnerable individuals and, 167–168
    Weber and, 142
morbidity, 116
motherhood, 157
mutual affection and identification, 69–70
mutual relations, viii–ix

Nagel, Th., 91, 171
narcissism, 183–184
The Narcissistic Epidemic (Twenge and Campbell), 183–184
National Health Budget, 132–133
National Health Service (NHS), 11, 179
    efficiency savings, 14
    marketisation of, 17

National Institute for Health and Care Excellence (NICE), 184
National Socialism, 15
naturalistic fallacy, 25, 48, 169
needs assessment, 118–122
von Nell-Breuning, Oswald, 50–51
neoliberalism, 174
    autonomy and, 17
    ideologies, rise in, vii, 109
    policies, 15–17
    states and, 26
neo-scholasticism, 7, 48–51
Netherlands
    health care background of, 110–115
    Health Insurance Act of 2006, 16
    long-term care and home care in, 27
    out-of-pocket payments in, 126
New Deal, 15
New Right, 83–84
    coldness of, 85–86
    libertarianism and, 86–87
    middle classes support for, 87
new treatments, 120
NHS. *See* National Health Service
NICE. *See* National Institute for Health and Care Excellence
normative claims, 142
Nozick, Robert, 42, 86
nuclear family, 147
Nuffield Council on Bioethics, viii, x
    on dementia, 1
    Dementia: ethical issues, 152
    partnerships encouraged by, 153
Nussbaum, Martha, 78–79
    Daniels on, 80–81

Obama, Barack, 29
obligation, 60
l'odieux individualisme (awful individualism), 37
On Compromise and Rotten Compromises (Margalit), 106
van Oorschot, W., 65
opportunity, 77
    approach to equality, 83
    Daniels on, 81
    lack of, 89–90

opportunity-egalitarians, 89–90
Oregon Health Decisions, 182–183
organic solidarity, 20, 58–60, 62
    148–149

Parmet, W., 3, 28–29
Parsons, Talcott, 65–66
participation-society, 123
Pasini, N., 101–102
Personal Budgets, 128
Pesch, Heinrich, 7, 168–169
  solidarismus of, 47–51
  Weber attacks on, 68
pharmaceuticals, cost of, 131
philosophical anthropology, 169
pillarisation, 111
Pius XII (Pope), 8
policy-making, 3
poor populations
  love of, 40–41
  shameful revelations by, 89
  undeserving, 83, 89
positive philosophy, 52
positivism, 53
poverty, 87
power, of health insurance companies,
  131
Prainsack, Barbara, 1–2
premiums, 126–127, 138
  unhealthy lifestyle paying more, 134
price controls, 119
primary goods, 74–75
  critique of, 78
  distribution of, 88
  health on, 75
priority-setting, 118–122
private health care insurance
  public insurance systems and, 128
  sickness funds and, 112
privatisation, 127–128, 134–135
  increasing influence of, 110
professional caregivers, 144, 151–154, 175
proletariat, industrial, 6
public constraints, 129, 137
public insurance systems, 10–11
  von Bismarck establishing of, 109
  private health care insurance and,
    128

public spending, 14
Putnam, R.D., 182

Raad voor de Volksgezondheid en Zorg
  RVZ. *See* Council for Public
  Health and Health Care
Radical Party, 43–44
rational decision maker as ideological
  construct, 91
rational egoists, 21
rationalism, 85
rationality
  goal and value types of, 67
  of modern era, 67
rationing by the purse, 126
Rawls, J., 85, 88, 139–140
  on collective distribution of basic
    goods, 171–172
  on redress, 81–82
  on self, 96
  Theory of Justice, 71–75
reciprocity, 69–70, 123, 173–174
recognition, 96
  of identity, 158
  of individual differences, 101–104,
    162
  legal recognition of rights, 102
  mutual, 94
  patterns of, 93
redress, 81–82
Reflections on the Revolution in France
  (Burke), 32
reflective solidarity, 158–163, 177, 185
reflexive modernity, 18
reflexivity
  individualisation and, 18–22
  modern life characterised by, 178
Reichlin, M., 101–102
Rein, M., 165
resources, scarcity of, vii, 138
Restoration (1814), 31
rights, vii–viii, 93
  legal recognition of, 102
  social, 112
  universality of, 102
  working class denied, 44
risk societies, 18–19
risk solidarity, 112–113

role captivity, 147
Romanticism, 31
Roosevelt, Franklin D., 15
Rousseau, J.-J., 31
RVZ. *See* Council for Public Health and Health Care

Saint-Simon, Henri, 33–35
Sandel, Michael, 84, 96–97, 155, 176
sandwich generation, 146
Scandinavian countries, 180
scarcity of resources, 12–14
Second Restoration (1815), 31
selective contracting, 131
self-respect, 88
Sen, Amartya, 77–78, 80–81
shared humanity, 173
shared utility, 92
Sickness Fund Decision of 1965, 110–111
Sickness Fund decree of 1941, 110–111
sickness funds, 110–111, 136
    premiums, 113
    private health care insurance and, 112
    regulations, 112–113
Simons, Hans, 131
social cohesion, 141
social contracts, 72
Social Darwinism, 39, 55
social democracy, 6
social groups, 159
social harmony, 5
    in organic solidarity, 60
social integration, 36
social personalism, 7
social philosophy, 25
social reform, 10–11
social roles, 154–155
Social Support Law (Wmo), 114, 121, 125
socialism
    collectivism of, 4
    core ethics of, 6
    solidarity and, 5–7
society. *See also* traditional societies
    Bourgeois on, 46
    cultural self-understanding of, 103

decent, 88
    egoistic tendencies suppressed by, 34
    heterogeneous, 20
    individuals reciprocal with, 7
    just and decent, 172
    moral debt towards, 68
    normative obligations of, 25
    task of, 105
    US centralisation of, 38
sociology
    Comte and birth of, 51–54
    concerns from, 20
    French, 3–5
    morality and, 42, 69
socio-political discourse, 4
solidarism, 7–8, 168
    Bourgeois on, 43–47
solidarismus, 47–51
Solidarité (Bourgeois), 44
Solidarity and Care in the European Union, ix
Solidarity. Reflections on an emerging concept in bioethics (Prainsack and Buyx), 1
Spencer, Herbert, 39
spiritual power, 52–53
spontaneity, 60
states. *See also* welfare states
    collective attitudes articulated by, 60–61
    evil tendencies suppressed by, 177
    individuals dependent on, 37
    minimal, 16
    neoliberalism and, 26
    paternalistic role of, 129
    solidarity enforced by, 10–11
Stjernø, S., 6–7
subsidiarity, 8–9, 174–175
Swaan, A. de, 23

tax based systems, 181
taxation, 11, 133
Taylor, Charles, 96–97, 105–106, 183
temporal power, 52–53
Thatcher-Reagan area, 86–87
Theoretical Medicine and Bioethics (journal), 1–2
Theory of Justice (Rawls), 71–75

The Theory of Social and Economic Organisation (Weber), 65
thin theory of the good, 75, 77
Third, Dean notion of, 161–162
tobacco, 133
De Tocqueville, Alexis, 35
    in US, 182
    views of, 37–40
Tönnies, Ferdinand, 21–22, 57
totalitarian control, 15, 155
trade unions, 15
traditional societies, 57–58
translation, 43
Treatise on Human Nature (Hume), 48
Trobrianders, 62
Twenge, Jean, 183–184
two-tier system of health care, 136
    moral argument for, 136

United Kingdom (UK), 14, 179
    Government Report *Caring about Carers*, 163
    2001 Census in, 145–146
    welfare state in, 15
United States (US), 29
    centralisation of society in, 38
    enlightened self-interest in, 69
    federal government services of, 181
    individualism of, 179
    self-understanding in, 183
    De Tocqueville in, 182
utilitarianism, 55, 184
    flaws in, 72–73
    justice as fairness and, 73
utopians, 36, 41

values, role of, 67–68
veil of ignorance, 72, 170

Veterans Health Administration, 181
volonté generale, 31
voluntary unemployed, 83

Wagner, Adolf, 48
waiting lists crisis, 119
Walzer, Michael, 99–100
warm family ideal, 125
warm traditional ideal, 125
Weber, Max, 5, 64–68, 150
    criticism by, 30
    moral connotations of, 142
welfare states, 175
    building of, 184
    decline of, 2
    European, vii, 2
    expansion of, 9
    humiliating procedures of, 87
    John Paul II (Pope) criticism of, 9
    motivations to support, 92
    in UK, 15
Wet langetermijn zorg Wlz. *See* Long-term Care Law of 2015
Wet Maatschappelijke Ondersteuning Wmo. *See* Social Support Law
Wirtschaft und Gesellschaft (Weber), 65, 150. *See also The Theory of Social and Economic Organisation*
Wlz. *See* Long-term Care Law of 2015
Wmo. *See* Social Support Law
Wolff, Jonathan, 89–90
women as carers, 145–146, 174–175
working class
    miserable conditions for, 36
    rights denied to, 44

Zorgverzekeringswet Zvw. *See* Health Care Insurance Law of 2006

Books in the Series

Marcus Radetzki, Marian Radetzki and Niklas Juth *Genes and Insurance: Ethical, Legal and Economic Issues*

Ruth Macklin *Double Standards in Medical Research in Developing Countries*

Donna Dickenson *Property in the Body: Feminist Perspectives*

Matti Häyry, Ruth Chadwick, Vilhjálmur Árnason and Gardar Árnason *The Ethics and Governance of Human Genetic Databases: European Perspectives*

Ken Mason *The Troubled Pregnancy: Legal Wrongs and Rights in Reproduction*

Daniel Sperling *Posthumous Interests: Legal and Ethical Perspectives*

Keith Syrett *Law, Legitimacy and the Rationing of Health Care*

Alastair Maclean *Autonomy, Informed Consent and the Law: A Relational Change*

Heather Widdows and Caroline Mullen *The Governance of Genetic Information: Who Decides?*

David Price *Human Tissue in Transplantation and Research*

Matti Häyry *Rationality and the Genetic Challenge: Making People Better?*

Mary Donnelly *Healthcare Decision-Making and the Law: Autonomy, Capacity and the Limits of Liberalism*

Anne-Maree Farrell, David Price and Muireann Quigley *Organ Shortage: Ethics, Law and Pragmatism*

Sara Fovargue *Xenotransplantation and Risk: Regulating a Developing Biotechnology*

John Coggon *What Makes Health Public?: A Critical Evaluation of Moral, Legal, and Political Claims in Public Health*

Mark Taylor *Genetic Data and the Law: A Critical Perspective on Privacy Protection*

Anne-Maree Farrell *The Politics of Blood: Ethics, Innovation and the Regulation of Risk*

Stephen Smith *End-of-Life Decisions in Medical Care: Principles and Policies for Regulating the Dying Process*

Michael Parker *Ethical Problems and Genetics Practice*

William W. Lowrance *Privacy, Confidentiality, and Health Research*

Kerry Lynn Macintosh *Human Cloning: Four Fallacies and Their Legal Consequence*

Heather Widdows *The Connected Self: The Ethics and Governance of the Genetic Individual*

Amel Alghrani, Rebecca Bennett and Suzanne Ost *Bioethics, Medicine and the Criminal Law Volume I: The Criminal Law and Bioethical Conflict: Walking the Tightrope*

Danielle Griffiths and Andrew Sanders *Bioethics, Medicine and the Criminal Law Volume II: Medicine, Crime and Society*

Margaret Brazier and Suzanne Ost *Bioethics, Medicine and the Criminal Law Volume III: Medicine and Bioethics in the Theatre of the Criminal Process*

Sigrid Sterckx, Kasper Raus and Freddy Mortier *Continuous Sedation at the End of Life: Ethical, Clinical and Legal Perspectives*

A. M. Viens, John Coggon and Anthony S. Kessel *Criminal Law, Philosophy and Public Health Practice*

Ruth Chadwick, Mairi Levitt and Darren Shickle *The Right to Know and the Right not to Know: Genetic Privacy and Responsibility*

Eleanor D. Kinney *The Affordable Care Act and Medicare in Comparative Context*

Katri Lõhmus *Caring Autonomy: European Human Rights Law and the Challenge of Individualism*

Catherine Stanton and Hannah Quirk *Criminalising Contagion: Legal and Ethical Challenges of Disease Transmission and the Criminal Law*

Sharona Hoffman *Electronic Health Records and Medical Big Data: Law and Policy*

Barbara Prainsack and Alena Buyx *Solidarity in Biomedicine and Beyond*

Camillia Kong *Mental Capacity in Relationship*

Oliver Quick *Regulating Patient Safety: The End of Professional Dominance?*

Thana C. de Campos *The Global Health Crisis: Ethical Responsibilities*

Jonathan Ives, Michael Dunn and Alan Cribb (eds) *Empirical Bioethics: Theoretical and Practical Perspectives*

Alan Merry and Warren Brookbanks *Merry and McCall Smith's Errors, Medicine and the Law: Second Edition*

Donna Dickenson *Property in the Body: Feminist Perspectives, Second Edition*

Rosie Harding *Duties to Care: Dementia, Relationality and Law*

Ruud ter Meulen *Solidarity and Justice in Health and Social Care*

David Albert Jones, Chris Gastmans and Calum MacKellar *Euthanasia and Assisted Suicide: Lessons from Belgium*

Lightning Source UK Ltd.
Milton Keynes UK
UKHW041108151218
334058UK00024B/464/P